Friends and Enemies

Friends and Enemies

The Past, Present and Future of the Communist Party of China

Kerry Brown

Foreword by Will Hutton

ANTHEM PRESS
LONDON · NEW YORK · DELHI

Anthem Press
An imprint of Wimbledon Publishing Company
www.anthempress.com

This edition first published in UK and USA 2009
by ANTHEM PRESS
75-76 Blackfriars Road, London SE1 8HA, UK
or PO Box 9779, London SW19 7ZG, UK
and
244 Madison Ave. #116, New York, NY 10016, USA

British Library Cataloguing in Publication Data
A catalogue record for this book is available from the British Library.

Library of Congress Cataloging in Publication Data
Brown, Kerry, 1967-
Friends and enemies : the past, present and future of the Communist Party of China/Kerry Brown; foreword by Will Hutton.
p. cm.
Includes bibliographical references and index.
ISBN-13: 978-1-84331-781-4 (Pbk)
ISBN-10: 1-84331-781-8 (Pbk) 1. Zhongguo gong chan dang.
2. Communism—China. 3. China—Politics and government—1949- I. Title.
JQ1519.A5.B76 2009
324.251'075—dc22

2009011716

ISBN-13: 978 1 84331 781 4 (Pbk)
ISBN-10: 1 84331 781 8 (Pbk)

1 3 5 7 9 10 8 6 4 2

The Communist Party is like the sun,
Wherever it goes there is light.
Wherever there is a Communist Party,
Hurrah, there the people are liberated.

'East is Red', Communist song written for Mao Zedong during the 1937–1945 war

...to become a Communist is not easy. It is both dangerous and alienating; for the idealistic Communist, it is even dangerous to be a Communist under so-called Communist regimes. It means exposure to persecution and bodily harm; this would be the fate of many who participated in the founding of the Communist Party of China. It means resignation to a sub-rosa existence, alienated from colleagues, friends, and even kith and kin. It means alienation from one's own values – the very values that justify Communist commitment but must be suspended temporarily in the name of long term goals. There is, in other words, a tragic element to Communism.

Arif Dirlik,
The Origins of Chinese Communism, (Oxford 1989)

China's democracy is a people's democracy under the leadership of the CCP. Without the CCP there would be no New China. Nor would there be people's democracy. This is a fact that has been borne out by history. The Chinese people won the right to be masters of the state only after many years of arduous struggle under the leadership of the CCP. The democratic political system in China was established by the Chinese people led by the CCP. The development and improvement of this system are also carried out under the CCP's leadership. The leadership of the CCP is a fundamental guarantee for the Chinese people to be masters in managing the affairs of their own country.

From the Chinese government white paper
'Building of Political Democracy in China,' Section One, 2005

Contents

Foreword

The Chinese Communist Party is the world's largest political party. With 76 million members and controlling every dimension of Chinese life since 1949, it has exerted more consistent political power than any other. Its destiny and that of China are inextricably bound together. Yet few, either in China or beyond, have the first inkling of how it functions and thinks, beyond recognizing its authoritarianism and strategic intelligence. Nor have they much idea of the Party's history and its surprising continuity with the past. This book aims to change that, and it succeeds triumphantly.

The task of holding China's 31 provinces and autonomous city regions together – most of which have populations larger than many middle-ranking countries – and driving them forward economically is extraordinarily challenging. The country over which the Party took control after, as the Party itself would describe it, thirty years of revolutionary struggle, was economically premodern and dirt poor. Today, it is the third-largest economic power in the world; its export volumes will soon overtake those of the US, Germany and Japan. Some 400 million have risen from poverty. Illiteracy and innumeracy have been vastly reduced.

Yet, for all this success, there is a fundamental ambiguity. A revolutionary Party has used the tools of the market economy over which, at the very least, it has profound misgivings if not ideological opposition, to create economic prosperity. Moreover, this generation of leaders, more than any of the previous ones (the first under Mao, the second under Deng, and the third under Jiang Zemin) lacks the political capital and revolutionary legitimacy for exercising power as did their veteran, warrior forebears. They are functionaries, technically managing the economy using decentralized price-setting rather than centralized planning as the core mode for allocating goods and services. But market economies are much more than that. They are populated by a web of institutions – companies, banks, auditors, lawyers, unions, media – that themselves have constitutions and purposes, that are autonomous. They hold each other to account for performance and behaviour. It is this linkage between capitalism and democracy – as much about a dense web of autonomous institutions and rich civil society as the right to vote, speak freely and assemble – that has been associated with economic success elsewhere in the world.

This is not the case in China. It has the technical apparatus of a market economy, and it has institutions that mimic those of other market economies; but they are not allowed to behave autonomously nor hold each to account independently of the Party and state. Instead, the Communist Party exercises ubiquitous control. When challenged, it ruthlessly crushes dissent. Today's China is the Party's creation. How has a revolutionary party made the transition to today? Can this and a fifth generation of political leaders, no longer legitimized by revolution, continue to control China? The Soviet Union's fifth generation of leaders were unable to hold the line. Will China's?

Yet, over and above the challenges that China has faced since the reform programme began in 1979, there is now the global recession – the first global economic contraction since the Second World War. China's exports have plunged, and the assumptions under which policy has been made for a generation – that the times are propitious for trade, inward investment and even peace, and that China can essentially assume that the responsibilities of managing the world's system will be done by others – are being undermined. China finds itself as crucially affected by the global economy as everyone else. As its economic growth falls away, there are fresh concerns about the capacity to create jobs and prosperity on which the Party's legitimacy depends. It is clearly in China's and the Party's interests to try and shape the global economy so that there is a quick recovery – and that similar shocks do not happen again.

The open question is whether China, given the ambiguities of the Party and its programme, can do what is necessary. At home, the economy has to be less dependent on savings and investment; abroad, on exports. Consumption has to rise by at least ten if not twenty per cent of GDP – an enormous leap that can be made only if consumers have the confidence conferred by a functioning welfare system and property rights. Internationally the world needs China to permit capital to flow more freely in and out of China, and for the reminmbi (RMB) to become a reserve currency freely convertible into others so that it takes its appropriate share of the burden of financing trade flows. Both moves threaten the Party's capacity to control China, opening up new sources of economic and political power. Yet, both need to be made for China's sake and the world's.

Brown shows how versatile the Party has been over the years, under Mao, Deng and Jiang Zemin, to do what needs to be done and still preserve its power – and that the West has an interest in its being versatile again. History's salutary warning is that the alternative is a potential breakup of China or a lurch to unthinking aggressive nationalism. Soviet communism lasted 73 years. Chinese communism will outlast it only if it breaches another limit of versatility, recognizing that there are limits to authoritarianism, and that China's success depends upon the Party planning what will succeed today's communism. China will need a network of economic, social and political institutions that look much like those emerging in the rest of the Asia – in other words, a progressive move away from a one-party state. The Communist Party's destiny is to manage that process and keep China together – and the West must allow the Party the room to manoeuvre while this long and slow process unfolds. Brown's book is an indispensable insight into the Party's mind, culture and history. Unless we understand, we cannot help. And this book helps that understanding.

Will Hutton, 12 March 2009

Preface

There are many books and studies on almost every aspect of the Communist Party of China (CPC), also known as the Chinese Communist Party (CCP). Its early history, development, final victory and the course of its control over China during the last six decades have been exhaustively studied. In many areas, despite this, the historic record is still unclear. And interpretation of how, and why, the Communist Party did certain things is still controversial. It continues to inhabit a world halfway between night and day. These obscurities are often things it cultivates.

Why another book on the CCP? About the history, I don't pretend, in what follows, to offer anything but a hopefully accessible narrative of how the CCP was formed, how it came to power, and how it has conducted itself while in government. Much that has been written about the Party is highly technical or specialist. This is a book for general readers interested in the forces that moulded and continue to shape the largest political organization in the world. But in addition to this, maybe acting more from folly than wisdom, I have also dared to look at the way the Party functions now, and, being even more foolhardy, how it might one day transform and change itself.

The CCP, to borrow Shakespeare's phrase, 'deserves studying'. It controls the destinies of a fifth of humanity, and its continuing existence (perhaps we could even dare to describe it now as flourishing) is to many an unfortunate incongruity in an age when democracies were meant to have swept all other alternative forms of governance from their path. The resolute continuation of a one-party system in China is a great inconvenience to those who prefer their history more logical – amongst them, perhaps, some followers of the master dialectician Marx. Like it or not, the CCP's success or failure, and its future plans, impact us all now. The following chapters will attempt to show why.

The Party – born from a 1921 Shanghai meeting of a group of intellectuals inspired by the Bolsheviks in the USSR (which was nearly eradicated in 1927, and again in 1935, and saved by a mixture of good luck and stubbornness in the 1940s) – now stands today as one of the key shapers of the modern world. It is a story of a remarkable past, an extraordinary present, and what will almost certainly be a fascinating future. This book tries to capture these three temporal aspects of the CCP and its journey into the century we live in.

Acknowledgements

I am grateful for the help of Professor Hans van de Ven, who sent me two very useful papers while I was preparing this book, and I have used them extensively in the second and third chapters. I am also grateful to Professor Joseph Fewsmith, Dr Ian Seckington, and Kate Westgarth for answering a string of questions about elite Chinese politics. Professor Rana Mitter, Nigel Cox, Professor Jeffrey Wasserstrom, Dr Temtsel Hao, Martin Andrew, Zorana Backovic, John Gittings, James Kynge, Elizabeth Corrin, Wang Tao, Michael O'Sullivan, Kelly Labar, Jasper Becker, Dr Bobo Lo and Professor Shaun Breslin kindly read all or parts of this work in manuscript and corrected many mistakes. I should stress that interpretation of the workings of the Communist Party vary widely, and all that is presented here is wholly my responsibility. There are many other people inside and outside China with whom I have discussed China and the Party over the last 18 years. Many of them, alas, I cannot mention, because of ongoing sensitivities about the history and the current development of the Party. But I am truly grateful for their insights, help and encouragement. I am responsible, of course, for any mistakes and failings that occur in the text.

I am grateful to Dr Lu Xinhua of Tongji University, Shanghai, for allowing me to use, in the fifth chapter, material that was previously published in October 2008 in 'China and Europe', which he edits.

I would also like to thank Katherine Peters and her family for allowing me to stay in her home in Wales while writing a large part of this work. Without the peace and quiet there, it would have been impossible to finish this work. I would also like to thank Tej Sood and Alexander Beecroft of Anthem Press for all their support.

I have used pinyin transliteration for all Chinese names and words in this book, apart from use of the older Wade Giles system in the names of Chiang Kai-shek and Sun Yat-sen, as these are much better known in that form.

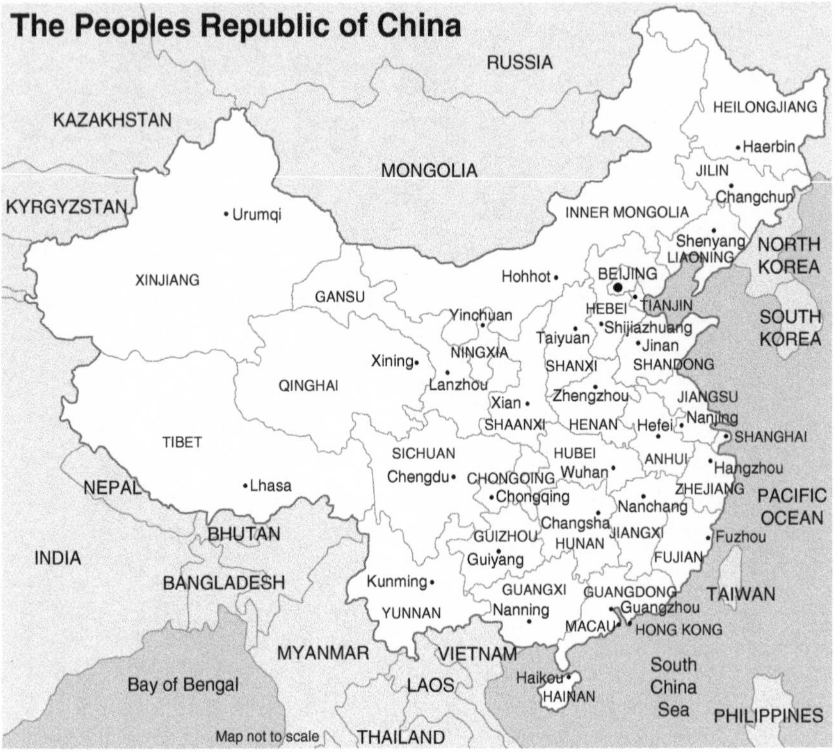
The Peoples Republic of China
RUSSIA
KAZAKHSTAN
MONGOLIA
KYRGYZSTAN
HEILONGJIANG
Haerbin
JILIN
Changchun
INNER MONGOLIA
Shenyang
LIAONING
NORTH KOREA
SOUTH KOREA
Urumqi
XINJIANG
GANSU
Hohhot
BEIJING
TIANJIN
HEBEI
Shijiazhuang
Yinchuan
Taiyuan
Jinan
NINGXIA
SHANXI
SHANDONG
Xining
QINGHAI
Lanzhou
Zhengzhou
JIANGSU
Xian
Nanjing
SHAANXI
HENAN
Hefei
SHANGHAI
TIBET
SICHUAN
HUBEI
ANHUI
Hangzhou
Chengdu
CHONGQING
Wuhan
Lhasa
NEPAL
Chongqing
ZHEJIANG
PACIFIC OCEAN
Nanchang
Changsha
BHUTAN
GUIZHOU
HUNAN
JIANGXI
Fuzhou
INDIA
Guiyang
FUJIAN
Kunming
BANGLADESH
GUANGXI
GUANGDONG
TAIWAN
Guangzhou
YUNNAN
Nanning
MACAU
HONG KONG
MYANMAR
VIETNAM
South China Sea
Haikou
Bay of Bengal
LAOS
HAINAN
PHILIPPINES
Map not to scale
THAILAND

It is the opening ceremony of the Beijing 2008 Olympics. An event it has taken a year to rehearse, involving over 18,000 performers. A world audience of 4 billion is watching. Eighty heads of state are in attendance, including the President of the United States, and the Prime Minister of Russia. The Chinese government has spent USD44 billion on the buildings, infrastructure and logistics for these games, more than any other host in history. Dozens have died in building the massive sports venues.

A man in a dark western-style business suit is sitting on a platform at the front of the VIP area, a bottle of mineral water and a teacup in front of him. He wears glasses. Despite his being in his mid-sixties, his hair is jet black, brushed back over his forehead. He wears a fixed, distant smile. From time to time he passes some brief comments, through an interpreter sitting behind him, to the head of the International Olympic Committee sitting to his right. When thousands of fireworks explode, the time for the games to begin, anticipated for years, finally arrives. Drummers, 2,008 of them, fill the air with noise. The man stands up and in standard Mandarin Chinese declares the opening of the 29th Olympic Games.

Hu Jintao, President of China, and leader of a fifth of the world's population, sits back down. No other human being in history has led so many people. But more importantly, not only is he China's head of state, he is also concurrently General Secretary of the Communist Party of China, an organization which continues, unchallenged, to hold a monopoly on the political control of the country he leads. He is the boss of 76 million Party members, the largest political organization the world has ever seen. But in this capacity, he has never given a one-to-one interview with a representative of any Western media outlet, despite being in office for over four years. In the West, he remains disturbingly unknown.

This book describes the history of the Party that he leads, and where it stands today. It describes how it came to be what it is, where it might be heading in the next decades, and what it feels its function is and the basis of its legitimacy. It sets out why the fate of the Party matters to the rest of the world, and where it must change to survive. And it also explains why – even for those Chinese who are not members and for people outside China – the way the Party operates, and what its decisions will be in the coming years, will fundamentally impact the world in which we all live.

Friends and Enemies

Introduction

This disturbance would have come in any event... They [the demonstrators] were attempting to subvert our state and overthrow the Communist Party, which is the essence of the issue. If we do not understand the fundamental problem, it means we are not clear about the nature of the issue... It all became clear once the incident broke out. They [the protestors] had two key goals. One was to overthrow the Communist Party, [and] the other was to topple the socialist system. Their aim was to establish a bourgeois republic totally dependent on the West.[1]

— Deng Xiaoping

In 1989 the rest of the world prepared to turn its backs on the leadership of China. The international press and media had gathered in Beijing in April to see the state visit to the People's Republic of China (PRC) by USSR leader Mikhail Gorbachev, the first between the two countries since the early 1960s. But at the same time as this momentous event, tens of thousands of students and workers assembled in Tiananmen Square in the centre of Beijing, demonstrating against corruption by government officials and rampant inflation, publicly airing grievances that had been building up for months. Many of them wanted political reform and saw themselves as heirs to the great current of Chinese student activism leading back to the 4 May Movement in 1919, when the slogan of reform for 'Mr Science and Mr Democracy' had first been coined. China needed change, they felt – radical change. The Chinese Communist Party (CCP), despite over a decade of economic liberalization and experimentation since the death of Mao Zedong in

1976, was moribund, and discussions about politics still highly restricted. The CCP needed to implement meaningful and extensive reforms. It needed, the students and activists dared to say, to allow political competition and the existence within China of other political parties capable of challenging the ruling party. The CCP's monopoly on power had to end.

The response of the main leadership of the Party is set out in some detail in top-level government documents, later leaked to the west.[2] It was brutal. On the night of 3 June they authorized the sending of tanks and soldiers with live ammunition into the city centre. Eyewitnesses saw people physically crushed. Crack troops from two ultra-loyal divisions of the People's Liberation Army (PLA) came from, amongst other places, the entrance of the Forbidden Palace at the north of the massive square, firing bullets into the remnants of the crowd of protestors left at the centre. The Taiwanese singer Hou Dejian was one of the last to leave the Monument to the People's Heroes, where the final few crowded. In a documentary filmed afterwards, *The Gate of Heavenly Peace,* he spoke of the eerie silence before the final onslaught, and the sense of defeat and deflation of those last students as they surrendered their space and exited.[3] Their departure, for many, meant the end of hopes for a peaceful transition to democracy in China.[4] According to recent research, many more killings occurred after the Square was emptied when troops panicked and went on a seemingly leaderless rampage.[5]

The CCP General Secretary in 1989, and ostensibly the leader of the country, was Zhao Ziyang. But as Zhao had admitted to journalists a few days before the Tiananmen Square event, the 85-year-old Deng Xiaoping still had a say in 'all major decisions and issues in China' despite resigning from political office a couple of years before.[6] Deng stated to troops a few days after the demonstrations that trouble 'would have come in any event'. He partly blamed international tensions. Subscribing to an almost fatalistic view of history, he told China to get on with business.

But the rest of the world, after holding out such high hopes for China in the 1980s and placing Deng's face not once, but twice, on the cover of *Time* as Man of the Year, were not so ready to forgive and forget. The image of a heavy tank stopped in its tracks by a single man with a plastic bag in his hands was relayed throughout the world. It was voted in 2000 one of the most iconic images of the twentieth century. To this day, no one knows what happened to the man, but the sentiment his stand expressed, of humanity holding out before a brutal system, seemed to capture perfectly the reality of the Chinese political system. Many who had followed and grown friendly with China during the early years of its reform and opening-up period since 1978 were bitterly angry and disillusioned. They felt as though a friend had suddenly been exposed as a liar, someone who simply could not change. Jonathan Mirsky, based in Beijing at the time and working as a journalist for *The Observer*, filed a number of reports expressing this disillusion well. China, under its surface, had not moved much further from the period of Maoist enclosure and darkness, when, in popular parlance, there had been rule of man, not rule of law.

European countries and the United State imposed embargoes. Some considered further sanctions, even to the extent of looking to break off all relations. Many temporarily withdrew their diplomatic staff. Foreign companies folded operations. Many investors hurriedly withdrew their money. Hong Kong people started to panic, remembering that, in only eight years time, this government, a government that had mowed its own people down in cold blood in its main public city square, was due to resume sovereignty over them. Many arranged passports to Canada, New Zealand or the UK. There was talk of China retreating once more into its shell, becoming, as it had in the 1960s and 1970s, an international pariah. The ten brief years of reform looked like an aberration.

Many commentators felt that the Party and its most senior leaders (the most important of them popularly nicknamed the 'Immortals') had finally lost the plot, and that they were facing historical forces and currents that they could not control. Their days were numbered, and they were at best rearranging the deckchairs on the Titanic. One-party rule was a busted flush in China. This sentiment was only strengthened when, later in 1989, the Berlin Wall came down and Eastern Europe escaped from the Iron Curtain and started a profound process of political and economic liberalization. The final blow was the collapse of the USSR and the rise of Boris Yeltsin in 1991. Never before had the CCP looked so isolated, anachronistic, and out of step.

Many analysts in the early 1990s (including such future enthusiasts for the Chinese way as renowned American economist Jeffrey Sachs) wrote a simple script. For them, the attempt by the CCP to introduce free-market economic reforms while doing nothing politically was a game only for the short term. As with the USSR and other countries, economic reform would inevitably lead to the creation of a middle class, which would in turn lead to the rise in demands for political enfranchisement and reform. They looked at China's long history of fragmentation, and foresaw scenarios where Tibet, Xinjiang, even Sichuan and the larger provinces, split away and went it alone, much as the Russian empire had fallen apart with the end of the USSR. They saw a China that was, despite all the bold talk in the 1980s of adapting Marxism-Leninism to a market economy, going along a fundamentally unsustainable path. No country had managed to avoid political reform after undergoing such far-reaching and deep-rooted economic changes. Since 1992, after Deng Xiaoping's famous final tour to the south, when he reaffirmed the Chinese government's commitment to opening up and pushing ahead with the reforms, predictions of the imminent collapse of the Chinese political system grew shriller, and more frequent. It was, for many people, not a case of if China would reform its political system, but when. The most trenchant critics felt that the Party had lost its purpose, as a deliverer of unity and stability, and had no mandate to rule.

This scepticism about the sustainability of the one-party system in China persisted throughout the 1990s. The democratization of Taiwan, culminating in the presidential elections in 1996 – elections that spooked the Chinese leadership sufficiently for them to undertake army manoeuvres off the coast of Fujian close to Taiwan – only confirmed many people's suspicions that the Communist Party was proceeding along a dead-end road. But no one could quite see an easy finishing point. Statements from within China about the country 'not being ready for democracy' increased. Taiwan had proved that there was nothing inherently impossible about a Chinese community being a democracy. But the Party ideologues in Beijing (and we will look at this complex and rich debate later) were adamant that China's conditions were not right for democratization. To those that agitated for reform, they produced the grim spectre the chaos and suffering that China had experienced in the 1920s and 1930s when it was fragmented. Stability was the Party's trump card, and they skilfully linked this to the need for China to have a strong, centralized, unified government. The year 1989 was dismissed as an attempt by 'anti-Party and anti-China elements' to destabilize and bring down the country, returning it to the weakness it had suffered in the past. Patriotic campaigns in the mid-1990s (promoting the merits of 'loving ones country') linked love of China to love of the Party. The two went together like teeth and lips. Those who tried to demonstrate, as dissidents like Wei Jingsheng and Xu Wenli did, that one could be fervently patriotic but anti-Party, were rewarded by lengthy prison sentences, condemned as enemies of the state and the Party, and, most woundingly, of the Chinese people generally.

As of 2009, those that foresaw the end of the Party's days have so far been proved resoundingly wrong. Well within the twenty-first century, the CCP remains fully in control of the People's Republic of China and of the political and economic destinies of a fifth of humanity. It has, at least so far, proved the pundits and doomsayers of the last two decades wrong. In fact, far from being weak and compromised, the Party has shown devastating instincts for maintaining its power base. It has allowed wide-ranging liberalization of the society and economy, but maintained an iron grip on the areas of power that it feels are non-negotiable. China is now home to more websites than anywhere else on the planet. Half a billion people carry mobile phones on which a proportion of them can, ostensibly freely, surf the Internet, and also, somewhat incongruously, text anonymously (people can still acquire mobile phone accounts in China without registering a name or address). Millions are engaged in chat rooms, and Internet forums. And yet, the Party has been able to face down any intellectual and organizational threat to its monopoly on power. This is one of the most remarkable feats of political organization and control of the modern world, possibly of all time. This book attempts to explain how this astonishing task has been achieved.

Hidden Giant: The Party and Openness

For all its success so far, the Party ranks amongst the world's most secretive organizations. With 76 million members (a figure that increases by two million each year), it would rank as one of the world's most populous countries in its own right. It could be even larger. Twenty million Chinese willingly apply to join each year. This is an extraordinary return for an organization that started life in 1921 with a few dozen members. And yet, despite, or perhaps because of its enormous size, the Party acts as though it were answerable to no one but itself, and its bunker mentality from the hard early days is oddly maintained. Its finances are undisclosed, its historical archives and the reports of the countless meetings amongst its members largely embargoed. It produces no annual report for its members. The closest it comes to this is when the Party Secretary speaks to the membership and the country at one of the full Congresses, held every five years. The Party disciplines its own, and sets its own standards.

And yet, despite, or perhaps because of this secrecy, it penetrates deep into the social and political life of China, and acts in many ways like an all-present invisible element, there, but not seen, except by those who consciously think of it. Those who try to understand the myriad contradictions and complexities of modern China will not get far without encountering and trying to understand the Party. In the secret recesses of the Party lie the closest we will get to understanding how the Chinese have, in a one-party state, succeeded as no other country has in creating a notionally free market economy that has become a major component of the global economy, but with no meaningful political reform.

Even looking at the physical urban landscape of China indicates the way that the Party is linked into modern life in China. Beijing is a city planned on socialist principles, a place which, after the revolution in 1949, ripped down most of its ancient walls to make way for the statements of progress, four-lane-wide inner city boulevards.[7] Standing in the world's largest open city square, Tiananmen, one can look west, to the museum of Revolutionary History, or east, to the Great Hall of the People, both of them built in a matter of months in the 1950s after the victory of the revolution. Ahead, there is the portrait of Mao Zedong, Chairman of the Party (but never President of the country) for over 30 years, and architect of the coming to power of the Communists. To the north of the square is the 'Gouanbu', the security agency that reports to the Party, not the government, and that undertakes its main work against elements regarded as corrosive and threatening, ranging from supporters of the quasi-spiritual Falungong sect, outlawed after surrounding the government compound in 1999, to lawyers who are seen as being too willing to support activists branded as having 'antisocial', unpatriotic motivations. At any one time, some have estimated that of every four people in the square, milling around, flying kites, sightseeing, passing the time of day, one is a security operative. Even taxi drivers have been reported to sometimes work for the security service, compiling reports that are based on conversations they have had throughout the day, catching the national mood. With the lack of a properly free press, this is perhaps inevitable, harking back to the USSR of the 1930s and the reports of 'minglers and whisperers' sent by Stalin's secret service to the Politburo, and the even grander ruse of Peter the Great of Russia, who would dress as a commoner and go about the streets of Moscow to eavesdrop on conversations. There have been no reports, yet, of someone matching the description of Hu Jintao or Premier Wen Jiabao milling around in bus queues. This work remains delegated, but it is very important.

Proceeding along the 'Road of Eternal Peace' (a road along which the tanks rolled, very unpeacefully, in 1989) one comes to the gateway of the Zhongnanhai Compound, living quarters and playground of the emperors in the imperial dynasties up to 1911 when the Qing fell, and, since 1949, the most sensitive seat of power in China. Here, at the court of Mao, the top leaders held their meetings. It was here that Mao himself had his living quarters, next to his swimming pool. According to the American journalist Harrison Salisbury in his biography of Mao and Deng, the very physical geography of this place inculcated an almost remote, imperial attitude in the leaders living there.[8] It is indeed a remarkably serene place, with large, well-preserved classical buildings, a peaceful and clean lake, and no nearby buildings visibly surrounding it overlooking the inner sanctum of power. Those that are granted meetings within this territory are ushered into reverently hushed halls, usually decked in grand floral displays, with huge, dominating Chinese-style pictures on the walls bearing down on them. It is a piece of political theatre that manages to move and effect even the most hardened of visitors. The understated main gates with the usual three guards standing in strict configuration outside have two slogans in Chinese, boldly written on across painted red brickwork at either side of the entrance. One side simply says 'Ten thousand Years to the People's Republic of China'. And the other: 'Ten thousand Years to the Communist Party of China'. The link is clearly declared at the entrance to the top seat of power. You cannot say you have not been warned.

Beyond Zhonghanhai, emanating from the heart of this Party universe, are a myriad of other buildings – from what look superficially to be think tanks to anonymous buildings tucked in back streets – which are all parts of the organization of the Party. In the Northwest part of the City, near the elite Qinghua University, from which many of China's top political figures have graduated, is the Party School, the key stomping ground for the Party's ideologues, those who are daily trying to square the capitalist circle with the Marxist square in 'market socialist' China. Their thinking will be looked at later in this work. But the Party school, reached along an anonymous-looking entry road, shares the same unremarkable architecture and look of bureaucratic stillness that so many other Party buildings do. It declares whatever power it has modestly. But its real influence is displayed by the so called President of the School – until recently Hu Jintao, who just happens to be President of China, General Secretary of the CCP, and Chair of the Central Military Commission. He was replaced in 2007 by Xi Jinping, a man widely tipped to be Hu Jintao's successor in his other positions at the next Party Congress in 2012.

This geography of Party power is replicated throughout the PRC's 31 provinces, autonomous regions, and cities directly under the central government. In the Special Administrative Regions of Hong Kong and Macau there are Party buildings, though far more discrete in deference to the 'one country, two systems' deal currently in place, where these zones have been granted a 'high degree of autonomy'. In the various regional capitals, from Lhasa to Hohhot to Hangzhou to Shanghai, there is a clear understanding that the Party Secretary is the key player in these places, and that the real power resides in the Party Headquarters, despite the fact that there is a parallel government function that is meant to take the lead in administration and organization. In each centre, there are the same provincial counterparts to central Party organizations, from organization committees, to regulation and inspection boards. At the township and county levels, down to the smallest village, the Party has its structures and its network – sending out messages, instructions and undertaking discipline – a system which, to all intents and purposes, was set up in the early 1950s, and continues to this day, although in the almost 3,000 county levels that constitute China, Hu Jintao's current government have implemented reforms to reduce the Party secretaries and their deputies in number and to standardize the arrangements in each place. These are the veins and arteries along which the blood that sustains modern Communist China flows, maintaining it in life.

Looking at the ubiquity of the Party's structure is a good way to appreciate one of its greatest strengths – its phenomenal focus and concentration on power. This ambition is such, that in recent years, think tanks in Beijing have been mandated by the government to look at the longevity of the Catholic Church, and how it has been able to survive as an organization for almost two thousand years. Commentators have variously described the Republican Party in the US, or the Conservative Party in the UK, as infinitely self-reinventing, able to recover from setbacks and assaults, and still remain focused on acquiring power. For these, the issue of ideology is second to that of being in power. The CCP puts even these fearsome organizations into the shade. Its monopoly on power, which started in 1949, has continued unbroken to the present day. This is all the more remarkable when one considers the huge diversity and the massive extent of the territory the Party rules over – much more extensive than previous Chinese dynasties, apart from the Mongol led thirteenth-century Yuan dynasty. It encompasses the isolated plains of Tibet, the densely forested and ethnically diverse regions of Yunnan and Sichuan in the Southwest of China, and the massive, modernist miracles of Shanghai, Guangzhou and Shenzhen. It is a territory that embraces over 100 million people living on less than a dollar a day, the UN standard of absolute poverty, and an emerging middle class that numbers anything from 40 to 150 million people. The Party rules over a population split between 50 per cent who still works on the land, in the agricultural sector, and the newly emerging group of super rich, the 750 people on Forbes and Hurun's database, who have made their money in property, manufacturing and finance.

Ideologically, the Party looks like it has jettisoned Marxism-Leninism. To many, it has created a country more capitalist than anything in the developed west. Many within China feel deeply disappointed that the CCP, which once ran a 'cradle to the grave' social security system, looking after health, old age and education through the all-pervasive work unit system, has now seemingly abandoned everything to the free market, meaning that individuals are responsible for all aspects of their lives from schooling to hospital treatment. They look at the wealth creation of the last few years, and see a country that has allowed many to prosper, and a similar number to languish in deepening poverty. They wonder how this can be called a 'socialist system' and what the founding fathers, particularly Mao Zedong, would think of such inequality and unbalance.

These people, along with many outside observers, listen to the words of modern Chinese party officials and politicians speaking about the country's problems, and feel like they are hearing people in a strange and severe kind of denial. Does the Party really stand for what its most senior representatives say publicly about socialism with market characteristics and developing the new level of Marxism? Do they really believe that this is compatible with the gleaming capitalist constructions of Beijing, and the highly volatile stock markets operating in Shanghai and Shenzhen?

Not a Tolerant Party: The CCP and Opposition

Whatever the controversy over what the Party really believes (which will be looked at in Chapter Six) there is one area in which the Party has been ruthlessly successful. In 1998, a group of intellectuals and academics in central China set up the China Democracy Party. They numbered only a couple of dozen, a similar figure to the founding members of the CCP themselves during the first ever Congress in 1921 in Shanghai (see Chapter One). Their demand was very simple. They wished to take advantage of the promise in the Chinese constitution to have freedom of thought and to set up a political party – with formal recognition from the authorities – that reflected their political views. Some of the members presented themselves at a local government office in Hefei, the capital of Anhui province where they lived, in order to complete the formalities. They were rewarded for their efforts by being harassed by secret police, then taken into custody, and, after several months of 'investigation', charged and imprisoned. Their crime? Sabotage and attempting to bring down the State.

The Party has reacted with similar ruthlessness to all other attempts to organize opposition. While Chinese society may be increasingly free and liberal, with whole areas of the economy and daily life largely devoid of political control, the Party had made it clear, by its actions, that any straying into territory leading towards organized political opposition will be met with total intolerance. A young blogger who, in 2001, tried to set up a group with just the word 'democracy' in the title, was rewarded for his efforts with a 12-year prison sentence. On this issue, the CCP shows no signs of giving in.

China does have parties other than the Communists. There are the so-called 'eight patriotic parties', amongst them the Nationalist Party Revolutionary Committee, and the Patriotic Party. Some of them have roots leading back to the period of turmoil in the 1920s and 1930s. They have leaders and party headquarters, and are wheeled out during the National People's Congress – the annual rubber-stamp government – that is held in Beijing. But it is widely known that these parties, whose memberships only numbers 130 thousand, are utterly without power, and serve as a useful façade for the CCP to pretend that it operates in a notionally democratic context.

The Party controls the key levers of power. And it does this in a highly concentrated and particular way. The National People's Congress may have grown more restive over the last few years, but everyone knows that the Party Congresses (held every five years since the death of Mao Zedong in 1976) are the most significant events, and these announce the conclusions of behind-the-scenes meetings, which then set the direction on which China travels simply by agreeing to the proposals of the elite leadership. The People's Liberation Army (PLA), combining the army, navy and air force, has been the power broker in China since 1949. And yet it openly admits that it is a servant of the Party, not the country. It reports to Party, not government leaders. Its senior leadership are all, to a man and woman, Party members, and anyone who enters it and wishes to rise above platoon commander level knows that they must join the Party to ease their way. Its loyalties lie there. The final instructions for the PLA come from the Central Military Commission (CMC), which is chaired by the General Secretary of the Party, Hu Jintao. In the current constitution, this line between the powers and responsibilities of the Party and the government is left vague. One of the themes of this book will be the thin, shifting line between the government, on the one hand, with its six to seven million civil servants, and the Party, of which the former is the servant.

The CCP's ruthlessness, its formidable organizational capacity, and its secrecy, mean that it is an entity that can never be taken lightly. Those that attempt to challenge it on issues that matter to it in China almost invariably pay a high price. In the last few years, there have been areas in which the Chinese government has welcomed criticism and comment – particularly the environment – where almost 3,000 non-government organizations have been set up. Those that wish to push the envelope of meaningful political pluralism a little further, however, are in danger of heading for a painful encounter with the full might of the state – a state which will defend, to the last breath, the monopoly of the Party to power. The Congressional Executive Commission on China estimates that there are currently 920 political prisoners in China.[9] In recent decades, the most prominent dissidents have simply been exiled abroad. Many lesser known ones have been sent into a form of internal exile. Since the horrible shock of 1989, not a single group, or individual, has laid a finger on the Party. It remains the only political game in town. This is an extraordinary afterlife for an organization believed to be on its last legs in 1990.

Part of the secret of the power of the CCP, I will argue, lies in its flexibility and in its strategic genius. The Party has responded to the needs and desires of its main constituency, the emerging middle class in the cities, and the increasing band of agricultural workers who have done well in the Reform period starting after 1978. There may well have been 87,000 protests in China in 2005 (the government ordered that these statistics were no longer compiled after 2007, as they were regarded as meaningless, though critics felt this was more because of the embarrassment they caused and the ammunition they gave to people who were critical of the authorities). But in a country of 1.3 (and probably closer to 1.5) billion, this is a tiny drop in the ocean. The Party has swept upon sources of potential dissatisfaction, like economic growth, or the rehabilitation of entrepreneurs, or the relaxation of agricultural taxes, and put in place measures to ease or eliminate these problems. It has enfranchised a new generation of young Chinese who barely know about the 1989 events or what happened before, and who see the existence of a central, single source of authority as a sign of strength rather than a weakness. The Party has controlled the territory it wishes to, and abandoned what is unimportant. Nowhere is this clearer than in the world of the Internet, the modern regimes of control (so far very successful) of which will be looked at in the final chapter. Most remarkably, a Party that was the product of one kind of society, the pre-1949 China, with a huge rural population, low levels of industrialization and urbanization, and only a tiny minority who had received any education, has now started to make the transition to being the main power in a totally different kind of society, split almost equally between cities and countryside, with high levels of industrialization, and a much more complex social composition.

The Party in Everyday Life in China Today

My previous book, *Struggling Giant: China in the 21st Century*, while it inevitably touched on the Party and its functions, was a more general look at the issues facing China at present and in the next few years.[10] It viewed these from a historical perspective, trying to map out how China had come to be where it is now, and how understanding at least something of its past behaviour and history might help to plot out its possible future path.

This book focuses on the single issue of the Communist Party. But in order to understand the Party, I have remained faithful to the model used in the first book, drawing on history, and looking at the themes history shows, and the patterns of behaviour it suggests. I have also used a great deal of personal experience in writing, and framing the arguments in this book. For almost a decade I worked as a diplomat, largely dealing with China. For two years I was based in the China section in London, and then for three-and-a-half years, at the British Embassy in Beijing. In my life since leaving the Foreign Office, at the Royal Institute of International Affairs, and in other areas – and for other reasons – I have been able to look at the power structure in China, and at various aspects of the Party, from many different angles. In the last few years, my familiarity and knowledge of the Party has increased. It seems that no matter what subject, area or issue one wishes to deal with in China, there is an element in it in which the Party figures.

I know the Party as the organization to which many of my friends and associates in China belong and, up to a point, which they believe in. It is a group the hospitality of which I have enjoyed, and the patronage of which almost anyone trying to transact any business in China needs to cultivate. To me, the face of the Party is the face of the many members I have met over the last decade and a half. It is the face of the Mongolian in Hohhot whom I grew to know well while I was based there in the mid-1990s, and who, despite the dreadful suffering he and his family had endured in the Cultural Revolution just two decades before, still proudly proclaimed 'Ten thousand years to the Communist Party of China'. It is the face of the young Youth League students I grew to know in Beijing, who joined it because of unspoken benefits they felt it brought, but who wore their membership lightly. It is the face of the many dozens of Party officials I met, hosted, and was hosted by, both inside and outside China, all of whom, for all their different perspectives and interests, were linked by this common but elusive element. The Party seemed to lurk under the surface almost everywhere. It truly was, as early propagandists for the Communists in China said, like the 'air in which you breathed, or water in which fish swim'. It was hard to imagine modern China, in fact, without the Party.

A businessman based in Beijing explained this ubiquity well, when I spoke with him in 2006. 'For me,' he said, 'my whole life doing business in China is spent trying to avoid the moment when I have to deal with Party officials. I've devised dozens of routs and ruses in order to put off the moment when I finally arrive at a place I know is the door to a Party organization. Of course, what I am always doing is deferring the moment, but I can never completely cancel it. I know that one day I will arrive at that door. In China, if you really want to get things done, you can never avoid it.'

For the uninitiated, therefore, modern China can be a highly misleading place. They will arrive on their planes from Europe or North America, or wherever else they have come from, to gleaming splendid airports, and be taken into the cities on trains that run on magnetic tracks at up to 450 kilometres an hour . They will stay in some of the world's tallest and most modernist architecture. It will seem like a place where the future has arrived early. They will deal with people who look and sound, often in fluent English, like capitalists from the West. They will do their deals, have their meetings, and it will all seem familiar and comfortable.

But in fact, while they may not be aware of it, they will often have already encountered the Party. Their counterpart may well be a Party member. They might be unaware of the strong links between the private enterprise they are dealing with and Party investment or Party leaders. Maybe the person who runs it or owns it is related to an important local Party official. After all, according to one recent statistic, of China's 3,000 richest people, 2,900 are closely related to high-level party cadres. Many of China's new wealthy have, since they were allowed, joined the Party. Wander into the largest employer of people in the city of Shenyang in the non-state sector, a lift manufacturer called Yuanda, and you will see the hammer and sickle plastered massively on the walls, next to and, highly symbolically bigger than, the company logo. For those that can interpret what is around them, the Party goes from being invisible to almost omnipresent in a matter of seconds. And this is particularly the case if businesses experience problems. While they have risen from literally nowhere over the last three decades, law courts are well down the pecking order when it comes to a straight playoff with the Party. Decisions issued by the courts that are deemed to negatively impact the Party's interests have a limited chance of even getting listened to, let alone implemented. And lest it not be forgotten, the majority of judges and lawyers and police are Party members. 70 per cent of China's legislation, in fact, comes from the government ministries. The so-called parliament, the National People's Congress, only accounts for 30 per cent. And in terms of initiating, formulating, drafting and then implementing law, the ministries take the lead – led, in all cases but two, by Party members (as of the time of writing, December 2008, only the Minister of Science and the Minister of Health are non-Party members).

Trying to Get Away from the Chairman

In the period from 1949 to Mao's death in 1976, through a combination of causes – some historical, some external, some internal – all of which will be looked at in Chapter Two, one man was able to accrue huge amounts of power and political capital. In the court of Mao Zedong, only the bravest, or the most foolish, dared take him on. He deflected numerous threats, large and small. A phrase, dusted off from the classical period, was often used at the time: 'He who dares to unseat the emperor must be prepared to die by the death of a thousand cuts.' President Nixon, during his groundbreaking visit to China in 1972, was awed by the sense of raw power emanating from the Chairman, and this at a time when he was physically ruined by Parkinson's disease and a mere shadow of what he had been like at his prime.[11] Mao's charisma still haunts the political landscape in China, and supplies the shadow in which all major politicians, to this day, move. Uniquely, despite his relatively privileged upbringing, he captured the imagination, and to a surprising extent the hearts, of the peasantry, the mass of people in the countryside who were his main constituency throughout his long political career.

The concentration of power in the hands of one person was, even at the time, seen as a major problem. One of the great challenges from 1978 has been how to create a more plural system. The Party has been key to this, with attempts to institutionalize its structures, and to create at least some level of transparency and accountability. Party Congresses, once held infrequently, and the top decision-making events, have now come to take place every five years. The formal organization of the Party has been streamlined, with specific levels and greater clarity of the responsibilities of each department and section. The Party has even made greater efforts with its own public relations, employing local and outside help to market and brand itself.

At the summit of the Party, and of the power tree in modern China, is the Standing Committee of the Politburo. A group of men (there are no women in the top leadership of China, reflecting the gender balance of Party membership, with only 20 percent being women), mostly in their 50's and 60s, with impeccable party credentials, these are the people in charge of the destiny of a fifth of humanity. The numbers in the Standing Committee have shifted from seven to the current nine. This reflects the complex interplay of forces within the Party and the broad views that the Politburo needs to reflect to be truly representative. In recent years, observers have traced factions, power groups, and parties within parties. This will be looked at in more detail in the final chapter. What is clear is that each current member of the Politburo has a deep Party hinterland. This generation of leaders lacks the political capital and credibility of their predecessors, Mao, Deng and Jiang. They are people who have spent the vast majority of their lives in the PRC growing up in a system in which the Party was already in control. In that sense, they owe their position, their authority and their mandate to this organization of which they are servants. Their attempts to set its agenda and shape its destiny are limited and circumscribed by the particular groups and sympathizers within the Party elite.

At the last Party Congress in October 2007 there were a few new faces allowed into the ultimate inner sanctum. One member of the previous Standing Committee, the mysterious and low-profile Huang Ju, former Party Secretary of Shanghai, had died earlier in 2007 after a long struggle with pancreatic cancer. Others, such as the influential Zeng Qinghong, had reached the formal retirement age of 68. This freed up four new positions. The new entrants, men in their fifties, were immediately hailed as the most likely to be what was dubbed the 'fifth generation' of Party Leadership. Two in particular, the ex-Party boss of Shanghai, Xi Jinping, and the head of Liaoning Province in the North East, Li Keqiang, were seen as being in pole position to become country president and premier, respectively, at the next Party Congress in 2012, when, according to the current constitution, President Hu Jintao and Premier Wen Jiabao have to step down.

Were any of these new people reform-minded or closet democrats? It was hard to discern this, looking at them as they trooped out, after some covert horse-trading and negotiations in the final days of the conspicuously extended Congress. They faced the flashing cameras with serene composure, lined up, to a man, in order of rank. The very best clue that Hu Jintao was able to give when welcoming the new members of the group was that they were 'young men of considerable ability'. Formal Chinese, at least in a political context, is not a language for emoting in.

Beneath them was the Politburo proper, a body of 24 people, with one alternate member. These were the representatives of specific regions (like, for instance, Xinjiang, or Guangdong province, still a massive economic engine for China.) Underneath this was the Central Committee, a group that consists currently of 204 full members and about 150 alternate members. The Central Committee is composed of the leaders of each of China's 31 provinces and autonomous regions, the heads of its armed forces and security details. At the 16th Party Congress in 2002 it even saw, for the first time, the election of the Head of the Haier electronic appliances factory in Qingdao, the first ostensibly partially non-state company president to reach such elevated political heights. Of the current 204 Central Committee members, however, there are only heads of state-owned enterprise (SOE) and state-owned banks. Nor is there a clear mechanism for the Central Committee for meeting and making decisions on day-to day-policy. As it has evolved in the last three decades, the Party has instituted systems led by the Secretariat of the Politburo, which carries on the running of the country. And the civil and military decision-making trees only come together when they finally reach the desk, through their separate routs, of Hu Jintao.

This structure is to an extent duplicated at provincial and municipal levels, and even the smallest county level. Currently, and for the foreseeable future, no Governor of any of China's provinces and autonomous zones is a non-Party member. Only at the Vice Governor level is there usually a token non-Party representative. There are, in fact, in the 76-million-strong membership of the Party, about 25,000 who can be said to belong to the real decision-making elite.[12] And within this, the Standing Committee of the Politburo ranks far and away as the strongest. Party membership, therefore, means different things to different people. Only a tiny proportion of Party members derive any real power from their membership. For some, in recent years, it has become a useful adjunct, something that assists their other work interests, and helps them get ahead. For others, it is part and parcel of what they do, especially if they work in the government. The training ground for the Party is the Communist Youth League, open to those from age 14 to 28, which has 87 million members, and which has supplied, through its central committee and president, some of China's top leaders in recent years, including the current president Hu Jintao. With a supply of fresh new talent on this scale, at least on the surface the Party looks in rude health.

For the vast majority of Party members, however, membership and the experience and benefits of membership are not something that fills their lives. Whether it is a local committee member in rural China, or someone in one of the various wards and districts in the great cities of Shanghai or Beijing, their attitude, like the attitude of many in the west, is that at very best, politics is a necessary evil, something for a specific time and place. They would regard a return to the highly politically mobilized society of 40 or 50 years ago, when responsibilities and declarations of faith to the Party filled every area of life, with horror. Most people, even those who are members, spend their lives skirting around the edges of political activity. The Seventeenth Party Congress in October 2007, despite the international interest it aroused, was regarded largely with indifference in China. Even the ever-voluble and opinionated Beijing taxi drivers were more exercised by the rise in inflation and the vagaries of the Shanghai stock exchange than who might appear as a new face on the Politburo Standing Committee.

Perhaps this is a good thing. Politics has led people to bad things in the past, at least in China. It is, in the modern parlance, a contaminated brand. Dai Qing, a famous Chinese writer and intellectual, and herself the daughter of a high-level Chinese army leader, complained in the 1980s that the 'greatest threat to peace and stability in China is the spectre of extreme leftism.' Even in the last two decades, as China has radically modernized, the argument by so-called new leftists that China needed to go it alone far more and return to some of its prime socialist values has lurked just beneath the surface, even though almost none of these espouse the extreme doctrines of Mao Zedong. At the 2007 Congress, Hu Jintao's comments that the 'path of opening up and reform started under Comrade Deng Xiaoping' was right, proper and irreversible was taken as a clear sign to leftists malcontents that there would be no chance of a return to the good old, bad old days of class stratification, complete state ownership and ubiquitous social struggle. This ideological battle will be looked at in more detail in Chapter Six, but its fierceness, and the residual power of leftism, should never be overlooked, no matter how peaceful things look on the surface in the PRC.

Never Forget the Past

The Party's greatest power and the source of its current legitimacy is history, the history of revolutionary struggle, the history of creating and then stabilizing a new Chinese nation, and the history of the Party being a liberator. This brilliant elision of the Party's good being the same as the country's good has been perhaps the greatest masterstroke by which the CCP has beaten back all political opposition, and maintained its iron grip on power. The argument is very simple: The Party, and the Party alone, delivered stability to China. The Party returned China to prosperity and unity. Without the Party, China could have been broken by the

Nationalists (KMT) or the Japanese, and might not now even exist. This is a powerful narrative to try to argue with, because many key elements of it are in fact plausible.

Those commentators in the West, and within China, who underestimate the Party and look at what they see as its ideological bankruptcy in the twenty-first century, have to remember the extraordinary history from which this organization grew, and the way that this history still acts as a powerful bond. The outlines of the Party's past are easy to sketch. This is an organization born from the frustrations at the end of the Qing period, a dynasty now regarded as stagnant and weak, which allowed China to be bullied and put down. It has its roots in the student anger in 4 May 1919, when demonstrations took place against what was seen as the iniquitous decisions visited upon China at the end of the First World War. The first Congress in Shanghai was attended, in 1921, by a handful of people. The importation of the new ideology of Marxism-Leninism was regarded as nothing more than a brief hiatus by those in charge of China at the time. As the Party grew in the 1920s, it shifted from idealism to a real toughness, tempered by the life and death struggle that it became engaged in to survive. Nearly eradicated by the Nationalists in the 1920s and 1930s, it created its own extraordinary mythology with the Long March in 1934–35, and the unholy pact with the Nationalists to defeat the Japanese in the Sino–Japanese war from 1937. Its leadership underwent frequent, and sometimes bloody and vicious, change. To add to its agony, there were numerous deep and debilitating divisions within its own ranks, adding to its fragility. The story of these early years, which still haunts the national memory, will be looked at in Chapter One. But by any reckoning, it is a remarkable narrative – at times moving, at other times horrific. The Party's survival after all this was little short of miraculous. The full story of Mao Zedong's rise from a relatively junior position to being the supreme political leader of the Party is still only partially understood. Maybe it will never be properly known. The Party, to this day, guards its archives fiercely. But by the start of the Chinese Civil War and the battle for final power over China in 1946, the Communists had experienced one of the harshest training periods for a political organization in modern history. Their mandate to be the ruler of a China rising from the ashes in 1949 was clear and overwhelming – final victory in a bitter and unequal war in which, till the final period, they were the underdogs. As Australia-based scholar Mobo Gao eloquently pointed out, Mao most certainly did not say, as he is often misquoted, 'The Chinese People have stood up' when he spoke from the Gate of Heavenly Peace in Beijing on the day the People's Republic of China was founded on 1 October 1949. He said 'The People's Republic of China has stood up.' And that new country was irrefutably the creation of the Communist Party of China. The current leaders of China are heirs to the revolutionary tradition that created the PRC, and carry the aspirations and hopes of a Party formed during this tragic period into the future. They live each day with the legacy of 1949, and could not, and would not, deny that they are servants of this tradition, however far their actions in the current time take them from what perhaps was hoped in the early flush of victory over half a century ago.

Plan of Book

The structure of this book is straightforward. In the first chapter, I will look at the early history of the Party, and the complex, impassioned political debates in the 1920s and 1930s, leading up to the final victory of the CCP under Mao in 1949. In the second chapter I will describe the path of the party in power from 1949 up to the 1990s, when it came close to almost annihilating itself during the Cultural Revolution, and was set against itself under the mercurial leadership of Mao. In the third chapter I will look at the debates in the 1990s and into the early 2000s, about which direction the Party needed to go in order to stay into power, faced with the rapid industrialization and modernization of its economy. The fourth chapter describes how the Party stands today, and how it operates and maintains control over this diverse, complicated and endlessly energetic country. In the fifth chapter some of the major global issues facing the Party as we go into the twenty-first century and the areas where it is most under pressure will be discussed. In the final chapter, I will throw modesty and caution to the wind, and will attempt to look into the future, to predict where the Party might go, what its steps to final political reform might be and how likely it is that it will achieve this in the coming two decades.

Whatever their political position or their sympathies, those who write about the CCP and its role on the creation of modern China cannot fail to feel respect, grudging or wholehearted, for what the Party has done and how it has maintained its role. Right from the beginning of the Reform process in 1978, China's attempts to create what many believe to be a square circle have been regarded with either heavy scepticism or outright disbelief. At each step of the way, pundits have predicted that what China was trying to do was, in fact, unsustainable and unsupportable. Imminent collapse has been warned of many times. The Party's days have been numbered. Yet, at least in 2009, we are still writing about and trying to understand the Party, and there is no alternative in China to look at. In that sense, to today at least, the Party has been successful and victorious.

But there are real issues about how long China can continue this extraordinary balancing act of having a free economy and a one-party system. Many in China share these worries, and are thinking hard about what the future might hold. The maintenance of the status quo is, in many ways, an embarrassing incongruity. In taking western economic models and brazenly applying them economically, but without the political structure of a multi-party system, China appears to rip up the rules of modernity. This was not how things were meant to be. This issue of China's vision of its global role and its own form of modernity is a key one for the immediate future. Can China have capitalism, but no meaningful political reform? And indeed, does it need the West's model of capitalism, a model that has made China richer, but destroyed its environment, and made it the factory of the world, without taking it closer to becoming a knowledge economy? After the shock of 1989, during the disturbances at that time, the Communist Party made a deal in which it tied its stewardship of the PRC to economic success. This was most powerfully symbolized by the visit of Deng Xiaoping, the paramount leader, to the south of China in 1992. If the Party made China rich, delivering prosperity to its people, then, the deal went, the political system could stay as it was. Changing this would cause instability and disruption, and return the country to the chaos of the past. Since then, the Party has introduced more local elections, and some so-called 'inner party' democratic reforms. The power composition of its elite is now extremely complex. In the twenty-first century, it will continue to carry out this balancing act – taking China from third largest to second, and then, sometime in the 2030s, to the world's largest economy. Every day it succeeds, is a day when the Party is proved right, and the pundits wrong. But the fear or anxiety that one day the final breaking point will come is never far away. There is a nagging suspicion that what the CCP is trying to do is, in some ways, fundamentally unsustainable, and that it can't carry on forever. The CCP of the USSR, until now the world's longest-lasting Communist Party in power, lasted from 1917 to 1991, a matter of only 74 years. The CCP has been in place from 1949. It remains a decade away from breaking the USSR party's record.[13] But every day forward towards this record also raises fears of whether its fate will be like that of the other Communist parties throughout the world, many of which simply died or were marginalized. Will China manage the kind of smooth transition to a democracy that it aspires to, the kind of thing former President Jiang Zemin referred to in 2000 when he predicted that in fifty years China would be a democracy (though there are valid arguments about what he, and CCP leaders mean, when they say democracy in this context)? Or will it continue with this system indefinitely, until the day that some grievance or social turbulence or nightmarish combination of environmental problems, energy supply breakdowns, and economic collapse finally brings it down? This is the fundamental political challenge for China in the next decades, as the Party finally comes to terms with how it can open up not only its economy, but its political system. If this succeeds, the chances are we will be still talking about the Communist Party in power in half-a-century's time, even in a democratic system. If it fails, it may well push the country, the PRC, off course, and send massive shock waves throughout the world. In that sense, the destiny of the Communist Party of China is intimately linked to our own destiny, whichever country we live in.

Chapter One

A History of Violence: The Rise to Power of the CCP

The Japanese are a disease of the skin. Communists are a disease of the heart.

— Chiang Kai-shek (Leader of the KMT)

The rise to power of the Communist Party took almost three decades to achieve. This history is one which is riddled with controversy, counterclaims and a mytholigizing process, meaning that getting back to the real narrative of how the CCP was formed, how it first established its membership, who the earliest and most influential leaders were and how it built up its power base, sometimes proves almost impossible. Even the Party itself, in 1945 and again in 1981, produced solemn Resolutions, trying to spell out to itself and its members what its past had actually been and what it had meant.

Its interaction with the main political competitor for control of China, the Nationalist Party (KMT), with whom it initially shared revolutionary goals, then had bloody fallings out with, and finally had to engage in a battle to the bitter end with (over control of the mainland), has meant that at least some material from the early years of the CCP is available in the more open archives of Taiwan.[1] Even so, key documents and sources of information are, if they are still available, kept under lock and key in the closely guarded archive centre on the outskirts of Beijing. One day, as with the USSR when it fell apart in 1991, the PRC might throw the doors of this resource open. But that hasn't happened yet, and nor is there any sign it will in the foreseeable future.

The rise to power of the Party is intimately linked to the figure of Mao Zedong. He was the victor, in terms of leadership struggles, in 1949. It is hardly surprising, therefore, to find that figures who had influence in the early years were to have their roles reappraised, rewritten, and in many cases either utterly falsified or modified so as to bare no real relationship to reality. Chen Duxiu, Li Dazhao, Wang Ming, Zhang Guotai, and Li Lisan, intellectually, or in terms of leadership, were to have clear, major input into the formation of the Party and its direction during its first decades in existence. But they were to fall on the wrong side of history. Mao, who had initially appeared as merely a side figure, a librarian at Beijing University, and an assistant and adjunct, an activist in the small but hardcore revolutionary base of Hunan, was to monopolize the power to tell the story of the Party for many years after 1949. This process has itself become part of the history of the Party, with many historians and experts both within and outside China in recent years trying to rediscover what happened, before Mao was pre-eminent. They are also gradually putting the pieces together again of how Mao succeeded in gaining ascendancy. Even so, Mao proved to be a genius in identifying himself with the Party and its goals, aspirations and purposes. The Party became his creature, and the fact that he succeeded in leading it to power means that, rightly or wrongly, until very recently, his shadow falls across much of the Party's past.

The Roots of Revolution

In the beginning, before the CCP even came into existence, there was a history of peasant and grassroots rebellion in China. Dynasties had been felled by popular discontent. The Ming (1368–1644) had been founded by a peasant, and ended with the Li Zicheng rebellion, which then precipitated an attack in the Chinese heartland by the northern Chinese Manchu, ethnically different from the predominant Han Chinese. They were, after the Mongolians in the Yuan dynasty

(1240–1368) to be the second non-Han ethnic group to rule the Chinese empire in the millennium leading up to 1911. The Qing dynasty, which the Manchurians founded in 1644, was itself to experience sometimes cataclysmic popular attacks. Its period of aggressive expansionism during the Kangxi reign in the late seventeenth century, leading to the conquest of Mongolia and Xinjiang (the new territories) in the mid-eighteenth century, created tensions and instabilities. A Muslim revolt in the early part of the eighteenth century predated the most savage and damaging of these uprisings, the Taiping Rebellion from 1850, which ran deep into the 1860s and killed over 20 million people out of a population of 350 million. The Taiping had famously been inspired by the quasi-messianic, apocalyptic claims of a failed applicant for the imperial exams that he was the brother of Christ. It raged throughout central China, pulling in 16 of the country's then 18 provinces, lapping at the gates of the newly enlarged city of Shanghai where foreign forces managed to repulse it, taking in a few lucky refugees from the chaos reigning outside the city gates. The Taiping leaders even made themselves a new capital in the city of Nanjing. The Nien, Tungun and Muslim rebellions that occurred around this period only contributed more to the disintegration of centralized state power. The Qing, weakened by this internal struggle, and by increasingly predatory and aggressive foreign intervention, was to feel the force of grassroots rebellion again, in 1900, when the Boxers, linked to an esoteric cult, turned on foreigners, brutally killing some of them. This reignited tensions with European and North American governments, resulting in swift military retaliation and equally brutal financial reparations. Half a century after many had predicted it, the Qing fell, over two messy years from 1911 to 1912. From this period forward, China was engaged in a battle to maintain some sort of unity, and to rebuild itself – a battle, the painful outcome of which was, 40 years later, after war, famine and devastation, the imposition of unity by the Communists.

Chinese Power Structures

Peasant rebellion has figured in Chinese history for centuries. But there are two key elements in understanding this counter-history of revolt. The first is the longstanding attempts to reform China's political model. And the second, and equally important, is the creation of the Chinese geographical and political entity as it exists today. Both of these involved complex historical processes. Both of them explain some of the context in which the CCP was created, and which partly it worked with and benefited from, and partly viewed itself as a solution to.

Explanations for the power system in China, and its historic genealogy, are manifold. A political culture which can put the sort of resources into constructing assets like the Great Wall (or at least the Ming Great Wall) betray a high level of absolutism and centralization. Scholars of China are fond of pointing out that the semi-mythical first emperor in the third century BC, Qin Shihuangdi, was to unify a Chinese nation, and then effectively bankrupt and destroy it with massive projects, in only three generations. Speculation over the decades has tried to understand the proclivity for highly centralized and hierarchical power structures in China by looking at both the need to have a strong unified political centre to deal with problems of water management (Karl Wittfogel in his *Oriental Despotism*, Oxford: Oxford University Press 1957, to take the most celebrated example) to blaming the civil service which grew up in the Tang and Song periods from the fifth century onward and which created a self-interested cadre of advisors and officials running a highly bureaucratic government. The longevity and robustness of these top-heavy power structures discernible in previous dynasties, and passing down almost seamlessly into the PRC, is striking. Just as China was largely to avoid the early processes of industrialization in the eighteenth and nineteenth centuries, so was it to only flirt with political reform. As Britain, France, and then most of Europe was to undergo various kinds of revolutions and power transitions from elites to more diverse new classes from the seventeenth century onward, Qing China rigidly maintained its political system, introducing superficial reforms, fighting to the death any attempts to dilute or compromise its central government's authority. As in the past with the ending of other dynasties, such brittle power meant that regime change was all or nothing. There was no gradual evolution or transition. Dynasties were blown away in a matter of months or years, leaving only a stain, and the same power structures, behind.

Attempts to strive for something different in China have deep roots. As far back as the late Song period a thousand years before, Ouyang Xiu, a major neo-Confucian intellectual, had been part of the Minor Reforms period from 1043–45. He had agitated with other scholars to strengthen governance and allow for opposition to be heard and not immediately castigated as insidious and inherently bad. This was unsuccessful. 'Loyal opposition,' as the historian of Imperial China, F. W. Mote has said, 'could not be acknowledged within a system of politics defined by ethical and personal rather than operational and institutional norms. China still struggles with the heritage of this eleventh century political failure.'[2] Legalists, and idealists, had contributed ideas for devising a new political system in China, where power was more diluted, right up to the end of the Qing. But the reigns of emperors were usually successful or unsuccessful, and China prosperous or not, according to the abilities of the person occupying the position at the top. Qing China was lucky in the eighteenth century to enjoy the long reigns of three exceptional leaders, the Kangxi, Yongzheng, and Qianlong emperors. The dynasty even forbade the formation of elite political organizations in 1651, only a few years after taking power. But its political stagnation was to start with the arrival of less gifted beings. The real rot set in with a series of fundamentally weak, compromised figures under the shadowy control of the infamous empress dowager, Ci Xi, from the 1870s onward. Her reactionary and conservative attitude meant that even when the opportunity for reform came, in the 1890s, towards the end of what was called the Self Regeneration Movement, bringing with it the chance to perhaps extend the dynasty's lease of life, it was not taken.

China historian Ray Huang of Cambridge, in his book about the Wang Li emperor in the Ming period, captures this element of the political straightjacketing of the imperial throne, and the stasis around it well.[3] Wang Li, who was to reign for over 40 years, was to withdraw into a cocoon, obsessed by a young concubine, literally, according to Huang's colourful account, disappearing into his own little world, regarding the structures and apparatus of authority around him with indifference, almost as though it had nothing to do with him. A tight bureaucracy ran things, on a day-to-day basis, and the rest of the China that existed then survived largely on local power structures. The emperor was impossibly remote, his powers negative, working within endless unwritten conventions and rules.

> [Wang Li] was too intelligent and sensitive to occupy the dragon throne. The more he gained an insight into its apparatus, the more sceptical he became. He began to realise that he was less the Ruler of All Men than a prisoner of the Forbidden City. His power was basically negative. He would remove or punish an official or a group of officials, but he could hardly promote a favourite or grant him an unusual request... Was the benefit of occupying the imperial throne worth so many restrictions? He had no say in deciding that either. He had become the Son of Heaven by birth, not choice.[4]

According to Immanuel Hsu's account, the emperor later in the Qing period 'decided all important state policies, made appointments, conferred titles, approved promotions, demotions and dismissals, awarded pensions, commanded the army, and ratified treaties... As the supreme legislator he enacted, annulled, and amended laws by decrees and edicts. Judicially, he was the highest court of appeal.' As if this were not enough, he was also a religious head, and the main sponsor for education and culture.[5] Such intense concentration of power in the hands of very few continues to haunt the Chinese body politic to this day.

Running beside this is the issue of how China was created, and the growth and evolution of the country over which this system of power was exercised. The shapes and territories of China prior to the one created in 1949 were radically different. The Yuan dynasty, once it had been founded, was to explode over a territory so vast it was to prove politically impossible to maintain for more than a few decades. Consolidation over a more manageable territory under the Ming was to precede the expansionist early era of the Qing, in which territories like the Northwest (now largely Xinjiang, conquered in 1759), Mongolia (conquered from 1685 to 1696), and Tibet (brought into a complex tribute relationship with China) were pulled into the sphere of influence of the Qing government. By the nineteenth century, the contours of the modern PRC are already clear – a territory that, with the addition of Tibetan and other border territories, was almost the size of Europe. After 1949 the PRC was simply to reassert and formalize control over these areas, upgrading some 'areas of special influence' into full sovereignty.[6]

The complexity and potential disunity that lurks beneath this superficial unity is ignored at any commentator's peril. US sinologist, the late John K. Fairbank and others in the introduction to the *Cambridge History of China* talk of the difficulty of treating

China as a unitary entity. 'The old notion of "China's cultural differentness" from the outside world, though it still strikes the traveller, is becoming fragmented by the variety of sub-cultures to be found within China.'[7] The period of expansion under the Qing, which in effect created most of the entity we now call China, was to embrace such a range of cultures and territories that it is entirely legitimate to ask whether there was really any meaningful political system or sense of nationhood that could mesh all this together. For the last two centuries, therefore, China has not only been battling with modernization and political reform, but also with the creation of a meaningful concept of nationhood that its highly complex and vast population can all feel they belong to and sign up for. This challenge remains up to the present day, and is the source for the anxiety that lurks behind many of the demands for allegiance that the CCP makes of its disparate territories. The CCP, as the party in power, were the re-creators and are now the custodians of this unity. They, more than any others, are aware of the fragility and vulnerability behind all this.

Intellectual and Political Roots of the CCP

The CCP was founded in the context of international conflict, and national breakdown. The first decade of the Republic Period, after the collapse of the Qing, had been chaotic – with a popular, but highly flawed election held in 1912, only for the victor to be assassinated, and the rise to power of northern Chinese leader Yuan Shikai after the brief presidency of Sun Yat-sen in 1912. Yuan was to declare himself President in 1915, but he was forced to resign before dying in 1916. Attempts to set up new structures of power embodied in a legislative council were accompanied by the continuing efforts to introduce industralization, at least along some of the coastal cities and in Canton (Guangdong). China was also an ally of the US and the UK during the First World War. But the granting of former German interests in Northeast China to the Japanese during the Treaty of Versailles in 1919 resulted in one of the seminal events in modern Chinese history, the May 4 Movement, in which students were to go out on the streets in Beijing and other cities and demand fairer treatment, and urgent political reform. Their catchphrase of wanting 'Mr Democracy and Mr Science' was to echo through the following decades. They would not have known what trauma and tragedy was to await them in the coming years, before only a small part of these reforms were ever introduced. Accompanying this was the New Culture Movement, introducing ideas into China from the industrialized West. Republican China has had a bad press. But as sociologist and historian Frank Dikotter has argued, this era marked down as the period of warlordism, banditry and instability 'might very well be qualified as a golden age of engagement with the world'.[8]

The foundation of the USSR in 1917, after the October Revolution, was to have a profound impact, not least because from this period the new leaders in the Soviet Union started to look for the signs of an international communist movement in other countries. China, because of its urgent need for reform, struck them as a major contender, especially in view of the decision taken at the Second Congress of the International in 1920 in Moscow that, as with other non-emancipated countries, the conditions for revolution in China were good and needed to be supported.[9] The relationship between the Soviet Union and China from this period on was to be a key one, right till the fall of the USSR, over 70 years later. Good or bad, the USSR was to be a critical player in the shaping and direction of the destiny of China, and in the opening years of the CCP as it grew powerful. Many argue that without its financial and political support the CCP would never have succeeded. Comintern Agent Gregory Voitinsky was to visit China in 1920 and finance the immediate precursor to the Communist Movement there, the Socialist Youth Corps. From these seeds, the Chinese communist movement grew.

There is passionate argument to this day about how Marxism was introduced into China. There were certainly young intellectuals who went to study in the USSR from the late 1910's onward. Zhou Enlai, Kang Sheng, Chen Boda, and others who were key in shaping the CCP later on were all students in Moscow. Some of Marx's works (albeit only a few) were translated from Russian or German into Chinese around this time and it was via this route at least, that they came to the interest of monolinguists like Mao.[10] Even so, Japanese scholar Ishikawa, in his study of the foundation of the CCP, has made a case for Marxism also being transmitted via overseas students from China based in Japan, of which there were many (including, again, Zhou Enlai, although, to be fair, he also studied or lived in Germany and France and visited Russia, before his conversion to Communism in 1922).[11] Marxism came, it is certain, at a time when there was a widespread interest in outside ideas and an anxiety to do something about China's perceived plight. Visitors to cosmopolitan centres like Shanghai in the 1920s included British philosopher Bertrand Russell (whose lectures, translated into Chinese, the young Mao Zedong read), American educationalist and philosopher John Dewey and even Albert Einstein. Waves of young Chinese intellectuals went, in the first great period of internationalization, to Europe, the US and Japan. In 1917 in France alone there were 150,000 overseas Chinese students. They could not have imagined that the intellectual import that would have most impact on the course of modern Chinese history, Marxism, was to be the product of a man who spent most of his life in Britain, writing about the impact of industrialization on its social system. Marx was to barely mention economic conditions in China, although he was to view the Taiping Rebellion as offering new possibilities for peasant revolutions.[12]

The early activists of the CCP were to be acutely aware that from the more purist perspective, Republican China fitted none of the Marxist templates. It was an overwhelmingly agrarian society, with only the vaguest hints of industrialization in cities like Shanghai. By 1921, it had barely two million who could be classified as proletariat workers, out of the population pushing towards 400 million.[13] This had risen from a mere 100,000 in 1894, only increasing to a million at the start of the First World War in 1914.[14] To explain how a workers revolution could be conducted here would be one of the major challenges for Chinese Marxists over the next few years. Mao's (and, to be fair, that of other's) success, in the end, is partly due to simply sidestepping the whole issue by claiming that the forces for revolution were in the countryside. This radical reinterpretation was to be the most significant contribution to the development of Marxism-Leninism claimed for Mao. It was also, of course, utterly heretical and deeply threatening to the USSR, and lay at the heart of many of his later, bitter arguments with the Soviet Union. But it was also his trump card. Had China waited to build up a proper proletarian class, it would still be waiting for its revolution.

Year Zero – the First Congress

Institutionally, and as a formal entity, the Communist Party of China started to exist from its First Congress in Shanghai, held from 23 July to 31 July 1921. Those that make their way to this sacred place in CCP history are rewarded today with the sight of a small, well-restored red-bricked house on the edges of the successfully renovated Xintiandi (New Heaven and Earth) area. They are only a few hundred metres from the People's Square, where the modern City Hall stands looking over a vast space, the 2000 skyscrapers of Shanghai crowded around. The current Party headquarters, in the second most important city in the country, is a vast, palatial and highly exclusive enclave. Those that look to explore where all this started are waived their three yuan entrance fee and ushered into a tiny room on the ground floor with a table, a lamp, a few chairs and a window looking out on what would once have been the street, but is now a white painted wall.

The Site of the First National Congress of the CCP was, after being made a national historic monument in 1964, anointed by calligraphy from 1980s paramount leader, Deng Xiaoping, and the President of China till 2002, Jiang Zemin. A large marble hall leads up to the entrance of the older buildings, with exhibition rooms plotting out the historical buildup to what was to prove one of the most momentous, but at the time subdued, events in modern Chinese history. Hanging on the wall are pictures of the British in 1842, sitting over the Chinese on a boat, as they are about to sign the first of what became called the unequal treaties: the Treaty of Nanjing. This stipulated the handing over of Hong Kong Island; and the opening of their markets for the first time to the outside world on terms the Chinese utterly opposed but had to endure. There are weapons and whips in a display case that the caption says were used by foreign police against Chinese in the British and French concessions in Shanghai. In one room is the facsimile of the document that the Congress passed, on its last day. They had been forced by this point to meet aboard a pleasure boat on the south lake in Jiaxing, in neighbouring Zhejiang province because the police in the French Concession had broken in and searched the Shanghai house. This document formally founds the CCP, acknowledging that 'the revolutionary army and the proletariat are unified, working to end the power of the capitalists, and the assist the workers in their struggle to create socialism.'

In one of the final exhibition rooms of the museum created to celebrate the founding of the CCP are wax models of those who were present at the first Congress, as it moved from Shanghai to Zheijiang. Mao Zedong, unsurprisingly, is shown standing above the other attendees, expounding from a sheaf of papers held in his hand. This was to be an iconic pose of leadership that was to reappear during the most intense period of the worship of him, the Cultural Revolution almost half a century later. Contemporary accounts show that Mao played no such seminal role in the early foundation of the Party, but attended as a representative of the Communist Movement in his native Hunan province. Of those thirteen that attended, representing barely 53 members, they were to share widely divergent and often tragic fates. He Shuheng was killed in Shanghai in 1935. Chen Tanqiu was murdered in prison in Xinjiang in 1943. Wang Jinmei died of illness aged only 27 in Qingdao in 1925. Deng Enming was executed by the Nationalists in 1931. Li Da was to die in suspicious circumstances at the start of the Cultural Revolution in 1966. Li Hanjun was killed in 1927. Chen Gongbo was executed in 1946 after claims he had become a traitor for the Japanese. Similarly accused of treason, Zhou Fohai died in prison in 1948.

Dong Biwu, Zhang Guotao, Liu Renjing and Bao Huiseng were to at least live longer. Dong was to prove himself one of the great survivors of the CCP, rising to become Acting President of the PRC before his death, only a year before Mao, in 1975. Expelled during the legendry Long March in 1934–35, Zhang was to flee to Canada where he died in 1979. Liu, expelled early on for being a Trotskyite, was to live till 1987, working for many years as a translator in Beijing. Bao, who resigned from the Party in 1927, was to be maintained as a State Councillor from 1949, and die in 1979. Mao, of course, rose to great and glorious things, and died in 1976, at the age of 83.

There were two others present at the first congress, a Dutchman called Maring (real name Henk Sneevliet), and a Russian called Nikolsky. Both of them died in the early 1940s, Maring shot by the Germans in Amsterdam in 1943 for being a Communist activist and Nikolsky as one of Stalin's many victims. The presence of these two indicates that at its founding the CCP was part of an international movement, and these international links, especially with the USSR, were an integral part of what it did and why it came into being.

To found a communist party in China, therefore, did not serve the health well of most of the members who attended that day. The political movement at whose birth they were all present, and which they helped bring into the world, was to repay many of them savagely. This was to be the pattern of the Party into the future. For while it expected fearsome dedication to its cause, it was merciless in its treatment of those it deemed to have erred. It is indeed ironic that the man who would prove to be one of its greatest persecutors, Mao Zedong, was also the one who brought it to power. But this lies in the story of the following five decades. There is one other common denominator for these individuals. They were all intellectuals. While they could look at the complex social changes around them, their backgrounds were typified by the two most famous leaders of the early Communist period: Chen Duxiu, head of the Party once it was set up, though himself not in attendance at the First Congress as he was formally then head of education in Guangdong province; and Li Dazhao, the first CCP leader based in Beijing and its most effective early propagandist, executed in 1927 during the first onslaught by the KMT. Both, though from different social backgrounds, were university professors. Both had spent time in Japan. Chen was to be the first to translate the full 'Communist Manifesto' into Chinese in the late 1910s, a document which was to be widely disseminated in the decade to follow. Both were keenly engaged, as polemicists and writers, in the intellectual debates about where China should go, from the 4 May 1919 movement onward, setting up small Marxist study groups. But they were also only parts of a complex initial moment of revolutionary activity, which stretched across China (Chongqing, according to van de Ven, had a party cell active in 1920 with 40 full, and 60 candidate members) .[15] The full of effect of the 1921 congress was to pull this disparate activity together. But it was to take many more years before the CCP had a truly unified front, and a single leadership.

The First Period – Growing Up Side by Side with the Nationalists

In its early period, the Party existed in an environment in which there was intense competition and intellectual ferment, both about the direction China should take, and how it should shape its national consciousness and identity and engage with the rest of the world. Throughout this period, it became increasingly clear that its chief ideological and political competitor was to be the Nationalists, founded originally by Sun Yat-sen, and then, from the mid-1920s onwards, increasingly shaped by the idiosyncratic, but highly effective rule of Chiang Kai-shek. Sun Yat-sen (1866–1925) was the most prominent influence in this period. A medical doctor born in Guangdong, he had lived in the US (he had an American passport), Japan and Hong Kong (where he had been baptized as a Christian) before returning to China in the 1890s where he was peripherally involved in the ill-fated moves led by reformers Kang Youwei and Liang Qichao to develop the Qing into a constitutional monarchy. Over this period he formulated his Three Principles of the People (democracy, nationalism and people's welfare), promoting these ideas in the years afterwards while based in the US, UK and then back in Japan. He was not even present in China to see the final demise of the Qing in 1911–12, an event precipitated by a military uprising. Returning soon afterwards, he was President of Republican China for only four months in 1912. The almost immediate fragmentation of China between north and south meant that as part of a unifying deal, he was to step aside. But his arguments were to have resonance for both the Nationalist Party, which he later founded, and the Communists, who were to bow to his principles and claim that he figured as an early revolutionary in the buildup to their own play for power.

Sun adopted a position of guided democracy. The Chinese people were currently not ready for full universal franchise. They were too backward and undeveloped. They needed to have strong government to take them towards this position. Sun compared democratic evolution in China to the tide of the Yangtze. 'Nothing can stop it,' he said. But in one moment of qualification, he also stated that 'just as the Yangtze makes crooks and turns, sometimes to the north, and sometimes to the south', so would China only reach democracy after a long, hard journey.[16] For years in the 1920s until his death he was involved in the attempts to unify south and north China, in the Northern Expedition. On this project, he was willing to take the USSR's counsel and work with the CCP. During the so-called KMT Reorganization Committee held in early 1924, the KMT adopted three new policies: Alliance with the Soviet Union, support for workers and peasants movements and, most fatefully, collaboration with the CCP. The collaboration was even to allow full, joint membership for CCP members of the KMT. Unified, the new United Front set out to conquer all of China in 1926, ushering in, through the success of its military operations against the War Lords who had been controlling large parts of China, the era of unified Nationalist Government.

Sun's premature death in 1925 meant that, like Lenin in the USSR, he exited before his influence could have reached its maximum. His legacy was to prove a battleground for future Chinese politicians. But the initial victor in this was the leader of the KMT military wing, Chiang Kai-shek, a native of Zhejiang province neighbouring Shanghai, and a former leader of the Whampao Military Academy set up by the Nationalists (another term for the KMT) in concert with the Communists to improve their discipline and military performance as part of the Northern Expedition. He was to ultimately win in a fight for the control of the KMT with Wang Jingwei. From 1927, he was the most influential political and military figure in China till the end of the Second World War, almost two decades later.

Chiang's impact on Chinese history in the twentieth century, and on the Communist Party, was to rank second only to Mao. In the last two decades in Mainland China, his reputation has risen again. Mao may have talked of the KMT as 'a bunch of bandits' but he always referred to the Generalissimo, as he was called by contemporaries, with respect. Chiang's political skills were to carry China through murderous decades. He stands responsible for the deaths of millions of his own compatriots. But he made the brutal choices in the 1930s to fight with the Communists against the Japanese, a war that nearly fundamentally destroyed China and, had the Japanese succeeded, would have carved the country up, possibly leaving it permanently fragmented.

The political patchwork of small kingdoms and warlord territories that China became in the 1920s was perhaps the most humiliating moment in its post-dynastic history. In the north, from late in the decade, the Japanese exerted greater and greater influence, despite signs that there was an intense debate within Japan about how much further, and how useful, this extension of their zone of influence was. In Western China, and the South West, the provinces of Sichuan, Gansu, Shanxi and Yunnan were run almost as separate entities. China was in a bad way.

Looking at the parallel development of the Communists and KMT during this period, it is easy to get confused about their identity because of the extent to which they were intermixed and intertwined with each other. Their preoccupations and challenges snake around and in and out of each other. Often there was joint membership of both organizations. In 1922, under the influence of one of the foreign attendees of the First Congress and Comintern advisor Maring, Party members were asked simply to join the KMT, which was viewed as having a stronger base and better organization, and to transform it from the inside. This was a move that was opposed by many of the Chinese in the Party at that time. But from 1924 to 1927 the CCP was simply incorporated into the KMT. The ruling Council of the KMT even had known and declared CCP members. Perhaps this indicated with what low regard Moscow looked upon their Chinese comrades.

The KMT was much stronger and, after the deployment of Chiang's brutal skills, it became more unified, effectively serving as the predominant government of China from 1927. Even so, as Mao was to sourly note many years later when, as Chairman of the CCP and clear supreme leader of the PRC in 1971, he was to meet the first Japanese Prime Minister to come to China; the Japanese attacks at least achieved what everything else had failed to – bringing about a painful unity of China's fractious provincial leaders and its two main national parties. Only the violent jolt of the 1927 purge of the Communists, where thousands of Party members were killed in Shanghai, started to place clear water between the two groups and make it obvious that, in the end, not only were they were after different final objectives, but they were fundamentally enemies.

Congresses and Comrades

National Congresses were to be key elements in CCP organization and the development of its political structures. For the last nine decades, ever since the Party was formally founded in 1921, the Congresses have been one of the main occasions through which leaderships have been formalized and important decisions made, or, at least in more recent decades, ratified. The two great exceptions to this are the period 1928 to 1945, when war and conflict interrupted, and the era of high Maoism, from 1956 to 1969, when Congresses, like most other elements of Party institutionalization, were jettisoned in favour of informal power clustered around the Chairman.

Looking at the Congresses held from 1922 onward gives an indication of the growth of the CCP, and its chief strategies and preoccupations. The Second Congress, held in Shanghai in 1922, almost exactly a year after its foundation, proposed anticolonialism and antifeudalism as cornerstones of its ideology. There were only 195 members to represent, with 12 voting delegates. The Third Congress, in June 1923, in Guangzhou, agreed to the fateful unified front with the KMT, largely through the prompting of Maring, who, as with the First Congress, attended as representative of the Comintern. It was at this congress that Mao Zedong was first voted onto the Central Committee, which was to serve, in effect, as the management committee of the CCP in the years ahead. The Fourth, back in Shanghai, over January 1925, was the first to talk of leadership of the proletariat, and of the unity of agricultural and factory workers, trying to extend its constituency beyond Shanghai and Guangzhou and looking to harness the rising power of the trade unions that had been established in other cities. The Fifth, in Wuhan in April 1927, just before the first dark night of the soul of the Party, set out the principles of this proposed rural revolution, and started looking more seriously at recruitment in the countryside. By this time, Party membership had risen to 57,967. Much of this had been prompted by the May 30th Movement in 1925, a series of demonstrations and uprisings provoked by the killing of ten demonstrators by police in Shanghai. As a result of the indignation created by this event, 10,000 joined the Party. But it was from this point that fractures began to appear in the leadership, a problem that would persist deep into the next decade, with arguments over how close it was necessary to stick to the USSR, and how appropriate its strategies were for conditions in China. The Sixth Congress shifted to Moscow (the only one till his death that Mao did not attend), where it was held June 1928, licking its wounds and reflecting on near annihilation after the onslaught by the KMT the year before. This was the first congress in which 'full' and 'alternate' membership of the leadership structure was adopted, something that has been maintained till today. It was to be another 17 years before the Congress would be held again, at Yenan in Shaanxi, the revolutionary base. But by this time the very nature and leadership structure of the CCP had changed beyond recognition.[17] Its membership had also boomed to 1.2 million members. And by this Congress, Mao Zedong ruled supreme and his era can be said to have truly begun.

For the first five Congresses, Chen Duxiu had been in clear leadership positions. The massacre of Shanghai CCP members in 1927, however, caused a backlash against his cerebral style of leadership. From 1928 onward, throughout the period of the Sixth Congress, a series of leaders held control before, in the late 1930s and into the 1940s, the power was finally distilled into Mao Zedong's hands. The brief tenure of Qu Qiubai in 1927 led to a three-year leadership under Xiang Zhongfa, with both Li Lisan and Wang Ming acting as General Secretary in the early 1930s, a symbol of the disunity reigning in the Party. Formally, the General Secretary up to 1943 was Zhang Wentian. But by the mid-1930s it was clear that Mao was the most influential and powerful. In 1943 this was institutionalized by the creation of the Party Chairmanship, a position that he was to occupy till his death in 1976, something that became so identified with him that, after the rather lacklustre occupancy by Hua Guofeng and then Hu Yaobang, it was simply abolished in 1982.

The great watershed of this period was the turning of the KMT on the Communists, after their initial period of unified action, and the shift the CCP had then to make, to survive, towards becoming a more militarized, and more ruthless, political force. Chiang had hinted at his desire to deal with the Communists, whose ideology he detested, long before the period in 1927 when he decided they should be expelled from the KMT and their main activists eradicated. Communist actions like the Canton Commune in December 1927 only confirmed Chiang's conviction that the CCP was after totally different ends. In a brutal period on 12 April 1927, Communists were massacred in Shanghai. Many had to flee underground. When some of the CCP leadership washed up in Moscow a year later, they were at a crossroads. Those that had survived had to contemplate either becoming ex-members of a movement that would soon be overtaken by history, a temporary political aberration that would quickly be forgotten, or trying to forge a new identity for themselves.

At least some of their Russian advisors had surprising faith, despite this massive setback, that they were on the right side of history and would prevail. Borodin, who had managed to flee China after the attacks, told a journalist that the CCP 'will go underground. It will become an illegal movement, suppressed by counter-revolution and beaten down by reaction and imperialism; but two years, five years from now, it will rise to the surface again. It may be defeated a dozen times, but in the end it must conquer…'[18]

The options facing the Party in 1927–28 were stark. But it made one critical decision that was to stand it in good stead for the decades ahead. It committed itself finally to violent revolution. This was no more than facing the political reality of a country as severely divided and dysfunctional as Republican China had become. It had grown to a membership of nearly 60,000 in 1927, from a mere 130 in 1922. It could suffer losses. As historian of the Party Jerome Chen put it, 'In any case, the situation in July and August 1927 was inevitable – the CCP had to have an army, a territory and a government. In other words, it had to make a state within a state.'[19] This it proceeded to do over the ensuing decade and a half. Some violence had figured in CCP strategy before this time. But it had been low-key, led by intellectuals who were more used to pondering cause and effect in their studies rather than looking at revolts on the ground. One aspect of Mao's genius was his true understanding of the role of violence and its deployment for political ends. His willingness to use this with few, if any, qualms also marked him out as exceptional.

The CCP's strategy from 1921 till the end of the first united front in 1927 had been to work with partners – to improve its membership and to get assistance and discipline. It did survive, just. But the cost had been that, from 1922, the CCP was, in effect, a branch of the Communist International with heavy direction and involvement from Moscow, the leadership of the Party being largely subservient to Moscow representative Pavel Mif. By 1928 the CCP's membership was rural. It had been swept from the cities. It became disunited, and went through a number of years in the wilderness. But it was in this period that it laid the foundations to becoming the tough, surviving and ruthless machine for political influence and power that lay in the future. The years 1927 to 1933 may well figure as the dark ages of the Party, where, even today, little is clear. But it was also the seminal moment when the CCP started to prove it could one day lead and be victorious. To compound its external problems, from 1930 to 1931, the CCP did not even have a unified leadership, finding itself instead under the direction of what came to be called the '28 Bolsheviks', a disparate group of individuals, most of them returnees from Moscow, carrying the authority of the Soviet Union's support, all of whom worked in a messy coalition without any particularly prominent individual, causing drift and slippage.

Revolution from the Countryside

The shift from power based in cities, where it was assumed the natural basis for a communist movement was, to the countryside was a crucial move, much of it down to Mao, who disagreed with both the Soviet advisors, and the mainstream of Party leadership led by figures like Chen Duxiu. In the late 1920s he had stated:

> In a very short time, in China's central, southern and northern provinces, several hundred million peasants will rise like a mighty storm, like a hurricane, a force so swift and violent that no power, however great, will be able to hold it back… there are three alternatives, to march at their head and lead them? To trail behind them, gesticulating and criticizing? Or stand in their way and oppose them? Every Chinese is free to choose, but events will force you to make the choice quickly.[20]

Mao had evidently already made his own choice. It was clear from membership drives that the CCP was popular, or at least more effective and more likely to survive, in the countryside. And despite orders from the Communist International to be harder on rich peasants, the strategic decision was made to create a number of isolated bases of revolutionary activity (soviets), rather than concentrate in the main cities. With the founding of the Red Army in 1927, the CCP now had the organizational structure to expand and develop. Its army was given orders to recruit from rural areas, which extended its franchise and support networks there. Disparate Soviets were established across China. Mao Zedong headed the Jiangxi Soviet in central China, eventually even having the temerity to be elected President there. For the first half of the 1930s, Chang Kai-shek's armies sought to eradicate the pockets of

Communist resistance. Extermination campaigns were waged with, initially, limited success. Armies were poured into areas, surrounding Communist groups, simply attempting to squeeze them of life and manoeuvrable area. The final such campaign in 1934–35 was to be successful, causing the Communists to up sticks completely and embark on a long journey to their eventual resting place in central Shaanxi province, at Yan'an. In this period, the Communists inhabited some of the starkest, least productive land in China. This was to be the incubator for their form of rule. They inhabited a political shadow land, operating with guerrilla tactics, simply aiming to survive. This was to leave a deep, and at times, traumatic stain on their collective memory, shaping the way that they ruled after 1949.

It was also to lead to the creation of powerful revolutionary myths, which were to shape the Party's consciousness of itself, its mission and its history for decades to come. The Central Committee had met in August 1927, and issued orders that the Party go underground. The deal with the KMT was self-evidently off. Mao's first base was in the Jinggangshan Mountains area, hard to penetrate and operate in. But it was here, fatefully, that he was joined by one of the other 'communion of saints', leaders from the early period of the CCP that were to last through to the 1970s, Zhu De, who brought a small military force with him. Mao compared their meeting together (betraying his aspirations as a poet) to the famous 'Water Margin' tales of banditry from classical Chinese. A failed semi-military action on the border of Hunan and Jiangxi provinces called the Autumn Harvest Uprising caused Mao and those around him to retreat deeper into isolated regions in Jiangxi from Jingganshan.

A History of Violence

One issue that the CCP Soviet governments did seek to address was land reform. Wherever they were based, they looked to unlock what was seen as the unfair distribution of land ownership in the countryside, where peasant farmers were crushed under both huge rents and unfair leasing arrangements. The first of a series of land reform campaigns was carried out in the late 1920s. Well intended at the start, they were to transform quickly into eras of stress and terror – afterwards labelled the first of the Red Terror campaigns.

The problem with offering an honest and comprehensive account of CCP history even up to the present day is perhaps due to this intimate link between violence and the coming to power of the Party. Mao, however, seemed unafraid of openly admitting this. In his famous phrase that 'power grew from the barrel of a gun' he simply confirmed what most knew – that before getting violent, the CCP was getting nowhere. The strategic deployment of violence was one of their strongest cards. His phrase has been interpreted in China at least as an admission that the CCP needed a military arm, and that the Red Army, after it was founded, was a key institution to be supported by, not support. The Party had to remain pre-eminent. But this was less palatable when it was clearly used against its main constituency – peasants, and Party members. The KMT were viewed as the murderers. The CCP was, after 1949, always portrayed as the good guys. In reality, however the CCP was often fighting, literally and figuratively, for their lives, and all too often they were slaughtering each other.

Historian Hans van de Ven has written extensively about this period. He has looked in particular at what evidence there is for how the Communists behaved from 1931 to 1934. Mao had talked of people's warfare, but it is forgotten how much war was waged upon people by the CCP. The Red Terror and mobilization campaign from 1931 to 1934 represented the extreme of this. Purges of those with claimed links or sympathies to the KMT (not that hard to prove in view of the fact that only four years earlier, both sides had been working closely together), along with a perceived need to toughen the Party and widen its support base, led to the use of terror tactics. These were, as van de Ven says 'an expression of the extreme paranoia that gripped the Chinese Communists as they came under attack, but was used purposefully as a device to secure military and political discipline and, of course, in internal CCP politics, to do battle in the internal struggle for power'.[21] Mao Zedong himself had said, 'War, this vile monster of mutual slaughter, will finally be eliminated by the progress of human society. But there is only one way to eliminate it and that is to oppose war with war, to oppose counter-revolutionary war with revolutionary war.'[22] One way or the other, there would be bloodshed, whatever the outcome.

A big recruitment campaign for the Red Army in 1933 saw almost 30,000 new members by the end of June.[23] A raft of new mass organizations was set up to gain yet more new members, ranging from the Workers Army to the Young Communist International Army. The army was brought deeper and deeper into economic and social life in the areas under Communist control. Purges and these mobilizations resulted in growing antagonism to Communist rule. Purges continued in the Party, even on the eve of the moment of greatest threat, the all-out attack by the KMT, on Chiang's orders, on the Communists, leading to their enforced march to a new base throughout 1934 and 1935. [24]

Violence was integral to how the Communists operated during this period. 'The Communists relied on the often brutal discipline of the Party to control organized local violence.' [25] History was to repeat itself a number of times over the coming decades, even when the Party tried to make the evolution from a group that waged revolution to the organizer of government. The mass purges in the 1950s and 1960s were all prefigured in these early movements, where tens of thousands of Party members and activists perished or were abandoned. As van de Ven rightly says, 'They derived from a revolutionary mindset that justified such campaigns as necessary to secure the project of the redemption of China, as well as to obtain military and political discipline, believed necessary to firm up the Party's control of the forces of history, whose outcomes, it believed, they understood.'[26]

Mao's role in pushing the Party in this direction is undeniable. After the threat posed by leaders like Li Lisan, a sophisticated and urbane Russian-educated intellectual, and Wang Ming, Mao, who had never spent any time abroad and was the most provincial of all the early leaders, was to rise to the top. Zhang Wentian's opposition in 1935 was to be as short lived as the others. By the end of the Long March, an event that has a number of question marks hovering over it about what actually happened, Mao was the dominant leader. Even so, he was to take many more years to build up the levels of authoritarianism needed for his actions after 1949. Attacked and criticized as a monster for what he did in the 1930s, it should be remembered that he was operating in a society with phenomenally high levels of violence, where there were powerful political forces that wanted his, and his Party's, annihilation. His masterly exploitation of peasant unrest and dissatisfaction with the KMT government, helping to shape and form its objectives, was to serve him well. Describing him as a sadistic monster doesn't help in understanding this process. Mao was interested only in the role of violence in order to fulfil specific political ends. He was inhumane, and uniquely blind to the impact of his decisions on the society and people around him, but, like Hitler, he sincerely believed that the ends justified these means. And in the end, in leading the CCP in its fight to achieve liberation for China from the Japanese, and then from the corrupt and exhausted KMT, he could offer powerful evidence for his leadership's success, even if many others contributed to this epic struggle. [27]

Mao also achieved something else. His grasp of Marxist-Leninist theory was basic and shaky, as anyone trawling through his sporadically brilliant writings sees clearly. But his ability to apply this ideology to the circumstances of rural China, the China that needed to be carried to make the revolution successful, was phenomenal. After the many years in which the CCP was the child of the USSR-led Communist International, and in which the KMT was to constantly question which master the CCP really served, China or the USSR, Mao was to link the aims of the CCP with national liberation, and national greatness. He was, in that sense, to prove British Prime Minister Clement Attlee's adage that if you ever scratch a communist you will find a nationalist underneath. Mao's nationalist credentials were undeniable. The CCP's skilful manipulation of Chinese nationalism has remained one of its greatest talents even to the present.

At the end of the Long March and the consolidation of Mao's position as the most influential and powerful figure in the Party, events which had been shaping for most of the previous decade came to overwhelm China, and push the Communists into the arms of the KMT again. The Sino–Japanese war, one of the most terrible in modern history, which resulted in over 20 million Chinese deaths and the displacement of perhaps ten times as many people, had been building up since 1931. By 1937, clear policy decisions were made by an increasingly militaristic government in Tokyo to resolve the issue of China, and unleash an all-out attack. From 1937 to 1945, China was dominated by this conflict. The CCP in many ways had seen war as inevitable and had laid their plans accordingly. But despite now being the most important and powerful leader in China and having almost reunified the country, Chiang Kai-shek was to be made to compromise once more, and to make a further pact with the party he regarded as fundamentally bad.

'A Good War'?

It sounds wrong to say that the 1937–45 war was a good war for the Communists. But many years later, Mao was to admit that without this devastating outside attack, the CCP might never have been able to unify, and recruit, the massive numbers it started to attract after 1937. Nor, for that matter, would the KMT have been so exhausted and weakened that after 1945 it was possible to bring it down and defeat it in civil war. As General Jacques Guillermaz says in his *A History of the Chinese Communist Party*, 'The deplorable policies of the Japanese… were to save the Communist Party.'[28]

Even during the war years, the united front between the Communists and the KMT was never as unified as it appeared. In many areas, the KMT infiltrated and worked against the CCP. In 1941 the unity almost stopped permanently. But while the bulk of the fighting against the Japanese was done by the KMT, the communists were to perform well on the battlefield, their tactics and guerrilla strategy effective in areas that the Japanese were never able to match. With the formation in 1937 of the Eighth Route Army and the New Fourth Army, the CCP was to pour its energies into rearguard fighting against the Japanese. The key to the Communist strategy in the early to middle period of the war was the formation of base areas, the most important of which was that around the headquarters of Yan'an, in the arid Shaanxi-Gansu region. In this period, China divided into approximately three of these Communist base areas, and then areas that could be regarded as neutral, or under KMT control – and the final areas, mostly in the Northeast or in the urbanized areas controlled by the Japanese. This suited the way in which the war unfolded. Massive military activity in the early stages over 1937–1941 meant that the Japanese, in effect, controlled all of the coast of China and territory inland in a line from Beijing, down to Nanjing and then into Guangzhou. This line didn't fundamentally alter till the final year of the war in 1944, when the Japanese, frustrated by attacks, started Operation Ichigo, probing along transport lines deeper into Chinese territory, using devastating air attacks.

Despite their unified objectives in defeating the Japanese, there were clear tensions between the KMT and the CCP and its armies from early on. The KMT put a blockade on the Yan'an base area as early as 1939. It also liquidated the Xinjiang Communists, killing Mao Zedong's brother in the process. CCP success on the battlefield ironically didn't help things, creating resentment. Chiang Kai-shek could see from early on that the war was an opportunity for the CCP to build up membership, continue to militarize itself, and to carve out territories in which it exercised control. There were dark murmurings that a victory by the Japanese, or an accommodation with them, would in many ways have suited his purpose. There were even dialogues via intermediaries about how such a cooperation might have happened. To the Communists, Chiang's appetite for power was confirmed in 1939 by him being named the 'Director General', a quasi-presidential position.

Talks between the two sides continued into 1940 and 1941. Mao in his *On New Democracy* spoke grandly of making a commitment to participate in multiparty elections and a constitutional democracy, working with the KMT. But the New Fourth Army Incident where retreating CCP forces were destroyed by KMT ones in 1941 undid this appetite to work in a coalition, especially as it seemed to some observers on the Communist side that the CCP were being annihilated even when they were obeying orders. Chiang's visceral distrust of the CCP meant that after the almost complete collapse of the Third United Front, there was heavy mutual infiltration and a breakdown of top-level dialogue between the two sides.

The CCP under Mao's leadership was to make crucial and successful strategic decisions in how it took on the Japanese during the middle to final period of the war, controlling the rural areas, operating behind Japanese lines, engaging in highly debilitating guerrilla tactics, never mounting massive operations for which it lacked the weaponry and infrastructure, but playing to its strengths. In 1940, the Hundred Regiments attack to force Japanese back into the cities met with brutal responses, prompting some to question whether Mao had agreed with what soon became a highly counterproductive move. The Japanese were to respond savagely, with their 'loot all, burn all, kill all' campaign, laying waste to whole areas of the northeast. Far from being looked upon as heroes and saviours, the CCP became, in the eyes of many peasants, the author of their devastation. But the Japanese military and political high command were aware that such levels of indiscriminate violence were unsustainable and in conflict with achieving their primary goal – the economic exploitation of China. Tired of skirmishes in the countryside, they were to concentrate their efforts and consolidate their positions in the cities from 1941 onward, largely abandoning the rural areas until their final onslaught three years later.

Cleansing the Ranks

Mao's influence within the Party increased throughout the war years. The war was the most significant event in bringing him ultimate power. But the master of contradictions knew that every progress brings with it negative side effects. The rapid increase in Party membership over the years of the conflict and the huge increase in its military and territorial strength had created an uncomfortably diverse membership whose ideological purity was, at best, questionable. His response to this was one of the first rectification campaigns, mounted in 1941 against Party members, with a following campaign that struck even deeper, the Zheng Feng Rectification, in 1942–43. This resulted in a wave of purges in the Maoist era, mostly of intellectuals. The most heated debates were about literature and its role in class struggle, with Mao arguing famously in his 1942 'Talks on Literature at Yanan' that all fiction had a class basis and had to reflect the real conditions of the people. This was to be a continuing debate over the next three decades of his rule, and the source of many of his disagreements with different groups of intellectuals. The Party, at least in Mao's eyes, was to reign supreme even in the world of make-believe.

All of this was finally confirmed during the Seventh Congress in 1945, anticipated since the dark days of 1928. The new Maoist lineup was to appear here in its full glory. The acceptance of the Maoist views of recent history was encoded in the 'Resolution on Party History', a document which was to prefigure that, over four decades later, it would explain the Party's own history to itself after years in power, struggling with the legacy of Maoism in 1981. Even at this early stage, therefore, it could be said that there were conflicts and battles over the interpretation of history, and the meaning of specific events. The new constitution, which was not revised till 1956, enshrined the position of Party Chairman. It was also to delegate more power to rural areas.

Perhaps this was simply because by this stage in the war, after the Japanese tactical retreat from the countryside, it was now irrefutable that in the rural areas resided the real strength of the CCP. With the entry of the US into the war in 1941, Japanese forces were to be redeployed in increasing numbers in the Pacific War, causing a lack of field personnel in China. The entry by Russian forces into Northern China and up to North Korea in 1945 only made it clearer that the conflict was entering a terminal phase. Japanese capitulation on 14 August 1945 marked the end of the international conflict, but only a pause in the battle to resolve China's own internal issues. Within a year, the country, exhausted after eight years of war, was embroiled in a civil war. The resolution of that war, quicker than the CCP or others expected, was to lead to the founding of the PRC and the beginning of the Party's reign of power in 1949.

The Civil War: The CCP's Prelude to Power

In 1946 few would have predicted that Mao's band of bandits, whatever the extra capacity and experience they had gained during the last few years, would have been in position to wage war, and win, in just over three years. They had experience in guerrilla conflict, but not in large-scale battle. They had far fewer military personnel than the KMT, and were weaker in terms of equipment. The US, despite claims of neutrality and the occupation of Japan, had already decided that Europe was its main sphere of influence, and had committed funding, help and capacity to the KMT, whom they viewed as the legitimate government of China and, from their actions at least, wished to see remain, as at least a stabilizer.

At the Seventh Party Congress, Mao and the top leadership had called for a coalition government. In August 1945, after much coaxing, Mao had even gone to the seat of the wartime nationalist government, the Southwest city of Chongqing (the first time he had gotten on a plane), and negotiated how the CCP and KMT could work together to achieve this. It was clear that the CCP was not willing to now quietly lay down its arms and disappear back into the shadows. The war had given them a taste of power, and a vision of their final mission in China. They had been able to implement fundamental land reform in some of the areas they had controlled. Despite initial skirmishes, a Political Consultative Conference, set up with the help of the newly arrived US liaison officer, George Marshall, brokered a ceasefire, and allowed the various parties to reach agreement on a constitutional government. But discussions on creating a national army from the disparate forces of both the CCP and KMT caused a quick breakdown, with both sides claiming lack of good faith and breaches of the agreement by the other side. The National Assembly may have been reconvened, and the 1939 agreement ostensibly implemented, but by the end of 1946, Chiang had already made the decision that, regardless of US prompting to work for national unity and maintain stability for China, he was ready to go for the final annihilation of the Communists.

He was to make two great mistakes in the battles that followed that were to bring about the final end of KMT rule in Mainland China and force him into exile. The first was to commit huge forces directly into the Communist strongholds of the Northeast, effectively sending them into an area where they had no easy routes of retreat, and overstretching them. The second was that he had tolerated corruption and fatally underestimated the anger and weariness of many Chinese towards this and the economic mismanagement of the KMT government. Perhaps some of this was unfair. Few governments would have been able to take the devastating onslaughts that the KMT had over the last decade and remain in one piece. Even so, the public perception was that the KMT looked after profiteers, speculators and corrupt elites and continued to bear down on the real entrepreneurs and workers. Inflation went through the roof in the late 1940s, causing a national economic crisis. Corruption and inflation were to be the final destroyers of the KMT government, which no amount of US support would salvage. The CCP-inspired land reforms had given many peasants a view of what a new power structure might look like. The age-old issue of more equitable distribution and control of the land and means of production needed to be addressed. Even so, many intellectuals, however revolted they were at the actions of the KMT, viewed final Communist victory with a heavy heart. To them, the signs were already clear that despite all the talk of coalition government, building consensus, and being committed to the new democracy, the CCP had shown a bias against the individual and a desire for control and heavy state intervention. For them, they were caught between two evils.

The general KMT onslaught began in July 1946. The KMT forces were to be successful in the early stages, fighting against the newly founded People's Liberation Army, which had pulled together the disparate Communist military forces extant till then. By the end of 1946 they had taken all the cities of Northeast China. The winter of 1946–47 was to be the final dark night of the soul for the CCP while out of power. With their territories compromised and retaken, many of the peasants who had enthusiastically participated in land-reform programmes found themselves abandoned to the KMT, who immediately allowed the old elites to have their land back and exact retribution. In many areas there was a feeling that the CCP had betrayed people, disappearing like smoke while those who had trusted them were savagely dealt with.

By May 1947, in a haunting duplication of the position of the Japanese after their initial successes, the KMT forces were spread too thin. It was at this point, in Manchuria, that they came face to face with the military genius of Lin Biao, whose campaign, over 1947, into 1948, and the very early months of 1949, was to devastate his opponents. Lin Biao, because of his 'disgrace' during the Cultural Revolution (see Chapter Two) and the sustained campaign to dishonour him at that time, has been less well served by history than he should have been. His leadership in the Civil War was to be one of the key components of the CCP being victorious, despite such severe disadvantages. He commanded some of the largest forces ever arrayed on a battlefield, taking almost one million troops into the final part of the campaign in 1948–1949. The character portrayed in post-CR material in China as a pasty, sick, and mentally disturbed malcontent, was, at least in this era, one of the greatest military tacticians the world has ever seen.

By January 1949 the CCP forces controlled most of the territory in northern China. They issued a sharp eight-point demand for peace. Gone were the talks of concession for national unity. Chiang Kai-shek was to be tried as a national traitor. The CCP was to form a new government. When these were rejected, the CCP forces pushed into southern China. By the summer, Chiang had retreated to Taiwan. Although it took till 1950 to pacify some of the areas in

Guangxi and Guangdong, the CCP had won. A final political consultative conference held in Beijing in September 1949 was used to prepare for the announcement, on 1 October, of the foundation of the People's Republic of China. 28 years after its establishment, the CCP had been victorious. Now it was no longer a group of bandits, good at waging guerrilla war. It was the sovereign government of one fifth of humanity.

Chapter Two

Revolutionary Administrator: The Party in Power

The Chinese people made a revolution led by the CCP, the most important leader of which was Mao… It was due to this revolution that the average life expectancy of the majority of Chinese rose from 35 in 1949 to 63 by 1975, in the space of less than 30 years. It was a revolution that brought unity and stability to a country that had been plagued by civil wars and foreign invasions, and the revolution that laid the foundation for China to become the equal of the great global powers. It was a revolution that carried out land reforms, promoted women's status, improved popular literacy and eventually transformed Chinese society beyond recognition.

— Mobo Gao
The Battle for China's Past: Mao and the Cultural Revolution

The Chinese Communists are not real Communists. They are margarine Communists.

— Stalin
Quoted in Lucien Bianco,
Origins of the Chinese Revolution 1915–1949

The CCP had won one of the most decisive mandates in history. After almost three decades of internal disunity and two decades of international and domestic war, the CCP's leadership was able to stand as the sole government of the People's

Republic of China. This was the beginning of a new era. But they were confronted by a raft of massive problems. China's infrastructure was devastated. The average life expectancy of its citizens was just over 30 years old. Millions had died or been displaced. The country was bankrupt and internationally isolated. It also had towering inflation. Chinese people were immeasurably, and needlessly, poor because of the war.

Its leadership had to make a number of immediate decisions. One of the simpler ones was where to locate the new capital of the country. After initially contemplating Chongqing (which was rejected as being too closely associated with the discredited KMT government whose headquarters had been based there for much of the war) and Xian (too reminiscent of China's imperial past), it settled on Beijing, the traditional seat of government for much of the last few centuries. But to be fit for the purpose, Beijing had to be reshaped, remade and modelled in the image of how the Communists saw the new world. Mao famously demanded that the old city walls be brought down, that the old central consulate area be levelled to the ground for a massive square to be built in its place (the famous Tiananmen Square, which remains to this day the world's largest public square in a city). He wanted to see large boulevards run through the centre of the city, with whatever stood in their way making way for them. Within a few years, most of this was done.

The energy with which Beijing was rebuilt mirrored the energy with which the Party, in the first few years, wished to reconstruct and rejuvenate China. The massive Great Hall of the People on the west side of Tiananmen Square was put up in ten months in 1958. New rail links that had been devastated by war were rebuilt. But the brutal fact was that after many years of conflict, China was bankrupt and weak. It did not help that within two years, it became embroiled in another war on its borders, the Korean War, with the UN forces coming up to the border between China and its neighbour. Hundreds of thousands of Chinese soldiers were poured in to assist their Korean comrades. One of these to die was Mao's son. By 1953, with the UN forces pushed back to the 38th parallel, the war came to a standstill, creating a situation that remains unresolved almost 60 years later.

There was to be one way in which China's new manifestation as the PRC was to eerily follow the march set by all of its previous forms. The CCP was to become, very quickly, a highly hierarchical organization, with a clear pecking order and an increasingly dense bureaucracy. Within a few years (maybe even from the beginning), much of this power was to be concentrated in the hands of only a few people. Within a decade and a half it was to belong pretty clearly to just one man. Mao's progression to imperialistic levels of authority, with its resemblance to the dynastic power absolutism of China's past, is one of the key stories of the first quarter century of CCP rule. The CCP, therefore, ostensibly started as a party of revolution, but became enmeshed in the same power structures as previous systems of government in China.

Building a New Future

It is easy to forget the optimism of the early years of Communist rule. The transitional years were hardly easygoing. From 1949 to 1951, the Party had to deal with continuing revolts against its rule in the Southwest, with one particularly serious incidence of opposition in Guizhou leading to the rounding up and murder of thousands of 'counter-revolutionaries'. The Party forgot its promise to the minority areas of Tibet, Inner Mongolia and Xinjiang to grant them quasi-independence, largely imposing the same policy as the KMT. Most remarkably, the city of Dalian, occupied by Soviet troops from 1945, continued to host a large Soviet military presence up to 1955.[1] Even so, China's exhausted population was willing to give the new government a free run. They wanted stability, and good governance, whatever their previous misgivings and apprehensions. The great city of Shanghai was famously cleared of its prostitutes and corrupt landlords. KMT officials were given an amnesty – initially. But even in this new history, there were scores to settle and clearing out work to do. One of the major tasks facing the Party in the first years of rule was to return to land reform, a process they had kicked off in the early 1930s, and been wrestling with ever since. The Rectification Campaigns first waged in the early 1940s were to return, only on an unimaginably larger scale. The digging out of the landlords, the rich property owners, was to be brutal, but effective. By 1955, China's land was in the hands of the state, and much of it had been redistributed. Large estates were now made into state-run farms. Struggle sessions against the rich landlords in which peasants were taught to 'speak bitterness' sometimes ended in violence, even death. Those who wished could look to the prefigurement of this in one of Mao's earliest writings, his 'Report to the Central Committee on an Inspection on the Peasant Movement in Hunan,' where it described how landlords were forced to wear dunce's caps and paraded through the streets. Such grim theatre was to return in the Cultural Revolution a decade and a half later, in a deadlier guise.

In these early years China, and the Party in particular, did not seem to have time to dwell. But there were signs already that it wished to address both the issues of class classification, and of how to unify China's diverse and complex population. It also wanted to do something about the personal allegiances of many of the most gifted members of its population. The first proper attack on those classified as intellectuals in Maoist terms (broadly those who were writers, teachers, scientists and some levels of officials) came in 1952–53, with, first, the Three Antis Campaign, and then the Four Antis campaign. It was a mere light prelude to those that were to follow throughout the 1950s, into the 1960s and 1970s, right into the current day (though in very different guises). Mao's relationship with intellectuals has aroused much discussion and debate.[2] His own intellectual credentials were clear. He was a poet, with a considerable knowledge of Chinese classical literature, and, where it had been translated, foreign literature. His calligraphy was judged by none other than the great sinologist Simon Leys as indicative of a strong and individual temperament. The Party's top leadership in the early years of the PRC were mostly people who had experience abroad, and who were highly urbane and educated. Zhou Enlai, Mao's right-hand man from the start, had been educated at university in Tianjin, and then in Japan, Germany and France. Liu Shaoqi had been to Russia. Figures like Chen Boda, who was to prove to be Mao's chief ideologue, and Kang Sheng, his chief hatchet man, had all studied in Moscow in the 1920s. Deng Xiaoping had lived for six years in France. In its early years, the Party had strong links to other Communist regimes in Eastern Europe, showing a level of globalization that was not to return till the 1980s, with links in particular to Yugoslavia and Albania and a steady stream of delegations and students there.

Returning intellectuals that heeded the call to come back to China to contribute to its new beginning and its future were to meet widely different fates. But many of them were to suffer terribly. Mao's uneasy relationship with intellectuals led to claims that he wished to brainwash and control his own country. The mechanism of control the CCP put in during the first decade of power was to be pervasive and long-lasting. China's lives with the result of this root-and-branch reform of the structure of everyday life to this day.

Communism in China and the USSR: Same and Different

China clearly owed a lot to the USSR. It had copied from the Russians its political model and much of its social and industrial policy (a push to industrialize quickly, and heavy state control of the economy). There were clear educational and technical links, and much investment, and aid, from the USSR throughout the 1950s. Mao's first and only visits abroad were to Moscow, immediately after assuming power in 1949 and again in 1950. But the gloomy look on his and Stalin's faces as they stood beside each other while their representatives signed an accord spoke of the massive cultural and ideological gap between them. At the end of the day, Mao was to place national (meaning what the CCP defined as national) self-interest before subservience to Stalin. 1949 was seen as a moment not of linking up with the global communist movement, but achieving long-needed national regeneration and showing that Communism was good for China because it served its national self-interest so well, rather than making it the servant of other outside powers. His deference to Stalin played much like his use of the KMT – something that was a means to an end, not a valid destination. By the time of Stalin's death in 1953, cracks were already clear. These were to break out fully by the time of Khrushchev's speech denouncing Stalin in 1956.

In the realm of Party organization, social organization and the new discourse that the CCP used when it came to power, the influence of the Soviet Union was clear. A fresh system was built, from village and county level up to national level, with new ministries created for governance and organizations, running from the cultural sphere right across to finance and security.

The Communists launched their first five-year economic plan in 1953, a clear sign that the state was now in charge of setting growth targets, allocating resources and managing every aspect of the economy. Infrastructure, provided and managed by state entities, was constructed and served large state-owned companies building anything from aircraft engines to automotive and machine parts. The aspiration of Mao's government's was to ape the Soviet Union in building up an industrial sector in record time.

Despite coming to power on the sweat and blood of the countryside, one of the great anomalies of the Maoist period was that, for a country ruled by a Party led in large by people from the Chinese countryside, it was to put in place policies which were highly unfair and place massive burdens on the agricultural sector. Internal passports and the '*hukou*', or household registration system much like in the USSR, were introduced in the 1950s. These were to set forth clearly different citizenship classes between the urban and rural dwellers, inhibiting the freedom of people to move from one place to another. The restrictions they created persist to this day. The countryside in China was to suffer badly under Mao, losing many million of its people to starvation in the late 1950s and early 1960s, bearing the brunt of highly unrealistic production targets, which, in Mao's logic, were justified because of the priority of supporting the efforts in the cities to build an urban, industrialized economy.

The results of the penetrating reform of China during this period can be seen in works like that by the great Chinese woman novelist Yang Jiang. In her 1988 novel *Xi Zao* (which translates as 'Washing', an ironic reference to the brainwashing that was claimed to be taking place over this period), set in a research institute in the mid-1950s, she described the tensions and conflicts between a group of well-educated, talented scholars who have to 'remake themselves' for the new country that some of them have come home from abroad to serve. This experience of returnees was often traumatic. One of her characters is exposed for being 'politically unreliable' and goes through an initial process of thought reform, needing to write self-criticisms and to appear before increasingly rowdy meetings defending themselves and admitting their mistakes. There was plenty of ground for literally anyone to be exposed and have questions asked of them. The years of war had forced many people to make difficult decisions of allegiance, with some switching backward and forward between the KMT and the Communists. Even Zhou Enlai, elevated after 1949 to the level of a saint in the PRC, had been an operative for the KMT in the 1920s. The 1950s were to see nothing like the mass purges in the Cultural Revolution, but there were plenty of events that acted as an ominous precursor.

The other interesting element of 'Washing' is the way in which it is clear that the new institute has been grafted onto an older series of institutes, and that despite these people and their organizations having new names, and being part of a new history, the past is only just below the surface. Importing Soviet style organizational and social models was well and good – but they were to be changed once they were set up in the very different social landscape and historical environment of China. There are few better examples of this than the choice by Mao and the top leadership to establish their main offices in the Beijing Zhongnanhai area, former seat of the emperors, beside the Forbidden Palace, a place thick with associations with the very China that supposedly the new Chinese leaders were trying to guide their country away from. Mao in fact did not wish to turn his back on this history, despite his revolutionary credentials, but often delved deep into it, seeking models and inspirations for his various new movements and ideas.

The Party also spent a lot of effort at this time in controlling the media that existed, and in creating a specific version of its past, which supported and enhanced its claims to being the legitimate government of China. In the 1950s, it established the *People's Daily* (*Renmin Ribao*) as the national newspaper, with firm control over its content, demanding that it be read in all work units throughout the country during allocated study sessions. Other papers like the *Liberation Daily* (*Jiefang Ribao*) and the *Guangming Daily* (*Guangming Ribao*) were set up to service the military and intellectual readership. But they all worked under the Ministry of Propaganda and were politically vetted. In *Doing Things With Words in Chinese Politics* (London: Curzon Press 1995), Michael Schoenhals describes how Hu Qiaomu, one of the editors of the *People's Daily*, took great care to present arguments in the paper's articles, changing words that might carry unfortunate or difficult political connotations, very aware that his chief readership was the upper leadership of the CCP. The media functioned as a means of broadcasting particular key messages to the population. It carried specific campaigns, and was viewed as the main way to broadcast these carefully honed and controlled messages across to a mass audience. Radio usage, while increasing, was available to very few – and television only from the 1960s – and to hardly any outside the main cities of Beijing and Shanghai. The role of the printed media, therefore, was key.

But the CCP's aspirations to control the language of political and social discourse went beyond this very tight regulation of newspapers. The Communists also introduced a whole new series of terms into the Chinese language, setting out concepts and ideas, trying to shape the way that people in China thought. As an early analyst of the Communists, Franz Schurmann, put it in 1965, 'The Chinese Communists have developed a rich vocabulary which has in many ways changed the Chinese language. Ideas and terms have come into popular usage which never existed before... One of the major contributions of this practical ideology of the Chinese Communists has been the generation of many new and useful categories and language. It has also given the Chinese a new way of thinking.'[3] The Party's real triumph, though, was to reinforce this by conducting a campaign to simplify Chinese characters. This continued the work of early language reformers like Hu Shi, the American-educated writer and academic who had, in many ways, performed the liberal opposition to the CCP during its rise to power before himself emigrating to Taiwan and back to the US. A national system for romanization (pinyin) was accepted, and hundreds of characters reduced from over a dozen strokes down to just a few. A mass campaign to improve China's literacy rates was conducted at the same time, along with a big push to improve levels of education. The net effect was that far more people were reached through newspapers and pamphlets.

Everyday life for a Party member in the 1950s started to show the levels of intense state management and interference that were to reach their climax during the Cultural Revolution. Study meetings were a staple, with articles from either the *People's Daily*, or what were called 'Red Top' directives issued from Beijing and circulated down to provincial parties, and then, depending on their classification, to specific work units. Many of these were speeches by Party leaders, or articles written by favoured writers, but often with almost total input by political leaders. The politicization of the everyday was to increase gradually (see the sections on the Cultural Revolution below). Even so, Party membership in the early days of the PRC still carried certain burdens, including the responsibility to be up to date on the latest campaigns, and being able to observe the Party line on matters like relationship with the USSR or economic issues like industrial production. Schools and universities were important places to make sure that students got the message, with political lessons being a fundamental part of daily study. By 1956 almost everyone in China, whether in the countryside or the city, was part of a work unit (*danwei*). Party branches reached into every area of organized social life, with the smallest possible being three people strong, and the average size about 100.[4] This meant that their healthcare, their retirement care, their education, their work, whether they went to university and where they went to university, were all decided not by themselves, but by the state, in service to the Party. The work unit system even decided when people could marry, and often whom they were able to marry. Such intimate involvement in the lives of its citizens made the Chinese state omnipresent. Those that tried to escape its reach, as, for instance, Bao Ruowang, the Chinese-French author of *Prisoner of Mao*, who wrote of his life in prison camps in China in the early 1960s, were to fall into a limitless black hole, isolated, disenfranchised and literally made into powerless slaves at the mercy of the security services.[5] Surveillance of people from this period started to also be a feature of everyday life, with neighbourhood committees being the main shopfront for a massive apparatus of state control that has probably never been equalled in any other society, before or since.[6] By 1957, the Party had 12 million members, the vast majority being peasants.[7]

It was through these mechanisms that from 1949 onward the Party was able to mould the creation, at least for those people under its control, of a specific revolutionary myth. This myth largely ignored most of the nuances of the past, presenting things in black and white, with the Communists as the good guys, and the KMT and Japanese as the bad. The Long March, for instance, about which many claims have since been made regarding what actually happened, became a story of unalloyed heroism and glory for the Party and the survival of it and the Red Army. Mao's rise to power was dealt with carefully, brushing away all the unfortunate problems about his compromises, relationship with the Soviet Union and the many that were murdered or dispensed with during his progression to ultimate leadership. This myth-making was a dynamic process. The guardians of the Party's retelling of its own past, largely the Propaganda Department, were to constantly need to retune the tales they told when there was a change in the political wind. For this reason, treatment of the USSR went from being largely positive in 1955, to being overwhelmingly negative in 1960. The USSR's assistance, through the Communist International, in setting up the CCP in the early days, was largely erased from the historic record. The KMT was to be given a particular role as historic villain and traitor to its country. The CCP was keen to stress the importance of ideological work, and the history that it told was to illustrate key truths, such as the role of dialectic in history, and the ways in which Chinese distant and recent past history fitted into this evolution from a feudal society, where one class oppressed another, to one where socialism was becoming victorious. As John Wilson Lewis commentated, in their desire to create what was called a 'mass line', unifying all social groups to a common modernizing purpose, they created not just an appropriate ideology, but also 'a new socialist morality to replace the traditional values of Chinese society and politics'.[8]

Leaders Together

In the early years of the CCP rule, the elite leadership was both stable and, from outside appearances, unified. From detailed accounts like those by Harvard-based scholar of modern China, Roderick MacFarquhar, prior to the Great Leap Forward in 1958, decisions on the Politburo were made collectively and there was a sense that Mao was merely first among equals. Even so, the formal apparatus for discussing and agreeing on policy was highly opaque. From the Seventh Party Congress held in the revolutionary base in Yen'an in 1945, China had to wait another 11 years for the next congress, convened in Beijing in 1956. Astonishingly, for Mao's 27 years in power, there were only three Congresses. He preferred less formal, personal ways of exercising power.

After so many years fighting, it was clear that the new leadership was committed to a unified, and a truly independent China. Apart from British-controlled Hong Kong, Portuguese-controlled Macau, and Taiwan, where the KMT leaders had fled, China was able to say for the first time in a century that it was free from foreign interference. The PRC absorbed Tibet into its territory by 1959, making Tibet, Xinjiang (which had briefly been an independent country under USSR influence from 1945 to 1949) and Inner Mongolia into what it called Autonomous Regions. These were, in fact, to have precious little autonomy.

Aware of the highly fragmented and potentially fractious nature of the Chinese political landmass, Mao's government ensured that Party structures were extended throughout China, down to the most local level. The Party therefore achieved what it had been aiming to for over two decades, becoming a state within a state, with its own governance, rules and systems, running alongside day-to-day governance. In effect, any person with a senior position in the executive government was almost certainly a Party member. The Party had regional structures, in which individuals mirrored Mao's powers at the centre, being Chairmen and Party Secretaries. Party members underwent extensive training educating them in the ideology of the CCP and in the responsibilities of membership. The PLA was also clearly set down as the tool of the Party, not the state.[9]

This period of relative internal stability was, in the end, to be short-lived. By the Eighth Congress in 1956 it was already clear that small fractures were beginning to emerge in the top leadership. Liu Shaoqi, born only a few miles from Mao in Hunan province, central China, was already national president. Zhou Enlai, as Premier, ranked as number three. But then there were a cluster of leaders around Mao, from former generals like Peng Dehuai, who now worked as Minister of Defence, to Lin Biao, the Head of the PLA, and Kang Sheng, the sinister head of the CCP's secret service. Peng Zhen, Deng Xiaoping, and Yang Shangkun, who were to figure so critically in China's later development, were also in senior positions at this time. All of them had slightly different perspectives on the direction China should now take. It was also clear that Mao was starting to grow restless and dissatisfied with some of the policies being discussed. The two events that were to most impact his attitude to the senior leadership of the Party and their success in governing were the Hundred Flowers Campaign from 1956 to 1957 and the Great Leap Forward that followed it from 1958 to 1960. Both were to be instrumental in setting him on a collision course with the very organization that he had been so instrumental in bringing to power.

The Hundred Flowers campaign was the first opportunity for the Party to hear the opinions of people on how they felt the last few years had gone. It was a bold move. As far as anyone knows, Mao sincerely expected to have some criticisms, but on the whole, felt the feedback would be more positive. More cynical observers merely see it as part of a long, demonic plan by Mao to create conflict within the Party for his own ends and to lure potential critics and troublemakers out early. Either way, the stream of criticism that flowed from intellectuals, Party members, even officials, over the few months the campaign was allowed took Mao and the top Party leadership aback. The most famous examples, by *People's Daily* journalist Liu Binyan, whose *'The Inside Story of Our Newspaper'* exposed a case of corruption in a party cadre in Northeast China, created immense interest and debate. This proved what many had been thinking to themselves: that Party officials were becoming complacent, corrupt, and falling for the same greed for personal gain as those during the KMT period. Writers like Wang Meng, who was to go on many decades later to be China's Minister of Culture, were to write similarly coruscating accounts of government misbehaviour, albeit in fictional garb.

Mao's initial response was simply to close the campaign down. Comments were no longer welcome. This was ruefully called 'the wilting of the Hundred Flowers,' and in some ways marks the end of the CCP's honeymoon period. In an internal speech in 1957, later issued as a fully-fledged pamphlet, 'On the Correct Handling of Contradictions Amongst the People', Mao identified the social classes and different standpoints that now existed in China, and were working against the success of the revolution. He ran through seven contradictions. That, between the capitalist and the bourgeoisie, took centre stage. But his trust in intellectuals, never that strong, had been dented. It was clear now that at some stage there would be conflict.

Mao had created the CCP as a Party of revolution. Its role up till 1949 had often been aggressive and destructive – attacking enemies, whether they were the KMT (who it had sometimes worked with) or the Japanese, and bringing them down. This battle mentality boded badly for a party that now needed to govern in peacetime. In the early years of the CCP's leadership, there was a little space for alternative voices. In 1957–58, during the antirightist campaign, some of the most influential writers and thinkers of pre-PRC China were attacked, and in some cases placed in jail for speaking out of turn. One of these, the theatre critic Hu Feng, a follower of Lu Xun, who had been based in Shanghai in the 1930s, was incarcerated for over 20 years for disputing Mao's belief on the need for all literature and art to serve a political function.[10] Others, like Shen Congwen, one of the major writers of Republican China, simply kept their heads low. He was to spend the rest of his career quietly writing about costume and clothing in imperial China, a subject free of political risk. The anti-rightist campaign also sucked in the young Zhu Rongji, later to be premier of China in the 1990s, who was jailed in the late 1950s. From the mid-1950s, the infrastructure of repression was already in place. Reform through labour camps was established, scattered in isolated spots across China. Psychologist Robert Jay Lifton was to write accounts of the process of intense thought reform and brainwashing that American service men had undergone when taken in as prisoners during the Korean War. He was also to look at the testimony of those who had then fled to Hong Kong and who were able to recount their experiences of psychological manipulation while still in the PRC. Their experiences were eerily similar. Initial periods of isolation, creating a sense of fear and vulnerability were followed by the deployment of moral blackmail, often involving friends, family members or close associates. All this was rounded off by an intense period of 'guided introspection' in which the 'patient' was brought around to admitting their errors and mistakes and started the process of reform.[11]

The Party that Mao led had only the weakest sense of legality. It continued to use the cell structure, in which every organization and entity in the country had a Party element, and a shadow-Party structure, but there was little sense of governance beyond personal patronage and relationships, and even less of any idea of 'loyal opposition'. Rules were written down, but almost completely disregarded. This highly personal model was to effectively mean that from 1949 to the late 1970s, China was largely without a system of law. Courts were merely the puppets of the CCP. Even the state itself was the creature of the CCP, despite initial conflict. The CCP was to place its roots deep into society and despite passing constitutions with high-sounding guarantees of individual rights, when the real crunch came these were meaningless. In some ways Mao can even be seen as the puppet of this utter concentration of power within his hands. This had, after all, been the pattern of power distribution for centuries in previous major Chinese dynasties. He was merely inheriting it. After a few years of initial resistance he became increasingly autocratic. Very ironically, the Party was to become one of his greatest victims.

The Great Leap Forward

The Great Leap Forward at the end of the 1950s can be interpreted two ways. The first is to see it as an attempt to build up China's national economic capacity, and to accelerate its growth. The second is to see it as part of the process of the falling out with the USSR, and the attempt to put clear water between the two major communist powers. China's economic progress in the 1950s had been adequate. But it had largely been rebuilding and reconstructing what had already been there before the war. From the mid-1950s, and the first Five Year Plan, there was an appetite to now push the state-led economy forward much more aggressively. This was also tied to clear strands of nationalism and to the increasing isolation that China felt as it moved into the 1950s. China was edging towards an almost autarkic position. The government agreed to a proposal that was largely Mao's, that they use highly unorthodox methods to increase industrial output. Most famously, backyard furnaces produced thousands of tonnes of substandard steel, all in order to meet the target of taking over the highly industrialized UK in steel production in 15 years. Enormous efforts were made for mass mobilization, with communes set up that cut across traditional family life, but were seen as the new way to create a reinvigorated China. The results were initially pleasing. But by the last years of the decade, something went badly wrong. A series of poor harvests pushed food from the countryside to the city. People became malnourished. Many died prematurely. By 1961, there was a large-scale famine. To this day, figures for how many died are still controversial. Mobo Gao has argued that the figure might be as low as 200,000. Jasper Becker and others have put it at closer to 30 million.[12] Recent internal reports put it as high as 50 million. Ralph A. Thaxton's magnificent analysis of what actually happened in one village in Henan province up to and during the

Great Leap Forward period proves that Mao remained fundamentally wedded to collectivization policies which were to lead directly to the smashing of the agricultural sector and the mayhem that followed. Tragically, there was plenty of evidence within China that the centralized policies were just not working. But Mao felt that once this period was endured, China would move on to a socialist paradise. This was one of his greatest mistakes.[13]

It was certainly bad enough for the Minister of Defence Peng Dehuai, on visiting the countryside where he had been born in Sichuan, to be struck by the levels of poverty and desperation, and to come back to Beijing and make a formal report on this. But by then the wall around Mao had already grown, and the distance in power between him and others in the leadership elite increased. The first major spat occurred at the Lushan conference in 1959. Mao agreed that mistakes had been made. Executive decisions were to be taken from now on by Liu Shaoqi and Deng Xiaoping, as Secretary General of the Party. Critically, Mao kept his position as Chairman. But for the following few years, he was less visible.

Beyond the economic impact of the Great Leap Forward and the famines was the deterioration and then breakdown of China's relationship with the USSR. The ideological differences between the two had been increasing for a number of years. Mao was willing to defer to Stalin. But Khrushchev presented different issues, and the reforms he was proposing were viewed as deeply threatening. This was not helped by the very poor personal chemistry between the two leaders. On one famous occasion Mao received the Soviet leader while swimming in his pool at the Zhongnanhai compound, and invited the Russian into the water beside him. The nonswimmer Khrushchev was forced to float in a dinghy while Mao paddled around him. By the late 1950s, the tens of thousands of Russian experts based in China began to withdraw. They had been instrumental in giving a great deal of technical help, some of which would be used to build the PRC's first atom bomb in 1964. They had provided expertise on construction, the building of airplanes and factories, and social organization. A generation of young Chinese had been trained in Russia. In the cities of the Northeast, like Harbin in Heilongjiang, there were Russian communities, even a Russian church. The largest hotel in the world at the time, the Friendship Hotel, was built in the northwest of Beijing to accommodate many of these Russian experts. But within a few years they were withdrawn.

By 1969, with a major skirmish across the border between Russia and China, they were almost at war, with both sides suffering casualties. There were complex reasons for the breakdown. But the result was that by 1962 China was almost alone internationally. It had only one ally in Europe, the small state of Albania. It was to aggravate this by presenting itself as the leader of the developed world, and starting to support revolutionary groups active in Africa and Latin America. This isolation was only to worsen during the Cultural Revolution.

Mao was similarly isolated. He remained titular leader of a Party that was straying into areas of economic liberalism that he fundamentally disagreed with. The leadership of Liu and Deng were to experiment with reforms that looked very similar to those that were finally introduced almost 15 years later. They allowed more freedom to agricultural workers, and started relaxing price controls and some of the state's overall direction of the economy. China posted growth rates in 1963 to 1965 for the first time in several years. Mao complained that he had been a 'Buddha put on the shelf' during this period, sidelined and ignored. But his conviction in his own rightness meant that by 1964 he was on manoeuvres, disappearing for several weeks to his home province, Hunan, contemplating the future.

Mao versus the Party – the Final Showdown

The Cultural Revolution (CR) continues to mystify people. The fortieth anniversary of its formal commencement in 2006 passed without much comment in China. This was despite the fact that only a few months earlier, one of those finally blamed for the disruption and chaos of the ten years of the CR period, Zhang Chunqiao, had died in his home city of Shanghai after spending many years in jail. Less material is openly published in China now with analysis and reasons for why the CR happened. It is becoming a forgotten period. But its role in the narrative of PRC history and the building of contemporary China is indisputable. The CR was a deeply traumatic experience for many Chinese. For others, it was fundamentally liberating, a political awakening. It remains a highly controversial era, for the same reason that the early 1930s also do – because during the 1960s, the Party was turned in on itself, and many of its faithful, sometimes long-serving and suffering servants were persecuted, removed from power, and all too often murdered. Admitting this self-punishment is, even now, a painful process for the Party, and one it wishes to avoid.

Mao had set his face against bureaucratism from early on in the Party's history. He had criticized its drift towards becoming a self-serving bureaucracy as early as 1935. That it had now become a multi-million-member organization, with structures all over the country, was raising this challenge to a new level. It had started, in his view, to lose its reforming edge. Self-serving power elites and systems that protected them were beginning to appear. The Party was becoming its own most relentless lobbying group. Mao's anxiety about it losing its mandate on power because of this process was ever present. His method to stop this was a simple but devastating one. He went over the heads of the Party, straight to the people, many of whom had shown in the Hundred Flowers period that they resented some of the high-handed treatment the Party had meted out to them, a feeling which had only been compounded by the tragic events of the Great Leap Forward. He reached this willing audience through a variety of ways, both personal and unorthodox. He tolerated the establishment of quasi-formal structures of power, and used the institutional strength of the People's Liberation Army as his final base. When China nearly slid into civil war in 1967–68, the PLA were pulled in to restore order, with some regions put under military leadership. He enlisted the support of the shadowy head of the PLA, the great strategist of the Sino-Japanese War and Civil War, Lin Biao. He built up an alternative power structure, which he then used to attack the Party structure that already existed. For the first three years of the CR, he tolerated profound purges of party personnel. While hard to understand today, the CR, at least according to contemporary records, was to enjoy high levels of support, largely because it appealed to people's sense of idealism, and, at least in its early stages, seemed to offer new forms of liberation. Only later was cynicism and disappointment to set in.

There were underlying themes running through the CR. These help make sense of what was to prove to be a highly complex and often contradictory period. At perhaps the easiest level of understanding, the CR was simply a power struggle. This figures in most of the narratives that were offered to explain it, both at the time and afterwards. Mao was frustrated with Liu Shaoqi, who offered an alternative power base. They had been comrades for over 40 years, but Liu still presented a threat. Mao's routes to destroy him were clear. His first victim was the Minister of Defence, Peng Dehuai. Peng had been removed from power in 1959, but left to his own devices. His criticisms of Mao still rankled. An opportunity to go for him came when the Vice Mayor of Beijing, Wu Han, wrote what appeared to be an allegory about a clean official from 500 years before who, for attacking the folly of an emperor, was removed from office. Mao had, in fact, had sight of this play and cleared it before it appeared in a literary magazine and was performed (though not very successfully) in the early 1960s. Perhaps one of the more opportunistic advisers around him drew it to his attention again. It served his purposes well. He authorized an exposure of the piece by a Shanghai writer called Yao Wenyuan; it was published in 1965 (after months of drafting and redrafting). Peng was to be one of the highest level victims of the CR, dragged back to Beijing from his place of retirement in Sichuan, Southwest China, and struggled against in large public meetings over a hundred times before being locked up in a public toilet and dying in 1972. It was an undignified exit for one of the greatest military heroes of modern China, and a man who had been instrumental in directing China's efforts in the epic Korean War.

Mao's real target, though, was clearly Liu, and by a dozen painful moves throughout the summer of 1966 and into 1967, Liu was little by little removed from power. It was not an easy process. Liu was respected, and had written the classic text of the Communist movement, 'How to be a Good Communist'. Even so, followers of Mao sanctioned the use of attacks on his links with the Russians. They accused him, fatally, of being a revisionist, and of treachery. Questions were raised over his past, and his links to the KMT. Like a masterly political campaign, which used heavy negative messaging, a number of questions were asked which simply raised doubts about what he really believed in. His family was coerced into participating in this process. By the middle of 1967, he was finished. While never directly physically attacked, his death two years later was the result of Mao simply doing nothing. In such a frenetic atmosphere, no one dared stand by him. He died, at least from later official accounts, because of lack of medical care.

Mao's calculation must have been that it was better to have him out of the way than serve as a potential lightning rod for rivalry some time in the future.

Institutional Chaos on the CR

The CR was labelled as 'ten years of chaos'. But at the heart of the second strand of understanding for the CR is the way in which the CR saw the establishment of alternative structures of power, sometimes competing with the Party or parasitical on it, and always challenging it. Perhaps it is possible to see the CR as part of an inevitable process. There were many unresolved issues from the past. Allegiances that had never been challenged were one of the most prominent. Many people had been accepted back into society, and some even into the Party, who had previously worked against it. Their fidelity and ideological purity had never been aggressively tested. Now the time had come for them to be fundamentally challenged. This part of the CR acted like a purgative, a means of cleansing society, and indeed, in much of the literature of the time, this comes across in the language very strongly. There were 'cleansing the ranks' campaigns, and 'digging deep' movements. Society needed to hunt for the 'enemy sleeping at their side'. In some areas where there were clear historic movements for separation from China, this movement to 'root out the enemies' became very intense. Tibet, Inner Mongolia and Xinjiang saw particularly savage purges leading to tens of thousands of killings, many of these Party cadres. The true story of these times is not even fully known to this day.

It became legitimate to draw out these various, questioned pasts and to hunt out those whose backgrounds gave rise to doubts. Many times, though, this was easy to manufacture and offered a good cover for other social resentments. There were plenty of occasions, too, when it became simply an opportunity for malevolence. Students set up rebellious organizations, often named after events in the CCP's past. They were encouraged to reenact the revolutionary deeds of the last generation. Mao sanctioned this by saying that the younger generation was becoming lazy, and distant from their history, and that they needed to relearn how to wage revolution. There was also great urgency over attacking the constraints of the Chinese past, what was interpreted as a history of feudalism. 'Smash the Four Olds' (old ideas, old culture, old customs, and old habits) was only the most visible of these attacks. Many young students writing at the time expressed a considerable sense of liberation and idealism. A plethora of pamphlets and booklets appeared, ironically creating something similar to a free press, in which once untouchable public figures were dragged down. Authority was attacked – though it seems in hindsight that the true core of the Party was able to survive this onslaught.

The Iconography of Mao, and the Creation of a Dream Past

In order to undermine Party authority, Mao set himself up, personally, as an alternative centre of power. He said at one point in the early CR that he would simply resign as Party Chairman, and then go down to the countryside again and refight the revolutionary wars with a new army, retaking power that way. His appeal to the people was through the creation of a profound personality cult. This was to outdo even that that had been created around Stalin, and rank alongside the saturating worship of Kim Il Sun in North Korea.

The Party had been wary of a personality cult from the early days. While Mao had been admired, there were plenty in the Party in the 1940s who were able to rein him in. A simple symbol of this is the brief, sporadic appearance of Mao on Chinese money during the early 1940s, only to disappear with the founding of the PRC, to be replaced by tractors, buildings and social classes. By the CR, however, Mao perceived that a personality cult would be a good means to an end. His picture began to appear exhaustively in newspapers, and public places. Statues of him were built in almost every provincial centre in China. A few of these survive to this day, such as the massive image of Mao that stands, arms outstretched, over the northeastern industrial city of Shenyang, or, more pointedly, the even more gargantuan one that stands in the unrelentingly bright sunlight of Kashgar, near the border between China and Pakistan right over in the Northwest. Over the years, many of the other statues from the CR have simply been discreetly removed.

Daily instructions were culled from the various writings of Mao, and placed at the top of newspaper articles. A seminal moment was the appearance of many hundreds of millions of copies of the *Quotations from Chairman Mao Zedong*, labelled the 'Little Red Book' in the West, a collection of Mao's sayings about society, struggle and the Chinese revolution. This had been based on a similar book issued by Marshal Lin Biao for PLA staff to ensure their ideological correctness. Cleverly echoing the gnomic remarks of Confucius from over two millennia earlier, it was memorized and quoted, ad nauseam, on every possible occasion.

Mao's image penetrated what little was left of people's private lives. His portrait stared down from the wall into living rooms and meeting rooms. There were new rituals to 'daily read and daily study Chairman Mao's sayings'. People performed ritual dances to honour and admire him. There were also extraordinary manifestations of this desire to prove that one 'belonged to the Chairman' by pinning badges of his image to skin, or repeating the phrase 'most most most most' before sayings like 'red sun in our hearts, Chairman Mao', until one was too exhausted to say more. This soon reached levels of absurd extremism. In one book, someone claimed that they could cure cancer with Mao's help. Millions gathered to see him during highly orchestrated campaigns in Tiananmen Square in 1966–67. These were written up in contemporary Chinese descriptions in a highly generic way, giving the impression that people were undergoing a semi-religious experience.

Perhaps Mao had reached new levels of manipulation and cynicism. But his strategy of using the people to attack the Party, and to reign in its power was to have one very clear result. It produced total chaos in large parts of the country, with a breakdown in organization and control. Schools simply stopped functioning. Many areas were locked in constant internal battles. There were waves of violence in areas like the coastal Fujian province, and in Sichuan and Yunnan. The worst was in Inner Mongolia where over 20,000 died. A battle between different rebellious groups in Wuhan in 1967 led to a descent into something approaching civil war. Shanghai briefly set up a people's commune, as a semi-independent government, in the early months of 1967. In what was labelled the February Counter-Current, Party leaders protested against the chaos, and demanded that Mao do something about it. While he allowed their persecution by rebellious groups and the extremists who had recently entered the revolutionary committee set up to run China around him, he finally authorized the PLA to impose some order. By 1969, military commanders were in effect in charge of most of China.

The CR was to also have a profound effect on another area – the resettlement of large numbers of people from the cities into the countryside. This campaign to encourage youths to go down to the rural areas and offer their services to the people there was to be called the 'sending-down campaign'. China, uniquely among large nations, was to undergo a deurbanization process, losing 2 per cent of its city populations back to the countryside. Despite having an internal passport system, where the state wished it, China's population was to prove highly fluid. Many from Shanghai were sent to Xinjiang. People from Hubei or Shanxi were sent to Inner Mongolia. Beijing students that could endure the high altitude sickness found themselves working in Tibet. A surprising number of these sent down never made it back to the places from where they had come.

A second impact on social life in China came through the establishment of communes, a process that intensified in the CR, though it had started some years earlier. The People's Communes, as they were called, were presented as a new, better way for Chinese to live. People ate and worked together. They shared their goods in canteens. They largely lived in male only or female only dorms, with times allocated for family life. Such massive rearrangement of social life was to prove very unpopular, and though it lingered into the 1970s, it was largely discredited by the very low productivity of the people working on these communal farms, and the general levels of human misery it created.

The 9th Party Congress – Night of the Long Knives

During all this turbulence, it was not surprising that there had been no Party Congress since 1956. But by 1969, there was enough stability for Mao to order the reconvening of what was left of the Party for a Congress, in order to elect a new central committee and politburo. After all, most of the former elite leaders had been felled, imprisoned, or simply killed.

The Ninth Party Congress was held in Beijing from the 1st to the 24th of April 1969. Regarded by the CCP now as an 'erroneous and mistaken' summit, at that time its main function was to confirm the commitment of the CCP to the direction of the CR, and to sanction the appointment of Lin Biao as Vice Party Chairman, and Mao's wife, Jiang Qing, as one of the key members of the Politburo standing committee. It was also to see an unprecedented number of members of the central committee replaced, with almost half brought in from the military. This was to be the team that Mao now hoped would take the Party forward in the direction he wished to go.

One of the more intense debates during the Ninth Congress was about how to enshrine descriptions of Mao's genius into the Constitution. This was the rather sycophantic suggestion of Lin Biao, who was, from this time on, described as Mao's closest comrade-in-arms and his chosen successor. His second suggestion, which was the one that aroused Mao's suspicion, was that Lin be named as country president. This position had been vacant since the removal of Liu Shaoqi two years previously. Mao set his face against Lin's idea. He also didn't like the notion of himself being described as 'a genius'. But it seems his main interest was in creating enough disunity around him to ensure that no one could pose any threat to his power. Bringing in his wife, despite clear undertakings several years before that he would keep her out of politics, was another method to create disunity. At the same time as all this was happening, he was also authorizing contact, through the Chinese embassy in Poland, with the United States. And initiating a military attack against Russia on the northern border. For a man in his mid-seventies, he had alarming levels of energy.

Lin Biao's Fall

In the seaside resort close to Beijing, on the coast of the Beihai Sea, at Beidaihe, there is a house that belonged to Lin Biao. It was reportedly here that he was to go, musing on how he needed to work his way up in the Party, ably helped (so the rumours created after the event of his ignominious fall tell it) by his fiercely ambitious wife, Ye Qun. Biographies in Chinese describe Lin as a man with a Howard Hughes-like fear of lights, dirt and lack of routine. His house was largely kept shuttered, and his rooms cleaned with scrupulous and meticulous care. It is hard to say how much of this story was created after his death to besmirch his memory. The propagandists did a fairly complete hatchet job on him. The effects of possible wounds from his long years as a soldier may have psychologically effected him, accounting for some of the weirdness he was imputed with. But in hindsight, he comes across more as the innocent victim of the Chairman's fiendish machinations, for which he was to prove no match. Lifted up when it suited Mao, in the mid-1960s, he was dropped again in 1970. The story of his attempted fleeing from China to Russia and the 'accidental' crash of his plane in the wilds of Mongolia is well known. Even so, both at the time and afterwards, there was speculation about exactly why he had gone, and whether, in the end, it was not the agents of the Chairman that had guided him onto the plane and launched him towards his fate.[14] Years later his body was recovered. Like Liu Shaoqi, it was a poor end to a distinguished and, at times heroic, career.

Even accepting the official Party versions from his death down to the current day in China that Lin Biao was a renegade and traitor who had planned, sometime in 1970 or early 1971, to assassinate Mao, it still left questions about why being the heir apparent to the Chairman was the world's most dangerous job. So far, two had been in pole position – Liu and Lin. Both had met messy, humiliating ends. After four years of relentless propaganda and worship, Mao's position had never been stronger. When he met Nixon in 1972, he struck the world's supposedly most powerful man as exuding raw power, the only possible equivalent being de Gaulle of France, who had similarly impressed him. Mao seemed to have something elemental about him. Their meeting, as described by Winston Lord, one of the attendees, left the Americans baffled. Mao spoke cryptically, in short statements, almost making jokes. But over the ensuing few days, as they negotiated, they noticed that everything happened pretty much in the order in which it had occurred in Mao's first meeting with them. Revealingly, the sophisticated, suave Zhou Enlai, who had impressed even the brilliant Kissinger, was to become a nervous, self-effacing bystander in the meeting with the Chairman.[15]

Lin's death highlighted a major problem for the Party, however, and that was what to do about succession. Mao was reaching 80.

His health was not good, despite highly adorned stories of him swimming against the Yangtze River and maintaining a ferocious daily timetable of activity.[16] He was showing the first signs of what would develop into full-blown Parkinson's disease and contribute to his death in 1976. And yet, there was still no clear successor and real fears that with his demise, the Party would be hamstrung, possibly even fatally weakened, by a bloody internal battle over who would eventually take control.

The Tenth Party Congress in 1973 did little to address this. It was overshadowed by the very visible absence of Lin. Mao was barely able to attend, such was his physical condition. The young Wang Hongwen, who would eventually be labelled as a leader of the Gang of Four, the group on whom much of the Cultural Revolution was blamed, was elevated to the politburo in his late 30s, gaining him the name 'the helicopter' because of his rapid rise. But this also succeeded in raising more questions about Mao's judgement. Wang had only the most limited administrative and political experience, running a revolutionary committee in Shanghai. He had no support in the Party, and very little even in his own city. From 1973 to 1976, there were clear divisions that were visible even to those outside. The radical leaders, which included Mao's wife, and the chief leftist ideologue Zhang Chunqiao, occupied one side, insisting on the dictatorship of the proletariat, deeply uneasy at the rapprochement with the US, and keen to deepen and further the radical reforms that they had seen kicked off in the late 1960s. It was hard to know what they stood for in terms of a positive programme, however. Against them was ranged the newly reinstated Deng Xiaoping, the previous Secretary General of the Party who had been sent to a factory in Jiangxi province for most of the CR, keeping a low head, but been summoned back and made a vice premier, probably with Zhou Enlai's support, in 1973.

Deng's return was a very covert admission that the experiments of the last decade had not worked, and that one of the key people who had been accused of being a traitor and renegade only six years before was now, in fact, acceptable and able to occupy high office. Deng was clearly not Mao's choice of successor, but just someone he saw as competent, who could be relied on to manage things. The leftists launched a bizarre 'Anti-Confucius Anti-Lin Biao' campaign in 1973, which was interpreted even at the time as a clear attack both on Zhou and on Deng. But it meant that there was utter confusion and bewilderment about what the Party direction was, even more about what would happen afterMao went.

In these years in which, in many ways, the Party had become Mao's victim, it had also lost control of its ability to explain both its past, and the reasons behind why it was doing things the way it was in the present. News of Lin's claimed treachery was only released slowly many months after his plane had crashed. Senior Party members were told in one wave, those lower in the hierarchy in another. Only after all this preparation could the news be slowly released to the wider public. Even so, it took some explaining. Frustration with the Party was already high. In Guangzhou in 1974, three brave writers working under the pseudonym Li Yizhe put up a Big Character Poster, one of the most popular means of communication at the time, demanding that there be more social democracy and representation of the people.[17] It was indicative of a deep cynicism and disengagement with politics, after the years of heady activism during the early CR. Those visiting in the early 1970s talked of a country that seemed to exist under a blanket, its people trapped in a rigid conformity, and very little action in its politics beyond arcane campaigns in which one faction in the elite political group attacked another. China was slowly developing economically in these years. It started the first of the reforms that would take off almost a decade later. But in 1971, what little foreign trade China conducted was via Hong Kong. There were few foreign visitors and very few links with foreign countries. The country's doors were permanently shut. Those peering at China across the border from Hong Kong saw only a sleepy, quiet backwater.

Party members themselves were as exhausted as anyone else by the continuous campaigns, and the chopping and changing of who was in power and who out. Many had been sent down to May 7th Cadre Schools, places that existed, in effect, as concentration camps doling out hard labour for those who were deemed to be 'problematic'. Most were located in some of the most isolated, harshest places in the country, where the winters were long and conditions savage. By 1976, the death of Zhou Enlai, after several years suffering from cancer, was enough to trigger demonstrations during the annual Qing Ming festival in April. People started placing memorials to Zhou on the Monument to the People's Heroes in the middle of Tiananmen Square. When these were cleared away by soldiers and police, more appeared, until there were violent clashes. The radical leadership, who were back in the ascendant now that Mao was effectively bedridden and out of action, labelled the demonstrators 'counter-revolutionaries'. In the summer, a massive earthquake in Tangshan, only three hours by train from Beijing, caused over a quarter of a million deaths. Its tremors could be felt in the centre of the capital. The radical leadership again turned their back on offers of foreign assistance, sticking fast to their principle of self-sufficiency. Mao's death on 9 September 1976 signalled a clear end of an era. He had been leader for 27 years, and head of the Party for nearly 40. Very few could remember the Party before he started to shape and direct it. This was a moment of immense importance for China and the existence of the project that Mao and his comrades had begun.

Mao had finally nominated Hua Guofeng, a native of the same province as Mao, as his successor. Hua was presented as the new Chairman of the Party. He quickly moved to incarcerate the radical leaders, having them arrested a few weeks after Mao's death. They were to be tried nearly five years later. Even so, Hua, like Wang Hongwen, lacked a proper power base in the Party. He was Mao's man, but in a very quick sign of the Party's instincts for self-preservation after being nearly wiped out by Mao, Deng Xiaoping, a man with far more formidable credentials, was quickly brought back (making his first public appearance at a football match). From 1978 he was clearly the most powerful leader in China and would remain so despite occupying no formal positions of power beyond being a member of the Politburo Standing Committee till 1987, and, till 1983, a humble Vice Premier.

Mao and the Party – An Assessment

Without Mao, it is questionable if the Party would ever have come to power. He made two critical decisions that decided its fate. The first was to base the power of the Party in the early years in the countryside. This was unorthodox if seen from the viewpoint of pure Marxism. But it was perhaps the only way in which the CCP could devise a successful campaign to gain power and avoid complete annihilation in the cities, which would have been its more natural base. The second was to work ruthlessly, and with great discipline, with different partners, from the Russians to the KMT, to promote the CCP's influence, and to ensure its survival after even the most devastating blows. Mao was to make the CCP a genuinely Chinese revolutionary party, one that was free of full Soviet dominance. His brilliant tactical sense ensured that despite these liaisons the Party was able to bide its time and wait till its moment came. He also understood the use of violence and force. Mao was no idealist. Everything he said and wrote showed that he understood profoundly the operations of power and the absolute priority of needing to acquire this before doing anything else. Even his forays into more abstract philosophy were motivated by profoundly practical considerations.

From the moment Mao became politically dominant in the Party, however, there was a ticking time bomb. Mao's method of operating from the early years was autocratic and intolerant. He demanded complete discipline. And he had been dropped into an environment in which power flowed towards the centre almost naturally. He embraced this historic trend with alacrity. Few emperors were as omnipotent as Mao. He had the great advantage of modern forms of technology and a massive state apparatus that grew from the partial industrialization of China. These he may not have understood (he admitted himself he was fundamentally ignorant about economics and science) but he knew how to manipulate them. Within a decade of Mao's coming to power, these trends became clear, and the early years of the more collegiate period of senior party rule were replaced with a 'winner take all' strategy in which people found they had to take up positions either of complete agreement with the Chairman or disagreement – with all the unpleasant consequences that entailed. The lucky ones like Deng were those who were allowed to exit the game a while and at least survive. There were many who didn't, and who perished. Amongst these was the man Mao had met many years before while at teachers college in Changsha, a fellow native of his own Hunan province, Li Lisan. Li's failed leadership of the Party in the early 1930s had resulted in him spending many years in the USSR, most of them after 1937 and the Great Terror as a prisoner in one of Stalin's gulags. He had even married a Russian woman while living there. His return to China in the late 1940s had been reasonably smooth. He had seemingly been forgiven his early role. Mao even gave him a position in government in the 1950s. But by the Cultural Revolution, he and his type were doomed. Carted off one evening, he was to disappear. It is unclear to this day whether he had been murdered or committed suicide. This was the reward for the young man, just after the Qing dynasty had fallen, who responded to an advert in a paper to discuss new political ideas and turned up with three others to be met by the young activist Mao Zedong. Mao had stated afterwards that the meeting really had three-and-a-half people there, as Li seemed unconvinced of the merits of the new ideology. His suspect status was to linger over him for the rest of his life, and contribute to his untimely death.[18]

By the 1960s, Mao had grown greater than the Party, and it became his victim. In many ways, he nearly destroyed it. He showed, in fact, that had he been pushed to do so, he would have turned completely on it and brought it down. In a few extraordinary years in the 1960s Party rule was routed and circumvented. The fundamental structures and functions of the Party stopped. Mao resurrected it when it suited his purposes to do so.

There are undisputable achievements under Mao. The first was to restore unity to China after the decades of disunity under a range of local leaders, many of them with personal and highly corrupt ambitions. From 1949 the PRC was stable and largely unified, despite worrying moments, especially during the CR when local leaders reappeared who looked similar to the warlords of the 1920s. China did rebuild much of its infrastructure over this period, repairing and then developing what had existed before the war and starting to post positive growth rates. The terrible famines of the early 1960s excepted, China posted large increases in life expectancy rates from 1949 to 1976, raising these almost double from 35 to 64. Illiteracy was massively decreased and a national health and security system constructed.

The human cost of this was phenomenal. Mao's ability to focus on political ends and aim towards them no matter what the cost in terms of lives or destruction is at the heart of the revulsion he inspires in many of his most passionate opponents.[19] He seems to have simply been born without the ability to see this aspect of any action he supported or took part in. To him, human life was an expendable commodity. For this very good reason, he will probably be remembered as one of the great tyrants of the twentieth century, alongside Stalin and Hitler. But he operated in much more complex circumstances and his legacy will take many decades to assess and understand.

The Communist Party survived him. In August 1977, almost a year after his death, it held the 11th Congress. Deng Xiaoping made a reappearance, as a member of the standing committee. Huo Guofeng was the Chairman. It formally announced that the Cultural Revolution was over. But the leadership at that meeting had to survey the devastation in their economy, in the infrastructure of their Party and in the political mood of the country. They had to embark on a second phase of the revolution, but this time without Mao. The era of the 'First Period of Leadership' was well and truly over. Very few regretted its passing.

Chapter Three
The Party in the Reform Era

It was from the Communist Manifesto and The ABC of Communism that I learned the rudiments of Marxism. Recently, some foreigners said that Marxism cannot be defeated. That is so not because there are so many big books, but because Marxism is the irrefutable truth. The essence of Marxism is seeking truth from facts. That's what we should advocate, not book worship. The reform and the open policy have been successful not because we relied on books, but because we relied on practice and sought truth from facts. It was the peasants who invented the household contract responsibility system with remuneration linked to output. Many of the good ideas in rural reform came from people at the grass roots. We processed them and raised them to the level of guidelines for the whole country. Practice is the sole criterion for testing truth. I haven't read too many books, but there is one thing I believe in: Chairman Mao's principle of seeking truth from facts. That is the principle we relied on when we were fighting wars, and we continue to rely on it in construction and reform. We have advocated Marxism all our lives. Actually, Marxism is not abstruse. It is a plain thing, a very plain truth.

— Deng Xiaoping
Excerpts from talks given in Wucheng, Shenzhen,
Zhuhai and Shanghai, 18 January to 21 February 1992

After the death of Mao, the Party went through a period of major readjustment. The Maoist years had left its personnel decimated and its structures exhausted and run down. The Party was an organization in search of a saviour. It was almost unimaginable that the saviour would prove to be a 74-year-old veteran of elite Party politics who had already been consigned to the political graveyard three times. Deng Xiaoping's return was popular, but hardly the harbinger of great things. His reappearance was neither marked by any great fanfare, nor by overt signs of mass approval, whatever the clues of quiet consent that observers noticed amongst Chinese people in the late 1970s during the power transition. People just wanted to see competent administration from their government. Deng was to prove himself to be one of history's great realists – a pragmatic leader for a pragmatic party. He was the chief creator of the final paradox of twentieth-century Chinese politics – an ostensibly free-market-orientated economy presided over by a politically one-party system. This unique arrangement continues to this day.

A Visitor from the Past

Those that attended the 17th Party Congress in Beijing in October 2007 were intrigued to see an ancient-looking gentleman, dressed in traditional Maoist garb, shuffle to his seat close to the current leaders of China, and take his place. Within a few minutes of the main talks starting, he was evidently soundly asleep, his head resting on his chest, slumped forward in profound peace. Only an irreverent photographer managed to capture this touching image.

Hua Guofeng is of interest, as he had been the top leader in China for four years. He was Mao's final chosen successor. There is a famous portrait of them both sitting talking to each other, the Chairman imperiously looking across the room, with the caption underneath, 'With you in charge, I am at ease.' (*Ni banshi, wo fanxin*). A scrawled note to this effect, reputedly from the Chairman, was produced as final proof of Hua's anointment by his predecessor.

Hua was evidently the lesser of many evils. He had very modest experience and little support in the Party. But Mao had already indicated his weariness with the leftists, led by his wife, but propelled by Zhang Chunqiao and others, who had been pouring out theoretical works, culminating in Zhang's snappily titled work from 1975, *On Exercising All-Round Dictatorship over the Bourgeoisie*. That they each looked like bad characters out of a pantomime did not help the propagandists who somehow had to sell their attractions to the Chinese public and the outside world. Their incarceration and trial was one of the great cathartic moments of modern Chinese history, provoking joy on the streets of Beijing, even though its conduct and outcome had very little to do with justice. As Jiang Qing rightly pointed out at her own trial, she was only the servant of Mao. Without his tacit and sometimes active support, she would have achieved nothing.

They were easy to dismiss. But Deng was a far tougher proposition. Mao had complained years before that he never felt he knew what Deng was thinking. Deng himself had cheekily said he was deaf in one ear, which is why he never managed to quite catch what either Mao or Marx were saying. Mao admired Deng's administrative abilities. But he felt he had seen Deng's revisionist tendencies in the early 1960s. Deng could not be trusted with the flame. This is given fulsome expression in Mobo Gao's rousing onslaught on Deng in his *The Battle for China's Past: Mao and the Cultural Revolution* (London: Pluto Press 2008), in which he states that Deng was a disaster for the Party, introducing reforms that have created inequality, instability, and ideological sellout. Perhaps these fears went through Mao's head when he elevated Hua to the Party leadership.

Hua's utter reliance on Mao was soon to prove a burden. Castigated as a 'whateverist' (based on his fondness for saying, 'We firmly uphold whatever policy decisions Chairman Mao made and we unswervingly adhere to whatever instructions Chairman Mao gave'), within two years of being in power he was effectively neutered by his popular and phenomenally able deputy. In 1981, he 'retired', maintaining his position on the Central Committee, and being an honoured member of the CCP. A few years back, I was being shown around a factory in Hainan and was astonished to see, amongst pictures on the wall of leaders who had visited the plant, one of the ancient Hua, incongruously dressed in a Mao suit again. The old man looked like someone who had wandered in from another age, seeing the final results of the process that he had been present at the start of, but had had nothing to do with. Ironically, he was to die during the Olympics, on 20 August 2008 at the age of 87. Without Hua's transitional work, where he at least managed to avoid China's falling into chaos and internal upheaval, China might never have been in a position to host such an event. He was modern China's quiet man, present at a crucial time, but seemingly almost having nothing to do with it.

Dealing with What Went Before

As though it did not have enough current problems, the Party had to deal with a few issues in its history. It had, to say the least, a somewhat complicated narrative, in which some of its former self-proclaimed great leaders had ended up being denounced as scabs. For ten years, daily campaigns had been waged against a series of enemies who had previously occupied the highest positions in the Party. Beyond this, the state was almost bankrupt, with no foreign reserves to speak of, factory output stagnant and a generation of students who had mastered the art of revolution but not actually been able to attend university and learn any other skills, as these had all been closed down. Its relations with the rest of the world, despite the rapprochement with the US, were at best tepid. And it had just discovered, during a brief disastrous military foray into Vietnam, possibly at Deng's deliberate prompting, how to show the PLA the hard way that they were weak, incompetent and not fit for purpose, that's its army was ill-equipped, and out of practice.

The Party was trapped by its own propaganda. For decades, the rural population (still the overwhelming majority of the Chinese people) had been fed a diet of constant praise for the utter correctness of the Party and its infallibility. Little did they know that, in fact, for most of the last ten years, it had been like a silent, suffering, battered wife. How now to convey the simple fact that Mao was not a god and that some of the policies implemented over the last quarter of a century had been mistaken? Blaming the Gang of Four, as Jiang Qing and her leftist comrades were finally labelled, went some of the way. Labelling extreme leftism and identifying it as a cancer at the heart of communism in China at least looked like an explanation as long as people didn't quiz this position too hard. The Cultural Revolution therefore was simply called a leftist error, led by a small number of people around the Chairman who had misled and manipulated him. This sat oddly with Mao's own consistency in explaining to whoever would listen that his two greatest achievements were the victory against the Japanese, and starting the Cultural Revolution with the insistence that similar mass movements be held every few decades to ensure that people did not lose their revolutionary edge.

In 1981, after months of drafting and discussion, the Party issued a resolution on its own history. It admitted and explained the leftist mistakes of the past. But it did not topple Mao from his place as a great leader. He was still too admired and revered in the Party. It accused him of being misled. The '70 per cent right, 30 per cent wrong' formula that became a popular distillation later, never, in fact, appeared in the Resolution, although it did appear in some of Deng's speeches and statements later. Instead, it admitted that errors had been made, but that the general direction of the party had always been correct. 'Comrade Mao Zedong was a great Marxist and a great proletarian revolutionary,' the Resolution stated. 'It is true that he made gross errors during the Cultural Revolution but, if we judge his activities as a whole his contributions to the Chinese revolution far outweigh his mistakes.... He rendered indelible meritorious service founding and building up our Party and the Chinese People's Liberation Army, winning victory for the cause of liberation of the Chinese people.' More grandly, the Resolution stated, 'He made contributions to the liberation of the oppressed nations of the world and the progress of mankind.'[1] This must have been news to the rest of the world.

Accompanying this declaration tidying up its understanding of its own history was a massive, and equally unsophisticated, rectification campaign. In one fell swoop, the Party blamed everything on the bad leaders of the past, a classic diversion tactic. It issued hundreds of thousands of notices to those once accused of being rightists and counter-revolutionaries, offering them rehabilitation and amnesty. Hu Feng, the close follower of the great Lu Xun, mentioned in Chapter Two, was let out of jail after languishing there for nearly a quarter of a century. Some of the youth sent down to the countryside were allowed back to the cities to become mature students. Small amounts of compensation were paid. People had no choice but to set aside the past and now carry on life as normal. This was a big task. Many had to return to work beside people who had betrayed them, and made their lives miserable for years. Some even had to work with people they either knew or suspected were involved in the murder of their relatives or friends. The Cultural Revolution was to leave lasting scars, but these were only dealt with in the early days by being buried.

Mao himself, after being embalmed, with advice from the Vietnamese and Russians, was placed in a newly built memorial hall in the middle of Tiananmen Square. There he lies to this day.

During the opening ceremony of the 2008 Olympics, many visiting journalists noticed that his image was absent from the festivities. He continues to exist as a 'respected', remote figure, but one who still exudes a whiff of danger. The publication of his unexpurgated works in Chinese has been an interesting, time-consuming, and controversial process. It seems even his propagandists in his own lifetime didn't quite know how to deal with the Chairman, and make him say the right thing.

Moving Forward

At the third plenum of the 11th Party Congress in December 1978, the new Chinese leadership, with Hua Guofeng still in charge, started to look at how they would move forward. They would return to the modernization strategy that had been one of the great themes of Chinese history since the late Qing reforms, the 4 May Movement of 1919 and the early 1960s. China needed to implement the four modernizations, in national defence, agriculture, science and industry. These were enshrined in new party statements. But it also needed to undertake internal reform, becoming more open to the outside world, letting new talent into leadership positions and becoming a late-twentieth-century party of government. Deng was clearly uninterested in long ideological arguments. He used Marxist terminology the way a businessman uses technical jargon, to convey a point, and then move on. By 1979, China had passed its first joint venture law, and Coca Cola was already being imported (though initially only for use in hotels where foreigners were allowed to stay). In the 1980s, China saw a raft of other reforms. The Special Economic Zones (initially four) were set up to exploit their positions near to international trade hubs (Hong Kong, Macau and Taiwan). China started to commit something like 45 per cent of its annual GDP to investment in railways, buildings and infrastructure. Airports were built again, and something was done about China's chronic lack of power and energy. Establishing formal diplomatic relations with the US under the Carter Presidency in 1979 was only symptomatic of a movement now to bring down some of the barriers that existed. The greatest reforms that were needed, however, were internal ones.

Back to the Countryside

Mao may have been called a peasant emperor, and he may have located his main power base in the countryside. The countryside had brought him to power, and farmers and their families fought and died by the millions in his armies. But he had allowed them to starve in the 1960s in order to feed the cities and to export grain to countries like Romania. And he had maintained their citizenship class where they were excluded from many of the social benefits of city dwellers. The countryside though, making up 90 per cent of China's population in 1980, could not be ignored. And they were to prove to be one of the main delivery agents of China's extraordinary development in the next two decades.

Deng's government (he was, after all, in this process only one of a group of leaders, including the father of current favourite to replace Hu Jintao as Party General Secretary in 2012, Xi Jinping, and the great economist Chen Yun, who in many ways could be called the intellectual father of the reform process) and his advisors decided that they needed to offer incentives to the agricultural sector to improve performance. By 1984 they had introduced the household responsibility system, which allowed farmers to sell surpluses to the public and back to the state at a small profit. This was the first kind of widespread, open, free market allowed in China since the 1950s and was a radical, bold departure from the past. It was to quickly prove a success. It dramatically improved the efficiency of the agricultural sector, freeing up people to work in the newly established town and village enterprises which remain, to this day, the major employers in China and one of the most successful parts of a partly privatized economy. All of this, as Deng Xiaoping was himself to admit, was largely unplanned.[2]

For a country that had experienced famine in living memory, China was to enjoy good harvests and excellent agricultural productivity throughout the 1980s. It was also able to look at attracting foreign investment to exploit China's plentiful supply of cheap labour and its raw materials and land. From the establishment of the Special Economic Zones (SEZ) in 1984 onward, China began to gain European, North American and Asian investment. Much of this was from Japan and Hong Kong, who were to be key partners in the early years of the reform process. Hong Kong in particular served as a conduit for capital and know-how, largely building on family links between people in Hong Kong and the Pearl River Delta and helping to develop the evolution of its own enterprises by allowing them to spread into China, where land was more plentiful and labour cheaper. As a symbol of this economic change, by 1989 Shenzhen, one of the earliest SEZs, had become a city of over five million. Deng's portrait was placed overlooking the new city, acclaimed as 'the chief architect of China's reforms'. A quarter of a century later, it stands there to this day.

All of this had happened without breathing a word about any kind of political reform. China's justification for this was that it was in the primary state of socialism (we will hear more on this later) and, therefore, hasty moves to instigate political reform were not wise. In the 1980s, though, there were sporadic bold moves to liberalize not just the economy, but society. This 'boom-and-bust' movement often meant that there would be powerful requests for China to open up its political system, followed each time by quick crackdowns of varying degrees of intensity and savagery. Deng may have become a more palatable face of the Chinese leadership – and during his visit to the US in 1979 he had won over many people by his seemingly avuncular, open-minded style. But he was no democrat. The Democracy Wall movement in 1978–79 had proved that, and during that period young and middle-aged activists had placed up big character posters and printed leaflets and unofficial newspapers criticizing the Cultural Revolution (which was then deemed permissible) and asking for reform, openness and the introduction of democracy (which was very much not permissible). The most famous of these, the poster produced by ex-Beijing zoo electrician Wei Jingsheng in 1979, demanded the 'Fifth Modernisation' – an open political system. Wei was rewarded for his labour with a 18-year prison sentence. But he was highly representative of a group of younger, urban intellectuals, many of them sons and daughters of Party members, or themselves Party workers, who had felt that after three decades in power, the CCP could have delivered more. Wei himself told the story of how, when he was a Red Guard in the late 1960s, he had caught sight of a nearly naked girl from his train as they passed a station. She was only wearing a top, with no trousers, because her family was too poor to afford clothing. He had asked himself how this sort of thing could happen under socialism. Wei's posing of the question and articulation of the problems was unwelcome. Democracy Wall was quickly closed down. Its site is now occupied by a massive shopping precinct. [3]

These brief outbursts were to occur throughout the 1980s. Many, finally free to write about their experiences in the CR, produced what was soon called 'wounded literature'. But they found that beyond testifying to their status as victims in the CR, and haranguing the Gang of Four for their crimes, they were unable to probe deeper into the causes for how this devastating movement had managed to happen. The writer Ba Jin, active since the 1930s, wondered why there was no museum of the Cultural Revolution, and that until there was, there would be no open reckoning in China.[4] He died in 2005 at the age of 101, and might have known that finally, such a museum did open, but only in the little-visited Shantou, in Guangdong, native home of Hong Kong's richest man, Li Ka-Shing. The Cultural Revolution gets little attention in the major national museums in Beijing.

Deng himself noted that when the windows were opened, flies sometimes got in. He sanctioned various attacks on spiritual pollution throughout the 1980s. During each one, a new batch of those who had spoken out a little too boldly, or old activists who needed to be reminded to remain being careful, were rounded up and given sentences in 'Reform Through Labour' (*lao gai*) or reeducation camps. Harry Wu was to painstakingly list the few of these that were definitely known.[5] Deng certainly didn't allow the sorts of mass imprisonments that Mao had – but there were still many thousands of incarcerations during the 1980s.

Ideological Headaches

In the 1980s, the CCP looked closely at other potential models. Its leadership, first under Hu Yaobang and then Zhao Ziyang, had records as reformists. As General Secretaries of the Party, they had sanctioned overseas visits by officials to look more closely at other forms of governance. They had shown an interest in northern European social democracy systems, impressed, like the rest of the world, at their excellent social security systems and their clean, transparent government. But they realized soon that such models needed a very high level of public investment. They were also very expensive. And they were catering to populations that were minuscule fractions of China's. Since the early 1970s, before the death of Mao, China had introduced forms of family planning. But with its population out of control, in the early 1980s it implemented a severe one-child-per-family policy. This, perhaps more than anything else, was to have a massive social impact on China, its outcomes very mixed (for the demographic headache this has caused, see the next chapter.)

The 1980s were a surprisingly adventurous time, looked back with some nostalgia by intellectuals and academics who now remember the period. Yasheng Huang has argued that it was the freest and most entrepreneurial-friendly period of modern Chinese history, with genuine liberty conveyed to business people, and many local governments making bold moves to develop themselves in ways that suited local conditions.[6] But the ideological problem would not go away. China still had a one-party system, enshrined in its constitution, and the frequent spiritual pollution campaigns waged in universities were sharp reminders that while the Party was changing, it had not gone away nor forgotten some of the lessons on control and fear that Mao had taught it.

Nor had it forgotten Mao's mastery of dialectics and his appreciation of contradiction. At the 12th Party Congress held in Beijing in September 1982, for the first time Deng Xiaoping announced the concept of 'socialism with Chinese characteristics'. This was to become the mantra of the new ideological position. In essence, it allowed market reforms to happen, opening up China to investment, and to some internal economic changes. Like Stalin's 'socialism in one country', it gave up the pretence of delivering revolution and liberation to the entire world's proletariat. Instead, it would strive to deliver a reasonable amount of wealth to China's own citizens. In later years the Party would grow bolder and call such an ideological position 'market socialism', blithely daring anyone to point out that such a concept was dangerously paradoxical. But Deng's leadership was consistent over the years in demanding that restraints to market growth be lifted and regulations and rules rationalized and relaxed so that the market could produce its magic. Such reforms were compared to those being introduced by Gorbachev in the USSR at about this time. But Deng was to prove to have no appetite for any reform that strayed into the key political territory of the Party. This he would prove in 1989. Perhaps the most famous exposition of this position was by one of the great architects of the reform process and a political sparring partner of Deng's, Chen Yun. He had described the Chinese economy as being like a 'bird in a cage', with the state supplying the framework within which people's economic creativity and energies could work – up to a point.

In addition to dealing with the ideology, Deng's administration also had to achieve two other goals. The first was to set up enough institutionalization to ensure that never again could one person control the Party in the way that Mao had. Deng should be accorded great respect for this. He never encouraged any form of personal worship. There were no Deng statues or cult of Deng, even though at the time the opportunity might have been there. He did not occupy grand formal positions of power like President or Chairman. He was marked merely as Comrade Deng in official announcements, one of a group of a half-dozen senior party elders who took an active interest in the running of the country. Of course, the world, and Chinese people, knew that Deng was the most important leader. This was let slip by Zhao Ziyang just before the events in 1989 when he said that Deng 'had a say in all major decisions made by the government and Party'. Such open admission by the man who was meant to be the General Secretary of the Party that he, in fact, danced to the tune of someone higher up, but not formally occupying any position, was unwelcome and one of the many sources of dissatisfaction that led to Zhao's removal. Even so, Deng at least went through the motions of taking decisions to the Party. From 1977 the Party Congresses have taken place every five years. Plenaries and National People's Congresses have also been regularly held. Deng stamped down on all forms of potential Deng-worship. The Party was great and glorious, not Deng. In this way, he proved he was a much better organizational man than Mao.

Secondly, in addition to the processes of institutionalization, Deng's government also worked on moving away from the 'rule of one man' to 'the rule of law' (*renzhi* versus *fazhi*). Setting up a legal system from scratch was no easy matter. China had a weak tradition of executive judiciary in any case, despite its history of legalism. There was no background in civil or commercial law. In 1979, moreover, China had no trained judges to speak of – most were either army personnel, or retired Party officials. The courts were regarded as 100 per cent supporters of the Party, and no cases that went to appeal (usually on the same day) were overturned. The Courts were the servants of the Party and the state. They had no credibility and the constitutional rights accorded citizens looked good on paper, but barely existed in the real world.

From 1980 China did its best to build a legal system from scratch. It looked closely at Japanese and Western legal codes and lifted much of their legislation onto its own books. It set about training a new generation of lawyers, and setting up a new court system. This was given extra urgency by the fact that, with foreign investment starting to come into China, there was the need at least for workable labour contract law, and the raft of legislation that would reassure outsiders that they had some level of protection in China. Even so, China lacked a basic Contract Law till 1999 (though it had had an Economic Contract Law since 1982), and had to leave the establishment of bankruptcy laws till much later. It also discovered early on that, while writing down and then passing good laws into legislation was relatively straightforward, implementing them was much harder. In the years ahead, there would also be clear problems in taking decisions from the central courts in Beijing and trying to have them implemented in any of the provinces or autonomous regions of China. This is still an ongoing problem, with marked differences between the quality of judgements delivered by a Beijing court and those handed down in places like Gansu or Xinjiang. Local interests came strongly into play in setting up a national legal system. While China increased lawyers from one per hundred thousand people in the 1980s to something closer to levels seen in the West today, the courts that were set up and the laws that were passed were never that far from political interference. The process begun in the 1980s, therefore, is still ongoing and it remains the case that the final arbiter of all important decisions remains the Party and that the courts are not free of political interference. The personal networks offered by the Party are a far greater guarantee of someone's protection and rights in China that mere legal process.

Starting to build a legal system was important not just for attracting investors to China, but also to encourage, for the first time, the seeds of a private sector. In the 1980s, China started to see people opt out of the state system and try to do business on their own. The roots of this were in the establishment of the town and village enterprises mentioned earlier. But people's options became more diverse, and their responsibility to manage their own future much greater, as the decade went on. Some simply set up roadside restaurants or small retail businesses. In the early years, there were many hundreds of thousands of these small individual businesses. A lot of them were run by people moonlighting from work unit jobs where they had nothing to do. Now that the market was more important, the state only set realistic work targets. Many of the massive state-owned enterprise's (SOEs) found that they had far too many employees and a very small customer base to buy their goods. This process was to intensify in the 1990s. But already, by 1986, there were many new entrepreneurs who were running their own businesses underneath the radar of the state, tolerated as long as they did not start to work towards more political directions (selling books with 'bad contents' for instance, or, as happened in Tibet and Inner Mongolia, setting up coffee shops which then became, it was claimed, covers for discussing political activism against the state). Work units still provided basic services, like education, healthcare and accommodation. But the restrictions they placed on people's daily lives lessened. And by the end of the decade, Party membership started to stagnate. Being a member of the Party, at least at this point, did not bring the sort of benefits once deemed important.

Searching for a Successor – the Recurrence of an Old Problem

Deng shared one common problem with Mao, although he handled it differently. He was approaching his mid-80s by 1989. His hearing and eyesight were deteriorating. He was seen less and less in public and had already declared, disingenuously, his retirement from politics. Even so, there was still the issue, as there had been with Mao, of who would be the main leader when he died. Those of the elite senior leaders were all roughly the same age as Deng, so they could not be put forward. Hu Yaobang, the lively, diminutive Party Secretary from 1980 to 1987, fell foul of Deng and the 'senior advisers' over a Party rectification campaign in 1986, and was unceremoniously removed from power, dying in 1989. His replacement, Zhao Ziyang, was highly regarded and, with his secretary Wen Jiabao, set about dealing with two immediate grievances. One was dissatisfaction with government corruption. The other was economic problems deriving from the supply of foodstuffs and grain and a recent bout of inflation. Both of these were to escalate over the next two years. But they were to be accompanied by something that the CCP was unable to control, which was the international collapse of fellow communist systems in the rest of the world, building up to the final implosion of the USSR in 1991. These were events that were largely unexpected, and which left the CCP highly exposed and isolated at the end, and with much of its credibility in shreds. As such, the buildup to 1989 can be called the most recent dark night of the soul for the CCP. It came uncomfortably close to losing power and Deng's legacy, while not wholly destroyed by the events of 1989, was deeply stained by them.

The year 1989 was to have been of great significance anyway. For the first time in two decades, the USSR and China had experienced a rapprochement. The visit to China in May by Gorbachev had occurred against a background of discontent in China, most of it directed at the Party and the corruption of its servants. This had focused around Hu Yaobang who, two years after being removed from leading the CCP, had died. While being no closet democrat, he was reasonably popular with the students, and it was this key group that started to appear in the streets, agitating for deeper political reforms and asking for elections and multi-party politics. Demonstrations spread from Beijing to Shanghai and then further inland to Xian, Chongqing, down to Guangzhou and even over in the far west in Urumqi and Lhasa. Tibet exploded in a sustained series of riots, stemming from dissatisfaction with the governance of the Party from 1987 onward, but these were to grow far fiercer in 1989. By the end of May, the Party was seemingly caught in the headlights, acting like it did not know what to do. Gorbachev's visit had happened under the glare of international journalists, but they had also had their attention attracted by the large groups of students, latterly joined by workers and other social groups and camping out in Tiananmen Square. Accounts of what happened over the final days leading to the night of 4 June are unclear. So is the number of casualties that were finally sustained in the events of that night. But by the morning of 5 June the square had been cleared of demonstrators, Beijing was under a curfew, there was a list of dozens of most wanted activists and an atmosphere reigned which came close to the sort experienced during the Red Terror purges of the distant past.

From highly credible-looking internal documents which were smuggled out of China several years later and issued as 'The

Tiananmen Papers', it is clear that there were some differences in the main leadership about how to deal with the disturbances. Elder leaders thought long and hard, but they interpreted the protests as 'counter-revolutionary' (ironically) and anti-Party. Once this label had been affixed, it became a simple matter of choosing between two options. Either the Party concede and see its power fundamentally compromised. Or come down hard on those it saw as causing the problems. Zhao Ziyang, one of the chief compromisers, was immediately a dead man walking. Removed from power, he was replaced by Jiang Zemin, till then Party Secretary of Shanghai, and a man, according to some reports, that Deng regarded with distaste. But at least in his handling of the protests in Shanghai, he had not had to resort to violence. The order to send the troops in was taken after several days of heated debate and internal discussions. Deng carried the day and bears the responsibility for what happened. For some, he was only seeking to prove to others in the Party that, in the end, when the crisis really came, he had the guts and hardness to endure even bloodshed to defend the Party. At least for this audience, his political credibility was intact when the events of 1989 were over.

Globally, the fallout from the crackdown was massive. Condemned almost universally, the CCP looked isolated and vulnerable. Things were to get even worse. By the end of 1989 old allies like Ceauşescu of Romania had been executed by his own people. Almost the same day, the Berlin Wall came down. None of this had been predicted or expected. By 1990, the CCP was researching what their reaction to this collapse of fellow communist systems was to be. A year later, the USSR imploded. China was alone as a large state with a one-party system.[7]

Starting Over

The student uprising and the turbulence of 1989 had rattled the party to its core. Students had turned against their own. Even more ominous, workers groups had also started to express deep dissatisfaction. The Party seemed to be only working for its own good. It had become a self-serving elite. Figures like Li Peng, the Premier at the time, typified this. A shrill autocrat, who had tried to enter into public debate with the student leaders in the days before the crackdown, it had been Li Peng who had announced martial law and demanded that students leave the central area. And it had been he, according to the Tiananmen Papers, who had followed a hard line with the Party elders, pushing them towards the final uncompromising position they took. Li Peng had impeccable Party credentials. He was taken under the wings of Zhou Enlai and Deng Yingchao after the death of his parents during the war. He had been educated in the USSR and was an engineer. He had a background in the power sector, and had worked his way up through the traditional technocrat's route, enjoying the patronage of Party elder Chen Yun in the 1980s. But he was perhaps the worst public performer in Chinese politics of the late twentieth century (a pretty hotly contested position, it had to be said) a man who inspired scorn and loathing in many Chinese, even if revisionists argued that in his later career he had been a quiet and persistent supporter of opening up and economic reform.

Deng must have realized this image problem. And while an immediate crackdown and rounding up of students and other activists could solve problems in the short term, the longer-term issues remained. China's development was too rapid. A sign of things to come was the extension of Special Economic Status in 1990 to Shanghai. In 1992 Deng undertook his famous Southern Tour. In some ways he was aping Mao, going straight over the heads of the bureaucrats and the officials to speak directly to the people. His visit to Zhuhai, Shenzhen and Guangdong was covered in the official press. He was able to speak, in his barely audible, thick Sichuanese accent translated into standard Chinese by his daughter, about the utter necessity of continuing to reform the economy and standing by the decisions made over a decade before. Socialism with Chinese characteristics still stood. Of course, there had been an international 'evil wind' that had disrupted things. But in the long term, the Party had been right. People now had to keep the faith.

Despite persistent lobbying, the event of 4 June 1989 is still categorized as a counter-revolutionary movement. An open assessment of what happened has not been possible and each year, around the anniversary of the event, there is great sensitivity and anxiety in Beijing and other cities that no small demonstrations crop up asking for rectification. Ding Zilin, whose son died in the event, has set up with others 'Mothers for Tiananmen'. But their lobbying for open discussion of who was killed in 1989 has fallen on deaf ears. Zhao Ziyang was to be kept under house arrest for nearly two decades, dying in early 2005. His obituary in the Chinese press was kept very brief. His secretary, Bao Tong, has been a persistent critic of the government's handling of the events of that year – and he too, despite being almost 90, has been kept under close surveillance.

The greatest shock for the Party in June 1989, or at least for the hard-line faction that had won the day, was the depth of dislike and unpopularity to which they had fallen. Even in the Party, there were many officials from the media and the Ministry of Foreign Affairs, amongst others, who had taken part in the 1989 disturbances. Under duress and coercion, people would fall in line. But at that time, there was little love left for an organization that had turned on its own people. Not even Mao's government had shot down students.

But in a deeper sense, it was also symptomatic of the Party's state at this time. Economic liberalism had been a pragmatic pact, to maintain credibility and popular support as a government without ceding its monopoly on power. But, in fact, economic liberalization and loosening of controls had let loose two particular demons. One was the problem of regionalism, with certain provinces and areas starting to develop faster than others, in the process articulating their own particular political ambitions and programmes (Guangdong falls into this camp). The other was the appearance of clearly visible factions in the Party.

The latter was a big problem. Mao had often spoken of the 'two paths', the two directions the Party could go in. This seemed to be etched in its genetic code, a contradictoriness pulling it in two directions, one towards the left, the other towards the right. This had been controlled throughout his period as leader by constant campaigns and rectification processes. But in the 1980s, these were not possible. The methods of the Cultural Revolution had been discredited and repudiated. They were too wasteful and destructive. Debate within the party was allowed. Groups formed within it, some of which wanted more reform, faster, and some that wanted to pull back. The conflict between these runs to the current day. The 4 June was the first sign of a violent struggle within the heart of the Party itself, with the reformist Zhao Ziyang sent into internal exile. In the 1990s (see later) the battle would continue.

Analysts in the 1980s called this 'fragmented authoritarianism'. The central Chinese government accepted a pact where, in order to achieve the sort of economic growth it was aiming for, it had to accept less control and looser restrictions than before. Regions had to experiment with different models. Some were able to get richer quicker than others– this was allowed in the famous statement by Deng that they would 'first let a few grow rich and then let the rest follow'. By 1989 there were signs of the inequality that would explode in the 1990s and 2000s. For a few years up to 1989, the Party even started toying with the idea of letting entrepreneurs into the Party. But 4 June interrupted this, and it finally happened 12 years later. There were periods when the Party seemed to change regulations every day, and some times when it wasn't in fact clear what was allowed and what not, because the pace of change was so quick. In any case, most people were doing what they wanted, regardless of who said what. From time to time there would be clampdowns. Then things would continue as normal.

Such fragmented power, though, meant that the Party had to have a strategy to deal with its own internal fractures and the complex society that it was stewarding. From 1989, and particularly from 1992, it recommitted to reform – but with a clear idea of the territory that it needed to control. It set its face against imprecations from the west to follow the Russians and reform as they had done. When the USSR fell apart and the Russia Federation went through tough economic years under Yeltsin the Party felt itself vindicated. The Party's argument to its own people was to remain simple and blunt: If China wanted to prosper it would need to remain strong and unified. If it started to fall apart, then it stood a good chance of returning to the chaos and external exploitation that had occurred in the past. From 1992 this pact kept the Party in power and till now there have been no further uprisings as there were in 1989. But they haunt the thoughts of many of the leadership, and play upon their anxieties. In that sense, the effects of Tiananmen can still be felt and the Party's reckoning with that traumatic time, while it has been postponed, has not been entirely consigned to history.

Chapter Four

The CCP from 1992 to 2008

Another reason for the deficit,' Wu continued, 'is illegitimate spending, the unspecified "other" expenses on the books. One of the abuses hidden under the item "other" is eating and drinking at public expense. It just cannot be stopped, no matter how many rules and interdictions are handed down. Mao Zedong said, "The revolution is not a dinner party." Now this has been transformed into "The revolution is a dinner party." Even the often-quoted lines from one of Mao's poems, "The red army fears not the long march, mountains and rivers they will take in a stride" has been changed to a popular saying, "The official fears not a drinking match, ten thousand cups he will down with pride."

From Chen Guidi and Wu Chuntao
Will the Boat Sink the River?: The Life of China's Peasants

The 14th Congress, in 1992, the first formal Congress after the 1989 'turbulence' (as it was called in official Chinese government discourse), was preoccupied with cementing the succession of Jiang Zemin. This was the final choice of an aging and very frail Deng, who made a brief appearance in the Great Hall of the People, and then, apart from a couple of fleeting reappearances, disappeared from view till his death in 1997. By this time, he had been a member of the Communist Party for over 70 years.

The era of Jiang Zemin, from 1992 to 2003, was dominated by two events. The first was the final entry into the World Trade Organization of the PRC, after almost 14 years of negotiations.

The second was a sustained campaign, called the Three Represents (*san ge daibiao*), to enfranchise entrepreneurs into the Party (and, for some commentators, to dismantle completely the intellectual legacy of Marxism – Leninism in China). Jiang's era saw a decisive shift away from one all-powerful leader to an attempt to institutionalize the handover of power from one group of leaders to another. It also saw a dramatic increase in the private sector of the economy, the challenge of seeing Taiwan democratize, despite its renegade status being still undecided, and the return of Hong Kong and Macau to PRC sovereignty.

Willy Lam, the Hong Kong-based veteran commentator on Party affairs, described the Jiang era as one that resembled the Brezhnev era in the USSR – noticeable for its complacency and for the failure to make big decisions. The greatest issue of the time for China was to resolve the status of Taiwan. Deng was, on Lam's reckoning, the only politician of his generation who might have succeeded at doing this. But he drew back, and by 1989 things were taken out of his control. Attempts to internationalize the economy in the late 1990s, while leading to spectacular rises in foreign investment, ended up creating a society more unequal and with more corruption than probably at any stage in the first forty years of CCP rule. These are the negative legacies of the Jiang era.

Making the General Secretary Happy

Jiang Zemin's extrovert nature made him a frequent and very voluble traveller. He was more politically astute than his opponents might have wished. One of his greatest victims was the Mayor of Beijing, Chen Xitong, who was removed from power in 1997 on the back of allegations of massive corruption around the building of the Oriental Plaza complex at the centre of the city. The suicide of a deputy mayor only made matters murkier. Chen had been presenting himself as a potential rival to Jiang, bringing back the problem of the various factions and divisions in the Party and the general lack of unity that lurked just beneath the surface.

Jiang himself was often accused of filling the Politburo with his own people. It was true that by the late 1990s the Standing Committee had several members with clear links to Shanghai, where Jiang had spent most of his career. This 'Shanghai band' included the highly rated Zhu Rongji, who was to serve as Premier and whose tough-talking style marked a totally new approach for a Chinese high-level politician. Famous for firing one Party Secretary of a province on the spot for failing to deliver on promises this hapless individual had made, Zhu's main task from 1995 onwards was to do something about the state-owned enterprises, which were dragging on the economy, creating mountains of bad debt and serving no useful economic purpose. Over the next five years, 60 million people were laid off. The pain from this process led to anecdotes about people who were unwilling to tell their family they were no longer employed, getting dressed up for their work and going out and spending the day in shopping precincts or parks till the time to go home at night, after 'a hard day at the office'!

The state needed to shrink, and its role in the 1990s went through a period of redefinition and readjustment. The average Chinese person's relationship with the government and authorities also changed. Once it was something that was omnipresent in their lives, allowing them to have children, marry, get divorced, study at university and then work in a specific place. By the end of the 1990s most of these decisions were left to individuals (with, of course, the exception of clear limits on the number of children one could have). Its removal from these key areas also called into the play the problems of who was providing housing, education and healthcare. As Jiang's period continued, it was clear that citizens had to bear most of the costs for this, with the effective breakdown of a social welfare system in many parts of undeveloped China and a multi-tiered system in the cities, catering for those with the cash to pay for it. This was to become painfully clear when the SARS (Severe Acute Respiratory Syndrome) crisis occurred in 2003, and people exited the cities to return to their home villages and find no healthcare for them there.

Ideological Matters for Jiang

China under Deng and then Jiang was a place in which Marxism-Leninism was seemingly a quaint term with no proper meaning anymore. This had been true up to a point since the repudiation of the

Cultural Revolution a decade before. The economic reforms, kick-started again in 1992, were working. It was common for those interacting with Party Members to laugh when someone mentioned Marx or Maoism. Maoism in particular seemed like a rather dirty secret that needed to be hushed away, despite the sporadic return of popular moments of remembrance of the Chairman, with taxi drivers hanging his image from cars and his picture appearing on bank notes and TV programmes. The Party had most definitely jettisoned class struggle. There was no more talk of rooting out the petty bourgeoisie, or drumming up support for the proletariat. Even so, for a system that had supposedly dropped its ideology, there still seemed to be a lot of talk about Marxism-Leninism. Political education remained a mandatory part of the school and university curricula. And there was a healthy rise in Party membership throughout the 1990s and into the 2000s.

The 1990s were littered with campaigns, most of them instigated at the behest of Jiang, some of them with the support of his chief ideologue, the wily Zeng Qinghong. In 1995–96 I recall a sustained patriotic campaign (*Aiguo Zhuyi*) waged in the small city in Inner Mongolia where I was living. Party members at my college had to attend doctrine lessons each week, reading chosen articles from the *People's Daily*, much as their predecessors in the 1950s and 1960s must have done. There were big character posters placed on the walls setting out the imperative of loving one's country, and massive red placards in the central square shouting out the need to give all to one's country. The world seemed to go on as normal around these verbal onslaughts. But at night, on the main seven o'clock news, the key phrases from the latest campaign would be fitted into each story. One leader of the politburo would be shown attending a meeting in some province or another where cadres discussed the importance of patriotism. Another was shown giving a lecture to an audience on the key element of loving one's country. To round it off, there might be a story of some common citizen who exemplified the qualities of patriotism, giving their all for their country, much in the spirit of Lei Feng, the PLA truck driver who had kept a diary in the 1960s that, after his death (in contentious circumstances – he might not have died a hero, but simply by being run over by a truck) was publicized and made into a everyman hero story. Lei Feng was to reappear, even up to the 2000s, used to propagate the virtues of selflessness and giving all to the Party.

Whether these campaigns, some of them relentless, helped steer people to 'healthy thinking' was debatable. Most people were more attracted to 'entering the sea' (*xia hai*), as the act of leaving government to become a businessman was called. Money became a constant and ubiquitous obsession. But it was clear that Jiang fancied himself as a thinker and produced collected speeches and papers, which were made available in cream-covered books piled high in the state-owned bookshops in every city throughout China and used in study sessions, even forming the basis for questions in some of the exams to join the Party. Jiang's 'Three Represents', mentioned earlier, was one such theoretical contribution, leading to the admission that entrepreneurs were also 'productive elements in society'.

The 'Three Represents' was also a partial admission that the social makeup of China was becoming more complex. In the space of only a decade and a half China had gone from having 90 per cent of its people in the country, to now having only 60 per cent. The household registration book, while it still existed, had little effect on stopping people moving to look for work in other provinces. Indeed, there was a crying need for labour in the coastal areas. Cities like Shenzhen and Zhuhai saw their populations shoot up. A new phenomenon appeared, the '*renkou liudong*' or floating population. The restraints and controls on this group were very limited. They were the people that built most of China's new, grand, modernist buildings and who worked in its factories and staffed its hundreds of thousands of new factories, shops and restaurants. While education had improved, only a tiny proportion went to university. For most, the best opportunities were to go and try their luck in the large cities. Shanghai's population at any one time was supplemented by as many as three to four million of this floating population. Beijing even acquired small enclaves, named after the provinces where the predominant groups came from. The most famous was the massive Zhejiang Village.

Indeed, it was one city in Zhejiang that typified both the new entrepreneurial energy of China and the evolving and complex relationship between the state and private enterprise. Wenzhou, in the northeast of the province, was also in one of its historically most outward-looking (being coastal) and entrepreneurial areas. It was in an area ill-served by public transport, with, until the 1980s, an economy that had fared poorly under the Communists.

All this changed with economic liberalization. Wenzhou people became famous for their ability to set up enterprises, almost indifferent to the role of the state in helping them, and their capacity to disperse throughout China, creating an extraordinary impromptu national network that was then used to service the commercial needs of Wenzhou enterprises. The wealth created from this process was to lift locals from poverty to being one of the best-performing and most equitably wealthy areas in China. Unlike many other places that saw a small number get very wealthy and a large number get poorer with only a tiny middle class, Wenzhou was to see a more 'diamond' effect, with small upper and lower classes and a strong middle class. Speculation on the unique character of the Wenzhou economy ranges from the comparative poverty of their area forcing people to be entrepreneurial, to a well-documented attitude towards the state as being a necessary evil and something to keep a distance from. These clear lines contrast to many other areas where the relationship between the state and enterprises was sometimes too close for comfort, with difficult issues being raised of collusion between the two.[1]

Throughout the 1990s and into the 2000s there were clear ideological debate lines in the Party marking out the new leftists from the reformers, maintaining the tension between the Party purists and those that wanted to push openness further. The year 1989 had been one opportunity for the leftists to call off the whole reform project, saying that it was leading to places that were inimical to the Party's hold on power. Economic scares in the mid-1990s and the pain from the laying off of workers only exacerbated this. Leftists were able to latch on to nationalism as a good rallying call, becoming particularly strident during periods of tension with the US, in particular around the bombing of the Chinese embassy in Belgrade in 1999 and the spy plane incident in 2001 when a US surveillance plane downed and killed a Chinese pilot and itself crashed on the island of Hainan. The Leftists, who largely felt that China had compromised too much to the outside world – particularly the US – were led by Party veteran Deng Liqun. Their demand that orthodox Marxism be introduced back in the Party, that the role of the state be expanded to ease people's economic pain and that the Party stop looking after people they viewed as capitalists and renegades, was to ebb and flow. Even in 2007, Hu Jintao had to make clear during his speech at the 17th Congress that the 'reform and opening up process is correct, and irreversible'. But the ideological influence of the new generation of leftists remains – people like Wang Hui, economist Hu Angang, Wang Shaoquang, and He Qing, who, while by no means desiring that China return to the vision of society supported by Mao, have argued that it needs its own vision of its future development and has to stop importing ideas wholesale from the west.[2]

The Basics: Party Structure at the Start of the 21st Century

The years under Deng of rebuilding Party institutions after the onslaught by Mao had resulted, in the early part of the twenty-first century, in a particular structure. The Standing Committee of the Politburo, which had expanded from seven members under Jiang to nine under Hu, was still regarded as the apex of power, through there was debate both inside and outside China about how extensive its powers were. The full Politburo itself consisted of 24 members and one alternate. This was serviced by the six-member Secretariat of the CCP and kept in line by the Central Discipline Inspection Commission, one of the most feared organs of Party intervention in China. To the question, therefore, 'Who runs the Party?' the simplest formal answer, at the highest level, is the Secretariat, headed by Xi Jinping, with one member of the military, and then Huang Yuning and He You, two of the most trusted advisers of Hu Jintao.

There was a range of other central organizations, including the General Office, the Central Organization Committee (in charge of personnel decisions), the Propaganda Department (now renamed in English the Marketing or PR department), the International Liaison Department and the United Front Department, which links with the eight 'democratic' patriotic parties allowed in China. Under this there are the various leading groups and work committees and organs, running from the Central Political and Legislative Affairs Committee, to the Central Leading Group for Party Building and Rural Work, to the Commission for Protection of Party Secrets (crucial work), to the Leading Group for State Security and the Party History Research Centre. The Party relies on the 'advice' of organs like the People's

Political Consultative Conference, and the National Peoples Congress, which meets each year. The Central Advisory Commission established by Deng Xiaoping as the means by which the elder Party statesmen 'advised' the current executive leaders of the Party was quietly erased when its members had either mostly died or were so ancient that they could no longer contribute meaningfully.

Under Jiang and Hu, the Party had attempted to be inclusive, reaching out to different communities and perspectives and talking about them contributing ideas to governance and policy. In 2005, 20 witnesses were selected from over 5,000 to testify before the National People's Congress. The Party and the government have also canvassed more widely for opinions on pieces of legislation. The Chinese Labour Contract Law, for instance, introduced on 1 January 2008, went through a process of formal consultations of several months, and underwent various reformulations and rewritings. One of the most persistent lobbyers in this process was the US Chamber of Commerce and the US China Trade Council, who were unhappy on behalf of some of their members with the rights to union membership encoded in the law and the way this would increase production costs in China. To some onlookers, it seemed contradictory for US companies to be fighting so hard against the conveying of basis work rights in China after all of the high-sounding rhetoric over the years from the US government of supporting the struggle for human rights and democracy in China.

How the Party relates to government is an often vexing subject. As US lawyer Randall Perenboom points out in his study of Chinese legal development in the last three decades, there is no clear distinction, even in the current Chinese Constitution, of the division of responsibility between the Party and the government.[3] It is not necessary to be a Party member in China's government bureaucracy, though in certain positions and functions it helps. Even Ministers have recently been taken from outside the Party membership, with two, as of 2008, being non-Party members. It is also becoming common for at least one Vice Minister in all ministries to be a non-Party member. Government is surprisingly light in China. China has a mere 6.37 million civil servants. This is less than 0.5 per cent of the population.[4] The key policies they implement however have to be according to Party guidelines. In that sense, government is the servant of the Party in China, despite the recent reforms.

Attempts at Reform

The Party knew it needed to increase its constituency, and its popular base. It was now serving an economy and a society that were far more complex and had access to increasingly different sources of information. While the control of the media continued with tight management of news on both television and in newspapers, there were increasing numbers of Chinese going abroad, and the new threat of the Internet and mobile phones, which made transmission of information far easier. The security services were still well resourced and well funded. But the initial success of the Falungong Movement (a form of spirituality based on breathing exercises), in the late 1990s in particular, with its use of mobile phones to arrange for people to meet and demonstrate had proved that the Party had to be vigilant.

In 1998 activists tried to register the China Democracy Party in Anhui as a formal political party. This was greeted with immediate refusal by the authorities. On the eve of its fiftieth anniversary in power, therefore, the Party had made clear that there was to be no talk of allowing its monopoly on organized party political power to be compromised. But Jiang's government did sanction the greater use of elections at the village level, a process started in 1988 just before he became General Secretary. They were heralded with great fanfare. In 2008 some 930,000 villages held elections, allowing three quarters of Chinese to participate.[5] But this process, according to the Carter Project, is marred by corruption and voting irregularities. In the 1990s, too, local community Party officials were also elected with the help of popular plebiscites, but the Party tightly controls those who can put themselves forward for this process, making sure all candidates are carefully vetted. This process has even been extended to considering allowing election of Party leaders in Shenzhen and other favoured designated locations.

The other area of reform was that of the Army. The People's Liberation Army had been the final arbiter of authority for both Mao in the CR, and during the 4 June Incident. Its loyalty to the Party, above the state or the government, was key. It had grown to being the world's largest fighting force, with over 2.5 million on active service and a million reserves. But there were major issues. Chinese military experts had watched the US actions during the first Iraq war with appalled admiration. They realized that their equipment was years behind. The payment of soldiers and their professional status was very low. It was realized in 1989, during the disturbances, that sending the army in with live ammunition to deal with civil unrest was not a good idea, and that using a better trained and prepared People's Armed Police, or riot units, was better and safer (both groups had failed miserably to fulfil their function in 1989). The final problem with the army institutionally was that it was involved in thousands of commercial activities, reducing its credibility. Army units owned seedy nightclubs, hotels and companies exporting toys and food.

Jiang dealt with this in 1998 by passing a number of restrictions, getting the army out of commercial activities. Part of the deal, though, was that he would allocate more money to them. He had already slapped the PLA down in 1996 during the elections in Taiwan, when there had been military exercises along the Fujianese coast facing what the Mainland government called the renegade province. This had backfired, with the electorate on the island giving pro-independence candidate (and *bête noire* of the Chinese) Li Denghui a massive 'yes' vote. The PLA was told to back down and let the politicians deal with the issue. Even so, the PLA made a valid point. It was ill-equipped, and was highly unlikely to be able to apply much pressure across the Straits if ever the government of the island really did cross the final red line and declare independence. If its budget was dealt with, meaning that it did not have to distract itself by engaging in money-making activities to fund itself, then it would be able to 'professionalize' and, to use the term favoured at that time, 'infomationize', improving their strategy and doctrine, and become a more effective fighting machine.

This was only what the rest of the world had been urging on the Chinese for some time. Contact between the Chinese army and the militaries of the US and of EU countries had ceased after 1989 as part of the condemnation of what the Chinese government had done. But the complaint by many of these powers was that the PLA was corrupt, riddled with small cliques pursuing their own personal interests, and was a highly unstable security force. It had had no combat experience since the 1979 debacle in Vietnam when the PLA had tried to invade the neighbouring country only to be humiliated and repulsed. From 1998 the PLA went through a process of reform. It maintained its role in the service of the Party. Deng Xiaoping, then Jiang Zemin, and finally Hu Jintao, were to sit as Chairs of the Central Military Commission (CMC), making clear that that link was the one that mattered. In fact, Chairmanship of the CMC was the last formal role that Deng relinquished, in 1989. Jiang Zemin held onto his chairmanship of the CMC a year and a half after 'retiring' as head of the Party in 2002, sparking rumours that he intended to hang around and be a political force for the years ahead. The CMC is a big deal. And in the last decade, the PLA had become a potentially much more formidable fighting force, ironically becoming more of a potential threat to the US than when it was busy running bars and nightclubs. Its soldiers are better trained, it has shed almost a million personnel (though it still ranks as the world's largest armed force) and it has upgraded its equipment, mostly with the help of the Russians who have sold it aircraft carriers, Sukhoi jets and other equipment with the sole proviso that it is highly unlikely to be used in any war against the Russians themselves. The PLA has increased its annual spending 17 per cent year on year for the last five years from 2003 onward. This is, according to the Pentagon's 'Annual Report to Congress on China's Military' in 2008, probably a massive understatement, with the overall Chinese military budget most likely going well above USD100 million. This doesn't come anything close to the US budget of over half a trillion USD a year.[6] But it still puts it in the top league of military spenders. From time to time, as the Chinese did when they shot down one of their own satellites in early 2007, the PLA does things that deliver a nasty shock. This reform was one of Jiang's most effective and may well have one of the biggest impacts.

A New Beginning, a New Story

With Deng's disappearance in 1992 till his death in 1997, it was clear that Jiang, far from being a stopgap leader, had now built up enough of a basis of power around himself to claim legitimacy. From the early 1990s, therefore, the Party narrative began to focus on the 'generations of leadership'. Mao had been the core of the first generation of leadership, and Deng the second. Jiang was named as the core of the third generation. He was described in analysis at the time as 'first among equals', answerable to a wider array of groups and interests in the Party, without the personal political clout of Deng, and very far from the sort of power exercised by Mao. Jiang was fairly typical of his generation of Party leadership. Like his Premier, Zhu, he was a technocrat. He had kept a largely clean nose during the Cultural Revolution. He was a princeling not because of wholly erroneous reports that he had been a son in law of former Chinese President Li Xiannian, but because his father had been a revolutionary martyr. And he had spent most of his career in the technical bureaucracy, in factories, and then in the Shanghai municipality. He had evidently never expected to be elevated to country leadership before 1989.

Jiang's weaker standing in the Party meant that, as W. F. J. Jenner was to point out in *The Tyranny of History: The Roots of China's Crisis* (Allen Lane, London, 1992), during discussions of matters at the politburo he had to build almost complete consensus and could not ram things through.[7] Whatever territory he picked to fight, he had to be very careful. His era has already become renowned for tolerating fantastic levels of corruption, with some figures almost proving themselves above the law. From fairly early on in his period, it was already clear that changes needed to be made to the structure of government and the Party to make it fit for purpose in the years ahead, but the perennial question before each change was whether enough of a coalition could be put together to get anything done. Upper-level politics in China often resembled a game of chess over this period, with any event preceded by dozens of moves and the final outcome clear only after long periods of torturous manoeuvring to get all the necessary allies in place and to clear those impeding a course of action out of the way.

Some of this was an inevitable response to the processes of internationalization that were going on. China continued its painstaking negotiations to enter WTO throughout the 1990s. There had been a deal available, according to some reports, when Zhu Rongji visited Clinton in the US in 1999. But thanks to Clinton's preoccupation with the latest fallout from the Lewinsky affair, he felt he didn't have the political capital on Capitol to push this through. Zhu was apparently appalled (see Susan Shirk's *Fragile Superpower* for a first-hand account of this – she was the undersecretary of state for Clinton in this period and had to clear up the pieces when the deal failed to materialize).[8] For much of the 1990s, China's being granted Most Favoured Nation Status by the US, exempting it from import tariffs and certain duties, had become a political football in

Washington, causing immense bad blood between the two countries. Allowing China to enter the world economic system through WTO would simplify and depoliticize this in one fell swoop. Beyond this, having hitched its wagon to producing decent economic growth for the Chinese people, the government now had to find ways to push its economy forward. More investment from abroad came in, particularly in 1992. Taiwan suddenly became a major investor. China allowed Special Economic Zones to make goods for the internal market (previously its factories had only made goods to be exported). It also allowed provinces to set up their own zones, and eased restrictions on import and exports. By 2001, when the deal on WTO was finalized with all the main partners, China had become a more open economy than Japan, and one with a high level of foreign investment (4 per cent of GDP, compared with 1 per cent for Japan).

The Party itself was also keen to reform and simplify government structures. Zhu Rongji undertook one massive reduction of ministries and government agencies, reducing them from over 40 to around 30. The government bureaucracy was reduced. Even so, as Anhui journalists Chen Guidi and Wu Chuntao observed, China still had one official for every 40 people, compared to historic records that showed that even during the Han period 2000 years before, there had only been one official for 7,900 people. China, on this reckoning, remained a country of big government despite the attempts to reduce government expenditure and roll back the frontiers of the state.[9]

At the 15th Party Congress in 1997 it was already clear that the Party leadership now had to change and that the old system of leaders hanging around, having influence literally till the day they died, was unsustainable. A retirement age of 67 was introduced for members of the Politburo. It was noted that this did not apply to the President and General Secretary, Jiang, but did apply to one of his main critics, Qiao Shi, who, to the surprise of many, was summarily removed in 1997. More importantly, it was already clear that there needed to be a smooth transition to a new generation of leadership, the fourth. The Party constitution stipulated that General Secretaries could only serve two terms. Jiang's time would be up in five years. Party consensus had already anointed Hu Jintao as the man chosen by Deng to be the successor. He had praised Hu's work very early on and been impressed by his handling of the situation in Tibet while he was Party secretary there (though he had largely been absent due to serious altitude sickness) from 1987 to 1989. Hu was already being spoken of as Party Secretary and President from the mid-1990s. He was appointed Vice President in 1997. Highly symbolically, it was he who delivered the speech during the demonstrations over the 'accidental' bombing of the Chinese embassy in the former Yugoslavia in 1999. By 2002, and the 16th Party Congress, he was a shoo-in.

The final strands of change seen during the Jiang era were a gradual appearance of civil society groups and an attempt to strengthen the role of the NPC. The National Peoples Congress, a consultative body to the government and the Party, had largely been seen as a rubber-stamp authority. In the Maoist period, it had hardly figured. Under Deng it had been revived, to at least give some impression of popular support and mandate to Party and government ministry executive decisions. The NPC first showed some truculence during the passionate internal debate over the building of the Three Gorges Dam along the Yangtze River near the city of Chongqing in 1992. In that year, an unprecedented number of NPC members had voted against the dam on the grounds of its predicted destructive environmental and social impacts. There had also been a high level of negative votes on the reelection of Li Peng to head the NPC and become, in the parlance of the government-backed, English language *China Daily*, China's 'chief legislator'.

Opposition to the massive Three Gorges Dam was significant for another reason. For the first time, debate was tolerated in the Chinese media on the rights and wrongs of the project. Dai Qing, a well regarded public intellectual, and the daughter of a high level General in the Maoist period, wrote extensively, and highly critically, of the project.[10] Civil society groups were set up to work against the project. Its significance was hard to overstate. Historians of China's imperial past have stated that those that control water in China, control China – period. Karl Wittfogel gave the most famous expression to this in his *Oriental Despotism: A Comparative Study of Total Power*, though Mark Elvin in his magisterial environmental history of China, *The Retreat of the Elephants* also makes clear that water was intimately linked to agricultural and political stability.[11] Water projects, from the time of the Three Gorges, have generated immense controversy. In a study from early 2008, US scholar Andrew Mertha talks of three much smaller projects in Sichuan and Yunnan, where there was bitter local opposition.[12] In one case, the project was overturned.

In the other two, it was either implemented, or at least the plans were maintained on the books with no final outcome. On the backs of these, a whole series of civil-society groups has come into being expressing strong opinions about specific projects. According to Qinghua University, there are now over a quarter of a million civil-society groups, although Nick Brown, a highly experienced development worker based in China for over ten years, puts this number more realistically at about 3,000.[13] In many ways, as Qiusha Ma shows in a study of Non-Government Organization (NGO) groups in China, the rise of these is no more than an admission that in many areas where the state used to be the provider, it has now withdrawn, meaning that there is space for other groups to operate. There is one important proviso.[14] Civil-society groups that stray into politically sensitive territory risk having all they have achieved, and all that they own, taken from them. The problem with this sensitive territory is that it has shifting boundaries, meaning that what was acceptable to do a few days before suddenly becomes banned overnight. In the last few years, too, many political activists have migrated into these areas of allowed and legitimate protest in the PRC, where they are freer to act.[15]

Hu

The quasi-institutionalization of succession was a major achievement under Jiang, bearing in mind that for both Mao and Deng, being chosen as heir apparent was a quick and speedy way to oblivion, and each time it had been messy. Hu had, in fact, been one of a younger generation of Party members that Deng had asked to be promoted and put into positions of power in the 1980s. He had gone around talent-spotting, and lifted a number of educated, hard-working people into higher positions, giving them a run at the upper reaches of the Party.

Hu can be seen as representative of the changes in Party membership since 1949. In the early years, the typical Party member had little education and often came from China's less-developed regions. There was a joke by diplomats working in Beijing in the 1970s that the higher up the Party echelon you managed to speak to people, the more you had to deal with their impenetrable local accents. Mao had a thick Hunanese accent. Deng spoke pure Sichuanese. Jiang bore the flavour of his native Jiangsu. Very ironically, much like Putin, who is the first leader of Russia since the revolution in 1917 who is able to speak standard Russian, Hu Jintao is the first leader of China since 1949 to be able to speak standard Mandarin though with a slight Jiangsu accent, according to some. Foreign degrees were a definite black mark in the highly xenophobic CR years. Deng valued education, and Party members in his period started to include more with tertiary degrees. Jiang Zemin's politburo was the first where almost everyone had some level of university education, many of them being educated (Li Peng, for instance, and Jiang himself) abroad, mostly in the USSR. For Hu, his Politburo was the first to include PhDs (Dr Xi Jinping and Dr Li Yuanchao), and the majority had masters degrees, although, unlike Jiang's politburo, none had studied abroad, apart from Luo Gan. He was to retire in 2007, meaning the current Standing Committee is the first to have all been purely educated in China.

Hu's path to the top typified what could be called the grass-roots route. A native of Anhui, it seems that he was, in fact, born in Shanghai, or Jiangsu. He joined the Party in 1964, the year he graduated from the water conservation department in Qinghua University, remaining in Beijing till 1968 but apparently taking no part in the savage battles that occurred there at that time (Qinghua was a hot seat of rebellious group activism and, according to some, the birth place of the Red Guard movement).[16] His career from 1968 onward was to be spent largely in the western regions of China, in the small, impoverished, but strategically highly important area of Gansu (where he laboured till 1982). He was Party boss in the southwestern area of Guizhou (still regarded as the poorest province in China) from 1985 to 1988. Finally, he occupied the same position in Tibet during the turbulent end to the 1980s. Only from 1992 was he based back in Beijing, in central party Positions. His rise was quick. By 1992 he was a Politburo member, and by 1997, Vice President.

There was an important central organizational link that Hu had in Beijing in the early 1980s, between serving in Guizhou and Tibet. He was head of the Communist Youth League (CYL), which was an organization both slightly older than the Communist Party (its predecessor, the Socialist Youth League, had been formed with USSR support in 1920) and with more members. Under Deng, the CYL had been seen as an incubator for future leaders, and just as people had talked of the Shanghai Group under Jiang, they settled later on the CYL group under Hu. Links between elite leaders and the CYL were closely noted. Even so, just as the Shanghai Group weakened and almost dispersed (its final fall being the moment when Party Secretary of Shanghai and alternate member of the Politburo, Chen Liangyu, was felled for corruption in 2006) the new lineup of Politburo members that appeared at the 17th Party Congress in 2007 showed only weak links to the CYL.

Deng and Jiang were keen to promote their ideological strengths. But Hu's contribution to Party ideology, beyond his theory of 'scientific development' enshrined in the Party Constitution in 2007, is difficult to describe. Where he has been markedly different to Jiang is in his attempts to reach out to the countryside, and to at least try to do something more about corruption, however questionable the results of this have been.

Grassroots Grievances

The China of Hu Jintao and Wen Jiabao is a place of increasing prosperity, but also great grievances. In 2001 two Anhui journalists, Chen Guidi and Wu Chuntao, a husband-and-wife team, wrote a report, called 'The Agriculture Report' *(Nongmin Diaocha)*, though somewhat confusingly translated into English with the oxymoronic title *Will the Boat Shake the River*.[17] Their work was immediately banned – which was an enormous favour to the authors, as they then managed to ship 10 million contraband copies. The picture they drew of conditions in the Chinese countryside was bleak, and disturbing. Farmers were still burdened with excessive taxes. Their land was being taken from them by local officials, to be sold for more lucrative building projects. Those that protested were beaten up, sometimes even murdered, with complete impunity by local thugs working with the covert blessing of the local Party. In Chen and Wu's accounts, the Party came across as little better than a lawless Mafia.

The book describes the Party as having lost its soul. In one statement, they refer back to the famous statement by Mao Zedong that 'revolution is not a dinner Party'. Calculating that cadres eat something like two times the cost of hosting the Olympics each year in food and official entertainment, they caustically comment that, in fact, the revolution has become exactly that – a dinner party.

Their report takes place against a background in which social protests in China have risen dramatically. The oft-quoted figure in 2005 of 87,000 protests throughout China was issued by the National Bureau of Statistics. Even the Bureau admitted that it was largely meaningless, covering anything from a few people waving placards outside a government compound in a small country to tens of thousands raging through the streets in a decent-size city. But it was clear to anyone wandering around China in the last few years that there are a lot of people who feel that they have lost out in the whole reform process. Amongst these are the 200 million who, according to the World Bank, live on less than a dollar a day, the UN standard of poverty. There are those who hold grievances against the Party for economic woes, environmental woes or, whatever the risk, political woes. The government might have stopped collecting social unrest statistics now, but in any one week there are more than enough reports to show that dissatisfaction amongst some groups in China remains high. In the week of the Beijing Olympics in mid-August 2008, for instance, Hubei police reported attempted bomb attacks on a bus. Two people were killed in a bomb explosion in Qinhuangdao in neighbouring Hebei. A suspected bomb was found in a shopping centre in Shanghai, and two people arrested in Guangdong and Shaanxi for threatening to undertake bomb attacks. For the designated protest spaces in Beijing during the Olympics, the authorities received 77 applications, though in the end granted none. They wished to protest over labour disputes, medical disputes and inadequate welfare. At the same time, a Shandong man was arrested in a park in Beijing for protesting the forced relocation of residents.[18] Such dissatisfaction can reach a greater scale. In the weeks preceding the Olympics, huge demonstrations in western China occurred when a young girl was raped and murdered, and there was perceived evidence of links to a police coverup.[19]

The Party has had to change, allowing some grievances to be addressed while facing down others. Petitions (*xinfang*) against the central government now stand at over 12 million a year, down from 13.7 million in 2004. The central government passed regulations aimed at lowering these further in 2005. However, only

0.2 per cent of petitioners received a response in 2005. A survey in 2007 found that 71 per cent of petitioners felt they had suffered intimidation or retaliations by authorities after their petition. Only 5 per cent were happy with the outcome of what had happened.[20] Hu and Wen were more than aware when they became General Secretary and Premier, respectively, that this discontent with the Party's internal governance and treatment of social issues was critical. They therefore used a discourse of 'social harmony', some of it cobbled from Confucian ideas of a well-ordered society. The return of Confucius must rank as one of the great comebacks of all time. Damned in the Cultural Revolution, he came to be used as a national brand in the 2000s with the opening of over a hundred Confucius Institutes throughout the world. That Confucius was used to justify the structure of power in China in the twenty-first century seemed odd – but the Party may have been looking to show that its mandate to rule was struck deep in the political traditions of China and Confucius was the best known candidate to front this.

Talk of 'harmonious society' and the 'socialist countryside' was a clear admission that the Jiang and Zhu period, for all the painful but necessary reforms it had made, had tolerated a level of inequality between the town and the countryside that was becoming unsustainable. By 2007 China's population, according to official statistics, had become split almost 50-50 between the two. China had undergone a massive process of urbanization. Cities like Shanghai had seen their populations shoot up to as much as 17 million permanent residents. Beijing had about ten million. But there was an immense floating population to add on top of that; they had mostly gone from the countryside to the cities to seek their economic destinies. More and more of China was becoming urbanized. The Jiang era had kicked off the 'Opening up the West Campaign' in 1999 (*Dakai da Xibei*) with great fanfare, proclaiming how it would see the sorts of massive developments that had happened on the coastal areas of China reach further into the country where poverty was more trenchant, the state sector still reigned supreme, levels of governance were much poorer and there was primitive infrastructure. Even so, the more cynical could see this campaign ending up being nothing more than a few large meetings (held in one of the two main western region cities, Chongqing or Xian) and little else. Foreigners, beyond those with very good reason (energy companies, for instance, or mining corporations) were loath to go to a place so hard to reach and with such an unknown track record in inward investment. The central government encouraged coastal provinces to 'adopt' a western province. This saw delegations from Zhejiang and Jiangsu troop off to Xinjiang and Inner Mongolia, to help their less-well-off compatriots. But on almost every level, from life expectancy to educational attainment to average GDP, the western regions were falling further and further behind. Average GDP in Shanghai per capita was over USD6,000 dollars a year by 2006. In Tibet and Gansu, it barely reached a thousand. Even so, commentators like Yasheng Huang could find evidence that, far from being located in the big cities, China's real entrepreneurial energy was strongest in the rural areas and in the tough western regions where companies had to fight tooth and nail to survive, and did not enjoy the pro-urban, biased policies of the central government.[21]

In 1984, according to the Gini Coefficient, which measures inequality, China was one of the most equal societies in the world. By 2006 it sat alongside places like Brazil and Argentina. It had seen its first billionaires, but, even on the official records of the government, over 23 million people (almost certainly a huge underestimate) were living in medieval squalor. Hu and Wen were aware of the potentially calamitous consequences of allowing this divide to continue. During the 11th Five Year Plan, running from 2006 to 2010, the government talked of putting more investment into the countryside. They also supported campaigns that built up social welfare infrastructure in the countryside and the less-developed areas of China. And they tried to repair the reputation of the Party by clamping down on corruption.

The Friend Who Never Goes Away

Corruption was a constant in Chinese political and social life throughout the twentieth century, and it looks set to figure in the story of China as it unfolds in the twenty-first century. A system in which large amounts of power lies in the hands of a small number of people, in which there are few transparent rules and no checks and balances, is set fair for trouble. Chiang Kai-shek's government was known for its fabulous corruption, something that meant its departure in 1949 was regarded by most as long overdue. Ironically, for all its chaos and political drama, the Maoist period was seen as largely incorrupt. As most people were at each other's throats for a good part of this period, this is hardly surprising. Mao himself earned money from his books, and could never have been accused of being an ostentatiously wealthy man. He left no billions, Suharto-like, to his heirs (though it could be argued that he left them priceless political riches, and his family still figures in the Central Committee). Deng lived in great simplicity, but from his period, the side effect of economic reform was the reappearance of an old friend; corruption came in many guises. Mostly it was linked to modestly paid cadres being in charge of authorization for massive, expensive projects. Sometimes it was because of an overly close relationship between business and government – in some cases, so close because the former owned the latter. Whatever form it took, a lack of legal process and real forms of investigation and prohibition meant that corruption in the vast majority of places went unchecked and unpunished. It seemed to be an accepted, unpleasant but utterly necessary part of the whole economic process, that without backhanders and finding connections ('going through the back door', as it was called) some things never got done.

In the twilight years of the Jiang-Zhu period, the most spectacular case of corruption was that of the Fujianese Mr Fixit, Lai Chaixing, who managed to work up a multi-billion-dollar smuggling scam that roped in everyone from customs officials, to senior cadres, right up, possibly, to politburo members. Lai was mean to himself, but lavished untold favours on those who helped him in his massive project. His office in Xiamen, for those favoured enough to visit it, was nothing more than a very high-class brothel. When he was finally tumbled, Lai fled to Canada, where he now awaits the result of a lengthy trial to decide if he should be repatriated back to China, despite the fact that for his level of corruption, the death sentence may await him.[22]

There are plenty of people still in high positions who would prefer that Lai continued to languish halfway across the world. One of them might be no less than number four in the current politburo, Jia Qinglin, who through his family and his wife is linked to Lai. His survival at the 17th Party Congress, where he maintained his position in the Politburo, was one of the surprises, in view of his unpopularity. But he typifies one feature of the contemporary high-level leader – the fact that, existing in a rich nexus of connections and with so much power at hand, they are usually best reached through their children or spouses. The Party has now got itself in a position of having an aristocracy. Sons and daughters of high-level cadres can sell themselves on the Party ranking of their parents (usually fathers). Some of them act as though they were untouchable. And in China, blood is most definitely many times thicker than water.

Premier Wen Jiabao, for instance, is probably a decent and honourable man. But his wife has grown wealthy, reportedly, on the proceeds of diamond trading. Jiang Zemin's son occupied plum positions in the telecoms sector. Li Peng's wife and family were up to their necks in the energy business and associated with the massive, expensive white elephant, the airport in Zhuhai (uselessly situated only a few dozen kilometres from three other major, already functioning international airports, so that it receives in its gleaming halls only few flights each day). Rumours about these things circulate in the Hong Kong press, which remains largely free, and some migrate across the border via the Internet and the blogoshere. It is almost taken as given, unfairly or not, that top leaders in provinces and those in the centre have some large hinterlands where they, or their families, are taking the state's riches. Hu's attempt to do something about this, with the felling of Shanghai Party Secretary Chen Liangyu when it happened in 2006, was linked not so much with the apparent embezzlement of billions of dollars from a social welfare fund into property, but because he belonged to the old Shanghai clique and had crossed swords with Hu and Wen on other political matters. Corruption was just the excuse. That, at least, was the popular take on this.

The Party has undertaken inspection and discipline campaigns, but of the many tens of thousands of investigations (there were 97,000 in 2006), only a few have led to any punishment. In the most severe cases, people have been executed. But on the whole, corruption has been tolerated, at least till now. Popular discontent and cynicism at this is growing. From what information from public surveys there is, corruption comes at the top of people's list of what they are most dissatisfied about, along with the state of the environment. The link between the poor quality of the school buildings in Sichuan that fell like cards when the earthquake happened in May 2008 and possible collusion between local government and construction companies was one of the most incendiary problems of the year. People want to see systemic change. But as long as the power structure is at it is, campaigns are likely to do little to fundamentally redress this.

The Return of the Men from Yesterday

The Party aristocracy goes further than simply meaning that elite leaders, and leaders almost all the way down the tree, look after their own. In the last Party Congress observers noticed in those that filled some of the key links in the top Central Committee the return of an interesting phenomenon – the princelings (*gaoganzi*), the sons and (very occasionally) daughters of former high-ranking leaders who themselves were now occupying senior positions in the Party.[23]

This was a upturn for the books. In the 1990s the Princelings had gone through lean years. Watched warily by the public, figures like Bo Xilai, the son of Bo Yibo (one of those reputedly called the old 'Immortals' and a key figure in the Mao and Deng years), who lived to be a hundred and died only in 2007, had spent time in less favoured provinces like Liaoning, or as mayor or Dalian. Jiang Zemin and Li Peng probably ranked as the only princelings in the Central Committee then, both being sons of Party revolutionary martyrs. There was a feeling, even within the Party, that it would look like out-and-out nepotism to reward these figures with very high office, no matter how able they were. Bo Xilai was to make a good job of Dalian, even though his success was to cause resentful grumbles from surrounding cities and even the province the city was in, because he took all the attention and seemed to ram through whatever proposals he felt were good for the city – and his own political career. Even so, it was enough to carry him to become Minister of Trade and then Party Secretary of the massive city of Chongqing. Relatives of Deng and Mao were kept out of sight. Deng's son, the disabled Deng Pufang, was kept busy being the head of the China Disabled Association, and his daughters occupied their time by writing adoring biographies of their late father, or doing business.

Xi Jinping, and Li Yuanchao, two of the current high-flyers who are destined for great things in the next Congress in 2012, definitely belong to the princeling stable, and their sudden upturn in fortune shows that now the Party is not only willing to trust those born into the stable of its former upper level leadership, but might even see it giving them a fillip. On the current Central Committee, there are at least nine princelings, including the son of Liu Shaoqi and Deng's daughter Deng Nan. A Party aristocracy is a hard thing to avoid and carries many dangers. It reinforces the idea of it being a massive self-serving clique. Even so, Xi's likely elevation to China's Presidency and the Party's top slot will mark a spectacular comeback. His father, Party Secretary of Guangdong in the early 1980s, was one of the key figures in the opening stages of the Reform process. Having his son carry on the flame is a nice historical touch. So far, though, no one seems to know enough about Xi Jinping to judge if he is up to it.

The Current CCP Standing Committee Politburo

Hu Jintao – President, General Secretary of the CCP; Chairman, Central Military Commission
Wu Bangguo – Chair of the National Peoples Congress
Wen Jiabao – Premier of the State Council
Jia Qinglin – Chair of the People's Political Consultative Conference
Li Changchun – Head of Information
Xi Jinping – Vice President, and head of CCP secretariat
Li Keqiang – Vice Premier
He Guoqiang – Head of the Central Commission for Discipline Inspection
Zhou Yongkang – Head of Political and Legislative Affairs Committee

Hu and Wen at the Midway Point

When Hu Jintao became President and Party Secretary at the 16th Party Congress in 2002, there were fond hopes that this would mark the arrival of a closet reformer. Perhaps observers misunderstood the nature of the Party. The idea of someone with Hu's background rising through the ranks and suddenly giving away everything the Party desires and wants with a simple shrug of the shoulders is preposterous. Hu and Wen have been reformers – but only in ways that do not cede the key ground to potential enemies. They have continued economic reform, fulfilled, by the end of 2006, and on time, the main stipulations they signed up to in WTO. They have undertaken legal reform and continued to develop the private sector. The Party seems to be able to survive without a grand patriarch like Deng to carry leadership from one generation to the next. It has its hands fully on the main levers of power. And yet, a little over halfway in Hu and Wen's tenure, there is a sense of nervousness and of vulnerability. In many ways, the easy work has been done – and that was hard enough. Now the Party has to look seriously at what it has had at the back of its mind for two decades – becoming a political party of the twenty-first century. And that means looking harder and longer at political reform, with the possibility of democratization. In the next chapter, I will look at some the key challenges facing China as a country as it moves into the twenty-first century, challenges the Party will need to engage with and find some answers to in order to stay in power. In the final chapter I will look at the challenges facing the Party itself as it tries to maintain power and develop. And in the conclusion, I will set out what I think will happen in the next two decades.

Chapter Five

The Challenges Facing China and What They Mean for Rule by the CCP

In China, no matter how big an amount is, it will be infinitesimal after you divide it by 1.3 billion; no matter how tiny a problem is, it will be enormous after you multiply it by 1.3 billion.

— Comment attributed to Premier Wen Jiabao

In the twenty-first century, there are some key areas about which the Communist Party must devise policy to help China face the challenges of developing itself, and remaining stable. Each of these has global implications. It will be on these issues that the Party's hold on power will depend. A failure in any one area will have massive and damaging political implications. These constitute the three 'E's' – the economy, the environment and energy. In none of these areas is China able to confront the challenges it faces solely alone. It will need significant outside help. There are signs already about how it intends to go about doing this. This chapter analyses each one, and looks at their importance for the stable future of the Party's rule in the coming decades.

The Economy

The reforms most closely associated with 1978 – moving China away from an agricultural economy, learning more about technology from the rest of the world, placing science, education and development at the heart of China's Five Year Plans – have created a unique economic model, one which, as of 2008, is highly reliant on manufacturing, and on export-led growth. As the years have gone on, however, it is clear that this economic model, whatever its undoubted successes, has had some major negative side effects. These can be divided into social, political and economic. Dealing with these in the years and decades ahead will be major challenges for the Party, and dictate how it now transforms the country it rules from a regional power to a major international one.

Deng Xiaoping himself admitted that one of the most productive effects of the reform of agriculture in the early 1980s had been unplanned – the success of the town and village enterprises (TVEs) which had been set up as a way of using the surplus labour freed from working in agriculture when this sector had become much more efficient.[1] Agricultural workers are, in many ways, the unsung heroes of the Reform Process. Their work and their contribution to the last 30 years have frequently been forgotten in the rush to praise entrepreneurs, the private sector and the government. The giddy heights of China's foreign-invested enterprises usually get disproportionate attention. But, as much as for 1949, the economic revolution that has been waged from 1978 had its roots in the countryside, even if the results have been to create the spectacular modernist cities that now line China's coast. Without the freeing up of the productive forces in the countryside, and the improved efficiency there, the modernization of China's economy and its move to a more industrial model simply would not have been possible. Ironically, it is now the workers from the countryside who constitute much of the estimated 200 million 'floating labour' population who are working on so many of the building sites that now exist in China, urbanizing its landscape.

Former Premier Zhu Rongji in the 1990s said, at the time proudly, that China was 'the factory of the world'. This underpinned its success in attracting inward investment. But a factory also produces pollution and uses huge amounts of energy. China's economic model, the result of at least thirty years of reform, is, at heart, one based on manufacturing. The country has also proved to be far less endowed with natural resources, or at least easily accessible natural resources, than was originally believed. It therefore imports the raw materials for this 'factory', large amounts of partly finished goods, or commodities, which it then processes by the use of plentiful, and cheap, human labour, and then re-exports. Since 2002, this has been behind the huge trade deficits with, particularly, the US and the EU. That in itself has become a political problem. The credit crunch and the international financial crisis from 2007 onwards might well have started to raise these fundamental costs. But the world has placed so much of its manufacturing capacity in China that it is hard to see where else so many factories and people to work in them might be found.

Such a manufacturing-based economy is certainly not what China really aspires to, at least according to official policy statements and the vision contained in its current Five Year Plan. The same Zhu Rongji said in the late 1990s that the country wished, as it journeyed towards middle-income status, to become a knowledge economy, strengthening its service sector, and producing strong financial sector brands. Just as it had studied, and in parts followed, the Japanese economic model used under post-war Prime Minister Shigeru Yoshida of developing its exports and then using these as a way of creating globally strong manufacturing brands which travelled up the value chain, so it also wanted to liberate its people from long hours working in factories in order that they could, as in the West, work in service sectors. Wu Yi, former Vice Premier with responsibility for trade, said as much to US Treasury Secretary Hank Paulson in late 2007, when he complained about job losses in the US being related to burgeoning imports from China. The US, she said, had lost five million manufacturing jobs in the last two decades. But it had created 15 million service sector jobs. China, too, would be happy to lose manufacturing jobs if these were to be mopped up by expansion in the service or technology sectors, with better quality jobs. Its people were weary of producing Barbie dolls for a few cents, which were then sold for twenty or thirty dollars in the US. And it needed good quality jobs to employ the many graduates who were coming out of Chinese universities each year, who aspired to something more than working in a production line or back in the countryside.

China's economic model is necessarily a work in progress, its ultimate objective to lift yet more of the population into work which does not involve long hours for very low pay in largely foreign-owned factories. The Chinese government, and Chinese economists, are aware that foreign investment has brought great benefits. It has created over 23 million jobs at a time when the state-owned enterprises were laying off many tens of millions of people. But 23 million people, in Chinese terms, is hardly anything. The real ambition is to create its own indigenous, strong, globally competitive companies. And the signs of this are very mixed.[2] The attempts since the 15th Party Congress to create global Chinese champions have been well-intentioned. But the results so far must be disappointing. Chinese companies, despite the appearance of Huawei and ZTE in the telecoms sector, who are very active abroad, are not seen as being global brand leaders, nor, despite the exposure of the 2008 Olympics for one of the new sponsors of the games, Lenovo, are they seen as being at the leading edge of technical development. China produces many fine mathematicians and scientific graduates every year. Many of these go abroad to study further (in a repeat, though on a larger scale, of the great outward migration of talent during the early Republican period), in order to learn new skills and (in some cases) then bring them back and use them at home. It is clear that one of the key impetuses behind the push for foreign investment in the 1980s and 1990s was to gain access to new technologies and know-how. But in 2005, of those exports classified as hi-tech, a staggering 88 per cent were made by foreign-invested enterprises.[3] This means that China still lacks a strong, innovative and internationally competitive hi-tech sector and that the policy to try to gain know-how through FDI has, at least according to that benchmark, partly failed. This lies behind the current emphasis on China as an outward investor gaining access to this (of which more later). Chinese companies, with some notable exceptions (the above-mentioned Lenovo and Huawei) still spend little on research and development. They are not known for investing in new areas, and are seen as being restricted by a largely state-led, and conservative environment and by poor intellectual property rights protection.

Expectations Towards the Private Sector

One of the most dramatic changes that has occurred in the Chinese economy over the last three decades is the appearance of a non-state sector, something comparable but not exactly similar to the private sector found in North America and Europe. The distinctive role of the state in China has been discussed in earlier chapters. According to the Organization for Economic Co-operation and Development (OECD), China's economy now splits almost equally between the state and the non-state.[4] After being effectively banned in the Maoist period and politically ostracized for the first two decades of the Reform period, Capitalists were allowed to join the Party in 2001.[5]

In fact, if there are heroes of the reform process alongside the agricultural workers, it would be this new 'red capitalist' class. What President Jiang did in 2001 in allowing entrepreneurs back into the Communist Party was in many ways merely being realistic and pragmatic. The role that non-state business people were playing in China's economic success was considerable. Over half of GDP growth was due to them. Business people like Li Dongsheng of TCL, who set up a joint venture with French TV manufacturer Thomson in 2002, and Jack Ma (Ma Yun) of Alibaba.com, a Yahoo partner, were both highly visible and also became ambassadors for Chinese business abroad. Letting them continue to live in a grey zone was unworkable.

China's entrepreneurs have come from extraordinary backgrounds and work in a unique environment. The British journalist James Kynge profiled one of them, Yin Mingsha, head of the Chongqing-based Lifan company, in his book, *China Shakes the World: the Rise of a Hungry Nation*.[6] Mr Yin had spent 19 years in jail from 1960 to 1979 for being branded a rightist just after the Hundred Flowers Campaign. In the 1980s, at the very beginning of the reform process, he was, in effect, unemployed, and only made a small amount of money to live on by selling books by the roadside. One day, he noticed people selling motorbike components. He bought some, and made his own motorbike, which he cheekily called 'Hongda', clearly mimicking the Japanese Honda. By the late 1990s his business had branched out into mineral water, cars and manufacturing in Vietnam. He had also bought the local Chongqing football team and reportedly looked at purchasing a share in the UK Leicester City Football Club. His story, remarkable as it is, is typical of a generation of tough-minded and hard-working Chinese business people who have now built, in China at least, successful companies.

The expectations towards the non-state sector have been high since the huge restructuring of the state sector under President Jiang and Premier Zhu in the late 1990s. This painful process, which saw 60 million people laid off, meant that the great state-owned enterprises of the past were radically slimmed down. Competition was created within some sectors, like aviation, which had been a massive state-run conglomerate till then. Parts of others, like the huge energy companies, were listed both in China and abroad, in London, Hong Kong and New York. But there is a political pecking order, with clear preference given to the protection of certain state companies from genuine competition from non-state new arrivals.[7] China remains a surprisingly fragmented economy, with some provinces practicing local protectionism and insisting, for political rather than economic reasons, in having their own automotive or aviation factories, even when these lose money. The clear political constraints within which a non-state business person works both challenges and impedes their aspirations. Chinese business people who have allowed themselves to become 'overly political' have been dealt with swiftly. In late 2008, China's wealthiest man for three of the prior years (according to Fortune Magazine), the Founder and Chairman of Goumei electrical appliance company, disappeared for 'stock trading irregularities'. But his sudden removal was all too reminiscent of the treatment of dissidents from an earlier age. Rumours abounded about what the real reason was for his being taken in. It is worth noting that in China's decision-making elite, as of 2008, of the full membership of the Central Committee, none are non-state entrepreneurs (though the heads of some of the major state-owned enterprises are there). And in the standing committee and the full committee of the Politburo, not one has a non-state business background.

The Environmental Cost of China's Economic Model

Even while China aspires to shift towards a more knowledge-based economy, it has to face two major challenges, and each of these has a definite global aspect. The first is the environmental impact of China's economic model over the last 30 years, and the second is its intense hunger for energy.

China's environmental problems, largely because of its manufacturing intense economic model and its energy usage (see following section on Energy Needs) have been well documented. US scholar Elizabeth Economy has dealt with these problems in some detail in *The River Runs Black*.[8] According to the World Bank, China has 16 of the world's 20 most-polluted cities.[9] There are major issues of clean water supply and of deforestation and desertification in the north of China. In 2007–08, though it has received little international press attention, northeast China, an area that has been experiencing something of an economic boom after years of being written off as a 'rust belt' after a concerted central government campaign, suffered a long drought. The city of Beijing is symbolic of this environmental unsustainability. It is one of the world's few major cities not built on a river, with a water table dwindling each year, a population creeping up and now largely dependent on water brought in from surrounding Hebei province. In past years, each spring, Beijing has suffered from bad dust storms, brought about by the conversion of grassland in the areas north of the city to cropland, stretching up to the border with the Mongolian People's Republic. The planting of a billion trees in the 1990s (called the Great Green Wall at the time) to try to redress this was only partially successful because of lack of water for the new trees.

China's environmental problems also derive from the intense industrialization of large parts of the coast this is now reaching deep into the country. The fact that 70 per cent of its energy comes from coal, of which the country is the world's second-largest holder of reserves (after the US), only aggravates this. The country has become, according to a European think tank (though the Chinese government disputes this), the world's largest producer of carbon emissions since 2007. The coal that it produces its energy from is often high in sulphuric content and mined from highly polluting sources, which are also very dangerous for the people working there (China had by far and away the largest number of people killed in mine accidents in 2007).

China's dependence on coal is a big problem. But it is a problem that the region and the whole world suffer from and are starting to want action about. In official surveys, Chinese people have said clearly that they are worried about the quality of their drinking water and the air they breathe. One estimate says that 400,000 deaths a year are due to bronchial problems directly attributable to air pollution. This is behind the hundreds of non-government organizations that have been set up in this sector in the last decade to lobby the government.[10] Premier Wen Jiabao is a geologist by training. He understands the science of pollution probably better than any other world leader. The central government he heads has made powerful statements on the need to improve environmental protection. At the National People's Congress in the spring of 2008, the State Environmental Protection Agency was upgraded to a ministry. Its outspoken deputy minister, Pan Yue, continued to say that the cleanup needed after 30 years of the environmental impact of its current economic model would cost as much as all the economic benefits that this process had accrued. The US State Department claimed that 25 per cent of the pollution in California could be traced back to China. Hong Kong Special Administrative Region, in particular, was to see the problems of outsourcing its manufacturing to the mainland, when, as became clear from the late 1990s onward, much of the pollution emitted from these factories was, because of wind direction, simply blown back into the Region, making it one of the world's most-polluted cities.

As with the economy, too, fragmentation and localism rear their heads. Central government might say strong things on the environment and show great political will, but provinces continued to react very differently to the need to clean up their air. Dalian, and then Liaoning, cleaned up in the early 2000s as a result of the efforts of former Party Secretary there, Bo Xilai. But other places like Inner Mongolia continued to allow highly polluting factories to be sited in their provinces for the economic gains these brought. In a playoff between economic growth and the environment, in too many places the latter lost out. It is clear, though, that there is a stronger and stronger movement amongst Chinese people to see improvements in their environment. Companies like the food manufacturer Mengniu have been in the lead in producing healthy food, though their record has since been blighted by the atrocious milk contamination scandal in late 2008, in which milk supplied to children and adults in China was found to contain poison, leading to dozens of deaths. Others have seen the marketing benefits, at least, in their being 'environmentally' friendly. Recent protests in Fujian about the planned location of a factory have shown that, just as in other places, Chinese do not want polluting factories near their homes. Environmental activists and the organizations they work for are becoming household names.

China's Energy Needs

China's environmental problems are intimately linked, as the previous section mentioning coal showed, to its energy needs. China's hunger for energy has rocketed in the last three decades. Industrial and private use of energy has increased almost exponentially. Despite discovering large oil fields in Daqing, northeast China, in the 1960s (something celebrated by Mao Zedong in his famous call in the Cultural Revolution to 'Study Daqing in industry') these are clearly nowhere near enough to satisfy its needs today. In any case, production in Daqing has peaked, and there is a need to look further afield. China became a net importer of oil in 1993. It now sources 20 per cent of its energy needs from oil, and half of this is imported, much of it from the Middle East (where it has signed long-term supply contracts with Iran and Saudi Arabia), and an increasing amount from Africa. Its energy hunger is partly the fault of energy inefficiency. The country is much less energy-efficient per unit of production than Japan and the EU.[11] The government rightly says that per capita energy usage is low. But when this is multiplied 1.3 billion times (as suggested by Wen Jiabao in the comment attributed to him that heads this chapter), then it soon becomes a world leader. It currently stands as the world's second-largest user of oil after the US – but it is catching up.

It is possible that there are more resources within China in terms of oil, but exploration, some of it in partnership with foreign companies like BP and Shell, has so far led to places which, while promising at the moment, would be highly uneconomic to exploit. The Bohai Sea off the northeast coast has deposits, but these would be hard to extract. Xinjiang, over in the northwest, also has deposits, but these are so far too small to justify full exploration. China is looking at other deposits, some of them in Tibet. But for the next five to ten years at least, it will continue to rely on imports, and its need for fossil fuels will increase.

There are solutions to all of this. In the latest Five Year Plan, clear energy efficiency targets are spelt out. So far, China has failed to meet these, but that is also largely true of targets set in the rest of the world by other countries. The main thing is that the aspiration is there and effort is being made. In addition to this, China is looking at the creation of new technologies that will be more energy-efficient. Car usage is a particular concern. China has gone from having nine cars per thousand people a decade ago to 18 per thousand at the moment. The growth of a successful middle class, especially in the coastal areas, means that this usage will increase. If it approaches the 500 per thousand of the UK or 800 per thousand of the US, then, in terms of pollution and congestion, there will be big trouble unless fundamental changes are introduced. Chinese automotive companies are looking at creating new, more energy-efficient forms of car technology. The automobile maker Chery, in particular, has excited interest abroad. Finally, China is also looking at renewable forms of energy. It is currently the world's largest user of solar energy, even though this contributes only 1per cent of its overall energy needs. It also uses wind power, especially in the north. It is building new nuclear reactors, and is also exploring more liquid natural gas, importing this from Indonesia and Russia. It has also worked with the EU on major clean coal technology projects. Even with a massive planned nuclear power station programme, with thirty new plants coming on stream by 2020, this will only produce 3 per cent of China's projected energy needs. On any calculation, China will remain fundamentally reliant on fossil fuels for the foreseeable future.

The environment and energy are global problems and it is clear, since both Kyoto and then Bali in 2007, that they need a universal, global solution. This debate, on which the future prosperity of humanity rests, is now at a critical stage. India and China argue, as developing nations, that they should not be punished by being given overambitious environmental and energy targets when much of the previous damage was done by countries like the US and UK during their early period of industrialization. They argue that the onus, therefore, is currently on developed countries to lead the way. As former editor of *The Economist* Bill Emmott says in his recent book, *Rivals*, about the impact of China, India and Japan on the coming century, everyone now recognizes that there is a problem.[12] Even the Bush presidency, after years of initial scepticism about climate change, finally acknowledged there was an issue. But no one seems to want to take responsibility. The Bali agreement sets a framework for developed and developing countries to work together. This will be one of the most critical areas for China's engagement with the rest of the world in the coming decade, and a place where it will truly be central to a global solution. If the Party fails to deliver here, its days will be numbered.

China as it Appears to the Rest of the World

Challenges don't just present themselves domestically. There are also challenges relating to how China links with the rest of the world. China has, as previous chapters have shown, been engaging with modernity and the modern world for a long time. In some ways, the CCP was one of the results of this. In the 1920s and 1930s, during its infant years, coastal China was a highly international society, at least in its great urban centres like Shanghai and Beijing. Just a look at the chapters relating to the history of this period in the monumental *Cambridge History of Republican China* testifies to the rich intercourse with the rest of the world at this time.[13] Frank Dikotter spells out the rich importing of culture and knowledge into China in the decades immediately before the Japanese invasion in 1937.[14] China wished to emulate Japan after the Meiji Restoration in the 1860s in modernizing and industrializing its economy. Unfortunately, it concentrated most of its efforts into building up military manufacturing capacity. As pointed out in Chapter One, the USSR's influence on China's politics, while still controversial and imperfectly understood, was clear – as was the American influence, for instance, in the setting up of universities in Shanghai and other urban centres, and the UK influence on trade.

Despite that, the country that has come from this process was very imperfectly understood till recently. The years of isolation during the Maoist period had created a clear knowledge barrier, some of it willingly continued by the Party in their desire to conceal their objectives and confuse outside observers. But by the 2000s, interaction with the rest of the world in the fields of politics, commerce, culture and education had become massive. For the UK alone, 80,000 Chinese students went to study there (out of a total of 790,000 who had been abroad since 1980), with 125,000 tourists in 2006. There is massive and increasing cross-border trade. More and more are studying Chinese. The country is no longer remote and mysterious. It has become part of a westerner's local environment, making many of the basic essentials they need to get through our daily lives. Whatever the impact of the global financial and economic crisis from 2007 onward, it is unlikely to change this.

Even so, there are still plentiful opportunities for miscommunication and misunderstanding. A few years ago, talk of celebrating 'the peaceful rise of China' (*zhongguo heping jueqi*), in English rendition, sounded ominous. This is because, in terms of the speed and scale of change, what China is currently doing is unprecedented. This process is greeted with very mixed emotions in other countries. For many years the international community, through the United Nations and other multilateral entities, was urging China to be a more proactive partner in international affairs. Now China is indeed active in places from Africa to the Middle East to the Asian region.[15] It has resolved all but two of its outstanding border disputes (conceding territory to Russia, in one case, in order to build good relations). Of the last 24 UN peacekeeping forces up to the end of 2007, China sent personnel to 16 of them, including playing a key role in the establishment of East Timor after a UN referendum in 1999, and sending 3,000 peacekeeping troops to Sudan in 2006. This proactive China is a different sort of challenge to the more inward-looking country, focused on its internal affairs, which the world had grown used to dealing with.

There are three ways in which China is impacting on the rest of the world, beyond its economic and environmental impact. The first of these is in terms of offering an alternative model of development and in changing the terms of globalization that have been largely accepted in the West. The second is in becoming an investor overseas through its state and non-state companies and through the recently established sovereign wealth fund, the Chinese Investment Corporation set up in September 2007 along with the State Administration for Foreign Reserves, which controls China's mountain of foreign exchange. And the third, through its participation in multilateral organizations like the UN and the IMF and its desire to see these changes and become more representative of a new world order where it is more prominent. All of these figure in the Party's ambition to stay in power by presenting a strong, stable China to the international community and being a credible standard bearer of Chinese nationalism.

China's New Global Role

First, we have to deal with the rhetoric created by the Party. China has, since the 1950s, adhered to the principle of 'noninterference in the internal affairs of other countries'. It's 'Five Principle for Peaceful

Co-existence', in which this noninterference was most fully articulated, were set out at Bandung in 1955. But in the era of internationalization, where issues in one region or country (like the Asian Economic Crisis in 1997–98) have profound and quick effects on other territories, noninterference becomes harder to stick by. China is one of the members of the UN Security Council Permanent Five, and has been since taking up its seat at the UN in 1971. This is recognition of the importance and impact of China and its regional and global role. The decision of the Association of Southeast Asian Nations (ASEAN) to create a new forum (ASEAN plus One, as it is called) to incorporate China is also recognition that discussion of issues of regional security and stability without it makes little sense.

But just as the Party wishes to engage, it is also the source of the key problems. The PRC's having a political model different from the other major nations is where things become difficult, and where a lot of the distrust finds its justification. The Party has been good at identifying the key strategic priorities it believes are best for the country. These are most famously expressed by the so-called '24 Character Strategy' statement by Deng Xiaoping in the 1980s, in which he said that China intends to be a cooperative member of the international community, keep a low profile and build up its internal economic capacity.[16] If ever the CCP had an international and national manifesto, this was it. But there is, however, a question mark over what happens once the country has achieved this goal. It has enjoyed a peaceful, stable international environment now for almost five decades. In the last thirty years, it has strengthened its economic capacity significantly. Now there is debate about what sort of global power China wishes to be. Is it one that wishes to support international law and which will take a major role in brokering agreement and consensus in global arguments? Or one that might be disruptive, offering an alternative model of how a country can develop, away from the more set templates of country evolution followed by most developed countries, and possibly antagonistic to them? Will the Party put its own survival before that of maintaining China's stability as a country, and could there ever come a time when the Party sees that its interests might not be the same as the country it rules over? At this point, would it willingly reform or cede power? What will happen if and when there is clear divergence between the good of the Party and that of the country? No one can answer this question till it actually happens.

The Party has put a great deal into China's development of its soft-power capacity in the last decade. In Southeast Asia, and indeed in the developing world generally, China's economic model has aroused great interest. According to public surveys, in the Philippines, India and other neighbouring countries, its image has overtaken that of the United States. Chinese investment in Africa is seen as delivering quicker, better results than western aid. This is connected to the collapse of the US's image internationally under the Bush presidency. Confucius Institutes have been set up throughout the world, promoting Chinese language and culture. China has over 16 million tourists a year from abroad. Its 'charm offensive' as one US journalist has called it, has resulted in some countries formulating what they see as a 'Beijing Consensus', a model where the state, rather than the free market, is in charge of development.[17] The spectacular collapse of the unregulated free market in 2008 only makes the system created in China of a world state-controlled free market more intriguing.

While it is unlikely that the US and China will come into overt conflict, the US under President Obama will need to react to and accommodate a China that is increasingly proactive beyond its borders, whose influence in some parts of the world may start to outweigh that of the US and which, politically, will be articulating positions led by a clearly diverse and complex domestic constituency within China. The challenge for the US will be how to respond to this, in its own interests, without creating conflict. One clear policy goal of the Obama presidency should be to rebuild the influence and credibility of the US in China and to show that the goals of freedom, dignity of the individual and rule of law, are still fundamental for the future, stable prosperity of the world community. It is imperative that the US and China work together within an agreed framework on energy and environmental issues. The US also needs to identify the very real constraints on China's development at the moment – from demographics (an ageing and increasingly male population) to its economic model and energy inefficiency. The US should not expect China to be able to step up to the plate and become a global leader when it is so clearly preoccupied with internal issues. But it has no choice but to encourage it to be a strategic partner and help spell out that shared strategy. To achieve that, at the very least, it needs to work with others to change the architecture of multilateral forums so that they are more representative, not just for China, but for other developing economies as well. The World Bank and the IMF are at the top of this list. That way, at least some of the tragic miscommunication that has marred the past might be avoided in the future.

China's role in trying to solve some international issues has been largely welcomed. Its key position as part of the Six-Party Talks with the Democratic People's Republic of Korea (DPRK) is part of the reason for the progress of these talks since 2006. China is also seen as having influence, and being willing to use that influence, in places like Myanmar (Burma) and Sudan. But perhaps the combination of these new influences and the lack of clarity about what the Party articulates as its long-term intentions, has caused some of the apprehensions and fears about its 'rise'. Critics, perhaps erroneously, see a long term plan where China exercises greater and greater regional and then global influence, attempting to export its political model. This is not likely, but it complicates dialogue in issues like the environment and energy, where the debate quickly becomes politicized. It also means that many are expecting a clearer leadership role for China. Weary of the interventionist nature of US or EU international diplomacy, they are seeking an alternative and looking towards China to provide that. It is unclear whether the Party would welcome taking up this new, international, prominent role. Its leaders remain, on the evidence available to the end of 2008, preoccupied with their own problems.

There is a dimension of this, too, which will see developed countries and those that have, in many ways, taken the lead in international diplomacy over the last few decades (the US, the EU, Russia) also needing to accommodate China and to compromise. This is particularly clear in the debates over the environment and energy usage, but it is also relevant in more traditional areas of international diplomacy. Some Chinese intellectuals have articulated a more assertive international role as leader of the developing world. China's specific formulation of human rights considerations (looking at the delivery of economic rights as taking precedence over those of civil or political rights for individuals) have also been used in countries in Africa and Latin America. China's influence has the capacity, because of its size and the speed of its development, to radically influence the global landscape. In many ways it can also aspire to be devising a new vision of modernity closer to its own tradition and intellectual heritage. Many Chinese are rediscovering some of China's rich intellectual heritage and seeing how some of these strands are applicable to devising a contemporary ethos that has global application. Just as Deng Xiaoping formulated the idea of 'Socialism with Chinese characteristics', so there is a clear belief that China has a specific culture and intellectual tradition, and that it therefore needs to formulate something which is relevant to this rather than importing ideas from the west. This will be looked at in the final chapter in more detail. Even so, the Party is now facing the quandary of needing to promote a good image for the country while being much quieter about the fundamental role of the CCP in running, and directing the country. It has been quite successful in keeping its own profile low while raising China's. The problems start when people start to ask questions about how China is governed and who runs the place. Then we end up back at the hidden doors of the Party.

China as a Global Economy – the Role of Chinese Capital Abroad

Having accrued almost USD2 trillion in Foreign Exchange Reserves through export sales and foreign investment, China now stands for the first time as an exporter of capital. The challenges of this new capacity to invest abroad have been dealt with elsewhere.[18] But it is a new phenomenon. In the past, China was never an overseas investor. This area, therefore, offers new challenges. And it also offers a powerful opportunity for it to acquire some of the management and technology know-how that its enterprises have said they need, and also to offer again a chance for much deeper dialogue between China and the outside world, where they can change each other.

In the last ten years, the Party has promoted a number of 'Going Out' campaigns to internationalize its corporations. In the very early period of the reform movement, China was not a large outward investor. It was, as Deng said, busy building up its own internal capacity. But since 1992, it has been investing increasing amounts abroad, particularly in resources like mines and energy. Now the non-state sector is also a player in this area, with companies like Huawei and Lenovo active overseas. Lenovo undertook the successful purchase of IBM personal computer division Think Pad in the US in 2005. The China Development Bank took a 3 per cent stake in Barclays Bank, UK, in 2007. The State Administration of Foreign Exchange (SAFE) also took a 1 per cent stake in BP, and a 1.7 per cent stake in French energy giant Total in 2008. There have also been reports that SAFE has taken similarly small stakes in over 100 British-listed companies, radically diversifying its portfolio.

All of this has culminated in the establishment of the China Investment Corporation (CIC) in September 2007. The CIC, the world's fourth-largest sovereign wealth fund, has currently USD200 billion at its disposal. It has made it clear it wishes to invest in commercially viable projects and has sought the advice of outside consultants like Goldman Sachs and Merrill Lynch. It even bought USD5 billion of Morgan Stanley, a 9.9 per cent stake, in early 2008. China's investment, at a time of global economic troubles, is suddenly important and helpful. But, as the China National Overseas Oil Corporation (CNOOC) discovered in 2005, when it bid over USD16 billion to buy US energy company Unocal, there are often political impediments to Chinese state investment, especially in the US, where they are viewed as being unwelcome in strategic sectors like national defence industries, energy and resources. The huge USD14 billion stake that the Aluminium Corporation of China (Chalco) has taken in UK-Australia mining giant Rio Tinto is currently the largest Chinese investment abroad.

China's investment in some developing countries and territories like Africa has also been viewed as politically problematic. It currently stands as the third-largest trading partner of Africa, after the US and France. It has a USD5 billion stake in the Standard Bank in South Africa, and has also invested in infrastructure and projects in Senegal, Botswana, Tanzania, Zambia and, more problematically, in Zimbabwe, the Democratic Republic of the Congo and Sudan. Its importance in the region was shown when it hosted a conference of African leaders in 2007, and the heads of state of 44 countries attended.[19]

Chinese overseas investment both poses challenges and opportunities. It offers a unique opportunity to work together with state and non-state corporations. Chinese investments in some areas of Europe and Latin America have regenerated those areas. It has also been a means to help Chinese corporations internationalize – 60 per cent of Huawei's activities now are abroad. But there remain issues of the transparency of China's sovereign wealth fund and the way these are viewed and received in the rest of the world. And while some countries like the UK, with highly liberal economies, have said that they are 'open for business' and wish to attract Chinese investment, in the US and in Germany and France, there have been signs that Chinese investment is only palatable in some areas, and there are general issues about the openness and conduct of sovereign wealth funds generally, even after the announcement of self-governing principles by the IMF on the conduct of such funds (the Santiago Principles) in late 2008. Once more, it is the role of the Party that is the problem. In the final analysis, it controls and sanctions major Chinese investment abroad. And it sometimes directs these with a strategy that can be clearly linked to political objectives – for which, see the evidence of Costa Rica shifting its allegiance from Taiwan to the PRC in 2007 because of 'investment' from the State Administration for Foreign Exchange (SAFE).[20] Those that receive Chinese investment, therefore, have to be aware of its political background and take a position on how comfortable they are potentially in the end, supporting not just China, but the political party that maintains full control of the country.

China and the Change of Multilateral Organizations

The emergence of China along with India, and the importance of their economies, has made it clear that the post-World War Two settlement, which saw UN Security Council permanent seats given to the victors – Russia, the US, France, China and the UK – is no longer fit for purpose in the twenty-first century. China's entry into the WTO in 2001 only deepened the process of it becoming part of the global economy and the international system. The convening of the G8 in the summer of 2008 made it starkly clear that having discussions about the global economy in a forum where India and China are only observers is incongruous. The creation of the G20 in late 2008 went some of the way to rectifying this, even if some commentators in China wryly noted that in their view the only forum that really mattered was what they called the 'G2' – China and the US. There is also the issue of China and developing countries having minor voting rights in organizations like the International Monitory Fund (IMF).

It is clear that the architecture of multilateral organizations needs to be changed to reflect the reality of the world in the twenty-first century. There needs to be reform of these organizations to reflect this, and to give them more credibility. China, as part of the 25-nation drafting group for IMF proposed rules on the conduct of Sovereign Wealth Funds, has made it clear that it wants to be taken as an equal member of this process, not as a participant who is viewed as passive and as needing to sign up to whatever is decided at the end of this process. In environmental and other areas, China has said that while it wants to be part of the debate, and is willing to act responsibly, it will not be dictated to.

These are the inward and outward challenges that China and the Party ruling China, the CCP, face in the twenty-first century. They are a formidable array of problems in their own right. The CCP could claim that it has the experience of facing down massive challenges from its own past. It survived through the 1920s and 1930s and in the early years of economic desperation of the Maoist period. It has shown that it can apply practical wisdom to the problems facing it. Even so, the Party needs to work in new ways in a rapidly evolving international system where it has had to drop much of the combative rhetoric of the past. Like it or not, there are many things that the Party is no longer able to control now. Is it really in the right condition and does it have the capacity and the resources to deal with these problems, or must it now seriously look to radically adapt and change? This is the question addressed in the final chapter.

Chapter Six

The Chinese Communist Party as it Moves into the 21st Century

We will, under the leadership of the CCP and in light of China's basic conditions, take economic development as the central task, adhere to the Four Cardinal Principles and persevere in reform and opening up, release and develop the productive forces, consolidate and improve the socialist system, develop the socialist market economy, socialist democracy, an advanced socialist culture and a harmonious socialist society, and make China a prosperous, strong, democratic, culturally advanced and harmonious modern socialist country.

— President and Party Secretary Hu Jintao
at the 17th Party Congress, 2007

...Chinese Communism did, during the time that it was a living faith and not just a discredited shell, provide the Chinese people with a story by which to live. With its current disintegration they face the loss of not just one but of two systems of belief and life-orientation within a single century.

— Mark Elvin,
Changing Stories in the Chinese World

Meeting the Party

Those who work in any field dealing with China will one day know that they will cross the threshold of a door that looks like it leads into a Party office, or that they will deal with someone who has a Party function or a Party background. The Party may well have retreated in the last decades, but it has certainly not disappeared. Encountering it in the twenty-first century is an experience to think over and remember.

A typical meeting will go something like this: A visiting delegation, from perhaps a western country, will be summoned at short notice. They have met all the people they expected to meet. But now they have been granted one final, special meeting. It's not something that happens that often. Even the officials shepherding the delegation around are impressed. Suddenly, the whole programme for that day is changed. Meetings are cancelled at the last minute. Things that took weeks to arrange are brushed aside. Those that have to be stood up don't seem to mind. The minute they hear that it is for a meeting with the Party Secretary, they are content. This is something you can never turn down.

Cars with flashing lights accompany the fleet through the city streets, clearing a neat path at the last minute through what looked like impenetrable chaos. They sweep into the large entrance of a walled compound, with soldiers in green uniforms saluting from the small podiums they are standing on. The chaos of the outside world disappears. You find yourself in a serene, well-kept garden, with beautiful lawns, perhaps some running water, and a large covered portico where the cavalcade stops, and the visitors are ushered into a large marble hall.

This is not the place where the final encounter will happen. Attendants in uniform usher the way towards a place deeper in the sanctum, behind a wooden screen, and through huge, partly opened doors. As you round the corner, there stands the line of officials. The Party Secretary is at the head, hand outstretched. You have a few seconds to shake his hand, and then you are moved on, towards your seat in the semicircle leading towards the two main seats in the centre where the Party Secretary and his main guest finally sit.

These meetings occur almost every minute of every day. They are recorded for the evening news and the state newspapers by cameramen and photographers. There always seems to be flashing camera bulbs and the scampering around of cameramen holding their cameras at the start of each of these occasions.

Those without much experience of these occasions – first-time visitors perhaps, or those who have never dealt with the upper levels of the Party before – are usually impressed by the sense of theatre, some of them even reduced to awed silence, unable to come out with the few lines they have learned in preparation for this encounter. The architecture, the setting, the bearing and manner of the Chinese officials, the build up to the event and then the actual performance itself, with all its stately formality, are impressive even to those who have been through this process many times before. They are, after all, joining a long line of many other delegations from years back, almost all of whom have come away from their formal encounter with the Party at least respectful and impressed.

Those that reflect on the way in which such meetings are handled may well conclude one thing: The distance in power between those in the heart of the Party, and the so-called common people, is massive. Western leaders might strain to appear like the common people in their talk and their body language and their way of acting. Current leaders of the Party, at least based on my own observations over the last two decades, are under no such burden. Their manner of speaking, their way of reacting to people, the way they interact with the public, all carries with it a great sense of distance. No one is much fooled by the pictures of high-level leaders, during big events or catastrophes, going down to the masses to sympathize with them. Wen Jiabao famously called himself 'Grandpa Wen' when he went to the site of the tragic earthquake in Sichuan that killed over 60,000 people in May 2008. His avuncular style at least makes him more approachable than the endlessly mysterious Hu Jintao. Chinese regard their leaders as remote, living in a world whose atmosphere is fortified by centuries of elitism and privilege. Those that enter this domain almost always pull up the drawbridge. As a friend of mine in Beijing who is a private businessman said in 2007, 'Words from the mouths of high officials are different to words from other people. They know about how they will be interpreted and understood. They speak with great care, and in a certain way.'

There is a very problematic side effect of this. Increasingly, over the years, people simply don't believe what Party officials say.

What is Power in Modern China?

The film director Zhang Yimou, who had started off as one of the Fifth Generation of young, rebellious directors in the 1980s with such films as *Red Sorghum, Raise the Red Lantern* and *Shanghai Triad*, films which had garnered international praise and won plaudits and prizes, but which had been banned and criticized back in China for promoting a poor image of the country, is living proof that it isn't just Party leaders who are changed by power in the PRC. Despite his past political problems, Zhang was probably the only artistic figure in the PRC who could be handed massively important and symbolic events like the opening and closing ceremonies of the 2008 Beijing Olympics and have a chance of carrying them off. Not that he lacked human resources; he used about 20,000 people for the two events.

During the Olympics, at least in the Chinese press, Zhang was candid. His work filming abroad had not been happy. Unions in France, for instance, had put up stipulations that sent his budgets through the roof. Their demands for safety and the strict, limited work hours for performers were 'western things' that compared badly, in his view, to the absolute authority he had in China to do with people as he chose. As he admitted, ruefully, China and North Korea were the only two countries in the world in the early years of the twenty-first century who would probably be able to put on the sort of mass performance people saw on the night of 8 August 2008.

The only previous Olympics on this scale that came to mind, in fact, was the infamous one held in Berlin in 1936. That immediately raised some unsettling questions about the nature of the authority system in China and possible parallels with the Nazi system. Journalist Jasper Becker, a long-term resident in Beijing, has said that there were many ways in which the current political system in the People's Republic could be described as fascistic, at least in its worship of pure power above anything else. Zhang Yimou's comments illustrate this, showing that the role of the individual and their relationship to power structures in modern China is too close to those systems in the past labelled as fascistic to be comfortable. Analysts like the late American Lucian Pye have written about the power system in the PRC over the last 40 years. They have looked carefully at the way in which power is accrued, used, deployed and challenged. There is one clear pattern. Power is still concentrated in the hands of a limited number of people, even in modern China, and the ways in which they can be held to account remain limited. They live in a realm of power very remote from those in the other side of the Party enclave walls. And those that wish to take them on are working against savagely ruthless, effective operators with all the levers of power in their hands.

Those who have even peeked into the world of power in China can see this everywhere. In any provincial city, the offices of the Party are far and away the most impressive and the most dominant. Their gates may sometimes have petitioners and demonstrators standing outside, but the security around them remains tight. Those that live in these sometimes walled compounds inhabit a world where their apartments, schools, even cars, shops and leisure centres, are totally different. Many in the non-state sector with money try to emulate this seclusion, being shuttled around in cars with drivers and blacked-out windows, living with bodyguards and flunkeys that minister to their every need. For these, the real meeting places are the various 'places of entertainment', the sorts of establishments run by renegade crook Lai Chaixing in Fujian, where the Party and the non-state meet in secluded relaxation to do their deals.

Does Anyone Believe in Marxism Leninism in China?

All of this behaviour raises one unavoidable question. The Party remains in control, and it is very focused on power. It has been very flexible in its approach to what it has allowed to be liberalized (economic and some areas of social life), and what it has maintained a tight grip on (media, political reform). In view of all this, in what possible sense could the Party be said to be following Marxism, let alone Leninism or Maoism, any more? The popular outside consensus is that China is no longer a society that believes anything. It is a non-ideological society, where in fact the Party and everyone else pays lip service to Marxism-Leninism, but carry on doing whatever they need to do, pragmatically, realistically and without fear or favour to any particular belief system. Proponents of this view quote the statements of Deng Xiaoping about it not mattering if the cat is black or white if it still catches mice, or the rightness of letting some get rich before the rest. Beyond questions of whether he actually ever said this thing, there is an uncomfortable issue.

Deng might not have been history's greatest theoretician. To his credit, he never pretended he was. But his selected, collected and complete works are informed in every word and phrase by the simple fact that, from beginning to end, he was a faithful servant of the Communist Party and of its ideology, Marxism-Leninism. Deng was a Marxist-Leninist. He was evidently much less of a Maoist. But he certainly had ideology, and the ideology was the justification for both what he did in the 1980s in promoting the economic reforms and in 1989, when he approved the sending in of the tanks. It was also the final justification for his southern tour in 1992 that restarted the Reform Process.

It is not that China is a place that now lacks ideology. The problem is that it is a place that is fundamentally too ideological. The issue is that as soon as anyone opens their mouth and talks beyond platitudes and the blindingly obvious, they stray into territory where the real issue of ideological conflict immediately raises its head. Ideological and social contradictions were behind the huge turmoil brought upon China by the Cultural Revolution. It was behind the massive rift with the USSR and the impetus behind the patently unsuccessful economic push in the late 1950s that contributed to the deaths of perhaps as much as 30 million people in a famine that was almost wholly human-induced. Ideology was at the birth of the PRC. It was ideological differences – profound differences about how China should reform and what it should do about its problems – that shaped the massive conflicts between the KMT and the CCP in the 1920s and 1930s, so much so that even when Chiang Kai-shek was engaged in a life-and-death struggle with the Japanese, he still had the energy and time, and thought it worth while, to continue his skirmishes with the hated CCP. Ideology was at the birth of the Party, and at the death of the Qing. And ideology still pervades the Chinese body politic to this day – witnessed in the elaborate justifications to let the non-state sector into the Party and the strains with so-called new leftists that rumble right up to the present time and, in the case of a bout of state instability or economic downturn, could very much come back in force.

This bafflement over what Chinese believe, at least for those from Europe and other cultures, is nothing new. The first westerners who went to live in China from the seventeenth century onward, particularly the great Jesuits like Matteo Ricci, and those that visited, came away with total confusion over what, in fact, the Chinese believed. They were not uniformly Taoists, or Confucians, or Buddhists or Christians, but a mixture. There were Muslims and even some who claimed that they were Jews (a tiny community most famously in Kaifeng). Europe, in good Orientalist fashion, imposed its own template there. Despite great schisms between Protestant and Catholic, Europe could be predominantly described, from over a thousand years before, as a Christian culture. The symbols and rites of Christianity, however contested, pervaded the intellectual, cultural and social life of people throughout most of Europe. The Islamic world, too, was, across states and territories, a unified belief system that was describable at some level, despite the schism between Sunni and Shi'ite (a theodicy). But with China, there was none of this. In the high period of nineteenth century ethnography, China was described as a system that saw the elevation of humans (the emperor) to god-like status – oriental despotism. Its political system was lazily described as Confucian. Those that looked harder at more remote Chinese history could even detect the vestiges of ancient Shamanism, and maternal cults in ancestor worship and folk cults.

In the modern PRC, things have not gotten any easier. The Party may well have the most members of any political force on earth – 76 million and counting. But, leaving aside debates about how many of these actually believe in the Party's current articulation of its creed, that is still less than 7 per cent of China's population. Even if the Youth League is taken into this, with its 86 million members, and we cut off those under the age of 15, we are still only looking at a fifth of the Chinese people being classified as believers in Marxism-Leninism.

The other Chinese believe in Buddhism (by one of the great ironies of history, the Buddha is largely without relevance in the country of his birth and teaching, but now has followers in China and Japan and the rest of Asia), which has made something of a comeback in the last few years, Confucianism (though more as a justification for forms of social organization and action than a real religious belief system), Islam (the Hui ethnicity, while highly assimilated to the majority Han, make up China's largest single minority group along with the Uighurs in the problematic 'autonomous zone' of Xinjiang) and finally, the recent dramatic increase in the number of Christians. Christians, according to some estimates, now number 100 million in China and are on the rise. The Party's discomfort with the Catholic Church's demand to place allegiance to the Pope above all else and to recognize Taiwan has been the source of massive friction over the last three decades, despite recent moves by both sides to come closer together. It is quite possible that China will have the largest increase in the number of Christians anywhere in the world in the next decade.

Mao may have talked of letting 'a hundred flowers bloom', but modern China is verily a massive vital mishmash of utterly different belief systems. This is not helped by the occasional appearance of wildcard superstitious systems, the way the Party angrily categorized the Falungong movement in the late 1990s. With its support for scientific development and its presentation of Marxism in particular as a scientific, empirical view of history, the Party regards with bitter distaste the underbed of popular, uneducated, semi-folkloric beliefs ranging from the enacting of odd little ceremonies after a natural disaster like that in Sichuan earlier in 2008 to the colourful world of fortune tellers, face readers, and mystics that lurk in the social underworld in any city or area of China. The Party was to round most of these up in the 1950s during its period of deep social cleansing. But the need for this sort of social activity never seems to let up, despite the Party campaigning vigorously against superstitious ideas.

Falungong will go down as a definitive case study of this – an idea, developed by a very junior official in the northeast of China, Li Hongzhi, which was to then spring utterly unexpected at the Party in 1998 and 1999 when over 10,000 people surrounded the government Zhongnanhai compound, protesting against the clampdown on their right to practice their beliefs. Linked to breathing exercises that were meant to deliver self-discipline and enlightenment, the way in which the Falungong started to edge towards more ominous forms of social activism deeply irked the Party. So, too, did the rumours that there were many faithful followers of the creed in the upper levels of the CCP, even in the Central Committee. A sustained campaign was undertaken in which believers were 're-educated', some of them, very unfortunately, ending up dead in the process. Falungong proved far more resilient than any of the brief unofficial Democratic Parties that had been set up. Some followers set fire to themselves in the traditional place of protest, Tiananmen Square. Others embarrassed senior Party officials abroad by shouting out Falungong slogans during public meetings (the most famous of which was a so-called journalist who managed to get in to the press conference between Hu Jintao and George Bush in 2004, and shouted out slogans condemning the communists). In a list of the 50 most influential Chinese in modern China, which I compiled for the website Open Democracy in 2007, where people were able to vote on who they believed exercised the most power in contemporary China, Li Hongzhi was the clear winner – no doubt more because of the zeal of his followers in registering a vote than for any real power. Even so, it was a potent and concrete piece of evidence for his influence and the way he inspires a core of followers.

The Party knows that these seemingly marginal belief systems can wreak devastating consequences. They look back to the Taiping Rebellion from the 1850s onward, which left more than 20 million dead, as the most pernicious example of this. How could a movement led by a man who claimed he was the reincarnated Chinese brother of Jesus Christ have almost brought down the Qing Dynasty, lapping at the gates of Shanghai and bringing ruin and havoc to most of inner China? The Party has been vigilant against these 'intellectual viruses'. Like the greatest of victors, it never underestimates its foe. Falungong was defeated in the end. But it was a nasty reminder of how these ideas can spread like wildfire.

And, after all, the Party has also seen, in living memory, the creation and exploitation of semi-religious ideas within its own ranks, something that almost caused it to implode. According to a long-term journalist based in Beijing since the 1970s, the Cultural Revolution is the only period in Chinese history that could be described as one of religious unity and fervour. Of a population of 800 million at the time, 600 million owned a copy of Mao's sayings. It was a movement that, at least for urban dwellers, reached deeply into their lives, whipping up massive popular fervour and excitement. As David Bonavia, a journalist for the *Times*, based in Beijing in the early 1980s, was to put it in his book, *The Chinese*, how was it that a whole population, seemingly with no real history of religious movements, could elevate one man to semi-God like status.[1] Even Mao himself was to find some of the extremes this led to disturbing. Chinese society seemed in search of a deity figure, a central core belief. Cults of Mao still reappear to this day, in the countryside particularly. In the 1980s, the Party had to repeatedly point out that Mao 'was man, not God', during the campaign to decontaminate them from his influence.

The Communist Party exists as a belief system in amongst a wide range of potential predators and threats. It has to stake out some system that is 'unifying' across this massively complex, heterodox society. But the Party takes ideology very seriously, and while it may be a doomed question in the Party School, and government sanctioned think-tanks like the Chinese Academy of Social Sciences and its various provincial sub-stations, it continues to try to square the ideological circle, relating Marxism to modern social development, even trying to devise a new, more sophisticated classification for social class. Ideological work is enough for it to insist that even its highest cadres attend sometimes lengthy training sessions on matters ranging from the understanding of the primary phase of socialism, which China states it is currently in, to the need to work more on alienation and the social superstructure. Bookshops in the main cities have special sections devoted to the exposition of ideological work. For the vast majority of people, this is of little relevance to their lives – a quaint background noise that they are most of the time deaf to. But to the power elite, it does matter. In it resides their claims to legitimacy and to having a mandate to rule. The worst crime in modern China is to set up organized political opposition to the Party. The second worst is to start to disprove and oppose its fundamental ideological position.

Li Jianru, current executive director of the Party School in Beijing, is the keeper of the Party's intellectual purity. A modest, quietly spoken man who comes, originally, from Ningbo in the ultra-reformist province of Zhejiang, he is in charge of a team who are representing and reworking Marxism for the specific conditions of China in the twenty-first century. At a meeting in London in November 2007, he sat politely through presentations predicting catastrophe and doom for the Chinese economy by such noted experts as *Financial Times* journalist Martin Wolf, and Will Hutton. After their dramatic words, he responded politely, 'It's odd that you don't think we haven't thought through all this, and worse. We have people from our school go out into the provinces and countryside of China all the time. They go everywhere. They see everything. We have thought through all of the scenarios, to the absolute extreme. And we still feel we can cope. You should be at ease. We have some clever people.' Here he pointed at a blushing professor accompanying him. 'Look at Dr Tian. He's a bright guy. We've got dozens of clever people like him. You needn't be so pessimistic.' And with that, he sat down, to silence. Li drafted much of Hu Jintao's speech at the Seventeenth Party Congress in October 2007. Such speeches are the pure distillation of policy arrived at by consensus. Nine months in the writing, with lengthy discussions and inputs from almost every angle, the final product is something that should definitely *not* take people in the audience by surprise. Twelve pages of this particular speech on the harmonious society had been deleted because of negative feedback during this process. What remained might strike most people as grindingly boring, but a dazzling speech, full of surprises, at least in modern China, is not a benchmark of success.

Searching for the Chinese Way

The Long March has been one of the metaphors shaping the CCP's narrative. China has been said to have had a long march to industrialization, a long march to stable government, a long march to prosperity and now a long march to becoming a global power. But one of the longest and most epic of all the marches undertaken by China in the last hundred years has been the intellectual one, to find a truly, authentically Chinese intellectual take on modernity, something that has not been imported to China from the developed world, something it can call its own. It is here that we encounter the great sleeping giant of Chinese politics – the force of nationalism, a force that shifts in and out of Chinese modern history like a massive, slow-stopping submarine, surfacing for a while then disappearing only to return, often when least expected.

Chinese intellectuals, that much-maligned group, were struggling with expressions of a uniquely Chinese form of modernity since the late Qing. The Meiji restoration in Japan in the 1860s proved that an Asian power could modernize – even though this was to lead, decades later, to horrible and tragic aberrations when it went along an ultra-militaristic, nationalist path leading to conflict with the rest of Asia and the US. The brief period of reforms in the 1890s was scotched by the acolytes of the Empress Dowager, Ci Xi. But the aspiration to create a new China, a China which was unified, strong, industrialized and fit to be part of the modern world, was strong and was to run through the New Culture Movement and the

4 May Movement of 1919, creating the intellectual ferment from which the CCP was to arise.

Chinese writers, thinkers and public intellectuals were uneasy at their inability to nail down what it meant to be a modern Chinese in the modern world. Lu Xun, the greatest of the writers in the Republican period, but someone who never formally joined the Party despite some of his sympathies lying with their political programme, wrote about the self-destructive, self-loathing aspect of Chinese culture. He particularly lambasted a conceptualization of culture and of a highly conservative sense of Chinese history and tradition that had become a stifling jacket, smothering attempts to reform and bring change. Mao was amongst the most radical of those who politically and intellectually challenged this cultural consensus, but with famously tragic results, only the most sizeable ones of which have been described briefly in this book. Mao was to state laconically, toward the end of his life, that his attempts to change China and terms in which China and Chinese saw themselves, had failed. People can only imagine the bloodshed unleashed if Mao had been able to give expression to his full ambitions.

Attempts to devise a Chinese form of modernity continued in the Deng era, most famously in his own government's 'socialism with market characteristics', but also in myriad attempts by intellectuals like Liu Xiaobo, He Xin, Gu Zhun (though from a slightly earlier period) and of writers like Wang Shuo, Zhang Xianliang, and directors like Chen Kaige and the aforementioned Zhang Yimou.[2] An aspect of the highly contradictory way in which this enterprise was conducted and the equally paradoxical results has been captured in Cambridge scholar Julia Lovell's description of the Chinese attempts to gain a Nobel Prize from the 1980s onward.[3] The Nobel Prizes for the various areas of economics, literature, peace, chemistry, etc., were regarded as worthy entities to aspire to, as a sign that Chinese intellectuals could rank with those in the West and that they were producing globally important ideas and intellectual contributions. In the 1990s, there was a 'Nobel Prize' fever, with the government putting resources into supporting writers like Wang Meng for the Literature prize. In 2001 the fever, however, was badly punctured. The award to Paris-based long-term émigré, Gao Xingjian, was seen as a massive slap in the face. His books, particularly *Soul Mountain*, were seen as 'un-Chinese'. The Nobel Prize was dismissed as yet another Western-biased piece of cultural and intellectual control, though a controversy in late 2008 – where members of the Nobel Prize committee in charge of awarding the science-related prizes were accused of going to China and lecturing (to high-level audiences for huge fees) on what it needed to do to secure its first award in the fields of either chemistry or physics – showed that a new bout of the fever had occurred. Chinese critics had a point. The Nobel Committee had only one member, Goran Malmqvist, who might claim any understanding of China. It had a history of passing over important figures in the developing world. But it was symptomatic of Chinese aspiring for something that the West, in the end, seemed uninterested in giving. While Chinese bookshops were, since the 1980s, full of translations of recent and current French, German, American and British writers, from Michel Foucault to Richard Dawkins to the economic wisdom of billionaire Warren Buffet, only very few Chinese writers or thinkers were given any sort of exposure in the West. When Jiang Rong's *Wolf Totem* got a huge advance before being published in English in 2007, it was a first. But reviewers disliked his dodgy politics (admiring the 'wild power of Mongolian wolves' during the Cultural Revolution period when Mongolians were being slaughtered wholesale). Harry Potter was a household name in China. In the west, the last Chinese person after Mao to enter the popular consciousness was Bruce Lee, and then Jackie Chan!

This is an indictment of the low levels of knowledge about China in the West until recently. Even so, Chinese were aware of their failure to produce ideas that took life outside of their own borders. He Qing's massive *The Modern and the Postmodern: A Brief History of Western Art Culture* (*Xiandai yu houxiandai: Xifang yishu wenhua xiaoshi*, Zhejiang: China Art College Publishing 1998), first published in Mainland China in 1998, is a splendid example of this – a book with over 439 densely argued pages about the introduction of Western thought into China, and a final epilogue, in which, in a mere 31 pages, He bemoans the lack of an indigenous intellectual tradition that it can call its own, and can project beyond its borders.

It was not that many of Chinese intellectuals had a closed mind. Many of them had gone abroad for periods of study. The Party School had accommodated 'thinkers' as diverse as Habermas and Derrida, who lectured to the cadres in 2001. They had even given a stage, briefly, to the architects of the Third Way, like Anthony Giddens and the politician Peter Mandelson, before having the sense to see that this particular new ideological path was leading nowhere. Books like Thomas Friedman's *The World is Flat* had been required reading in Party School courses and even in the city of Chongqing. But this was hardly stuff to radically transform the intellectual agenda of the modern world. Most Chinese political science, criticism or economics, whatever their quality, were hemmed in by the cultural context in which they was being written and needed massive contextualization to make sense to outside readers.

China aspired to make its contribution to international debates. In the early 1970s, it had devised the idea of the 'third (developing) world', about which, in one of his political come backs, Deng Xiaoping had lectured the UN General Assembly. This was to return in the 2000s, when there was talk, admittedly not by Chinese, of a 'Beijing Consensus', a model of development which was much more state-led, rather than the 'Washington Consensus' which was to allow the free market full control.[4] With the failure of international banking corporations, and the denting in confidence of the western free market, perhaps the time for China's model had come. But talk of China's political system being preferable to that of the US or UK was at best bold, and at worst fanciful. There was more interest in what China was doing, but Chinese thinkers were not those that Western economists and leaders were likely to call up to seek new ideas about how to critique and mend their failing systems. And this despite the appointment of Chinese Justin Lin as Chief Economist of the World Bank.

Cambridge economist Peter Nolan, in his 2004 book, *China at the Crossroads*, argued well that, in fact, China's constant looking outside its borders for insights and intellectual resources, however laudable, was only part of the story. China has a rich intellectual tradition, some of it reaching back centuries. Joseph Needham's multi-volume *Science and Civilisation in China* since the 1950s had documented the many ways in China's previous dynasties had been innovators, creators and leaders in invention. Chinese intellectuals could mine this rich and largely unexplored territory, looking to the legalists of the Tang and Song dynasties, the great political theorists of the Ming and early Qing, even up to the debates that had occurred amongst Chinese intellectuals and writers in the early twentieth century. With this intellectual tradition, Nolan argued, there was no need for a cultural cringe, a sense that has hovered below the surface since the time of Lu Xun that China is not quite up to the modern world. This was partly proven by the increased interest in Chinese philosophy, culture and art in the west. Western academics looked upon working with Chinese as rewarding, stimulating and challenging. In mathematics and physical sciences, the Chinese academic community proved itself internationally competitive. They were part of the international exercise to map the Genome in the early 2000s.

But there was a nagging feeling that while the Party looked on all of these debates nervously and proved itself quick to intervene if things were taking a turn in an unwanted direction, then China would always be participating in these debates with a massive disadvantage. Chinese intellectuals like Fan Gang, the economist, were to find themselves prey to occasional withdrawal of state approval and support. The more daring still needed political patronage before they could say the unsayable. There were some bold ideas in the 'webosphere', but putting these into written form was a high-risk activity. And the Party, or at least its faithful servants and agents, proved itself wonderfully dextrous at picking territory it wasn't going to allow to ease up, or become over-liberal in. The era of Dengist 'spiritual pollution' campaigns might be over, but the cold hand of the Party could easily descend on those who stray too far.

The Internet in China: A Case Study of Control

In 2008, China became home to more internet users than anywhere else on the planet. With over 200 million surfing the web at home, and about another 300 million doing so on their mobiles, China was a veritable boom zone for cyberspace. This should have been good news for the supporters of free speech, intellectual democracy, and human rights. But there was a problem. In the late 1990s, when the Internet was in its infancy in China, it had been viewed by many as a place where we would see the start of some bold reforms. The Chinese press had been ruthlessly and very effectively controlled up to then. But the mechanisms of even publishing a paper or magazine, distributing it, selling it, were much easier to control, in theory, than material on the Internet. Falungong had proved that emails and mobiles were wonderful means of social mobilization. In the late 1990s, the Party had a rethink.

China had proved itself historically adept at staking out territory and control through constructing walls. From the late 1990s, it built a new kind of wall – the great firewall of China. Websites that were deemed to have unsound content, like the BBC's, were blocked. The real red line was material in Chinese. English content, was mostly let be – though to this day, except during the Olympics, Amnesty's and Human Rights Watch's China sites are still blocked, no matter what language they are in. The Chinese authorities reportedly employed 50,000 inspectors of web and email content, with some highly elaborate and effective detection software, working in Beijing. Not satisfied with this, entrepreneurs who had opened up thousands of small Internet bars in cities and towns throughout China found that a raft of new regulations demanding that they inspect and record the identities of anyone using their computers cut their customer base down, and forced many out of business. Yahoo brought opprobrium and revulsion on its head in 2004 by giving the details of an account user who had posted information considered sensitive about former President Jiang Zemin. Chinese journalist Shi Tao was given a lengthy prison sentence. The great firewall of China, as it came to be called, proved to be remarkably effective. Those that tested the waters by posting sensitive content, usually remarks about political leaders of the 'three T's' – Taiwan, Tibet or Tiananmen 1989 – found that often in less than half an hour, their chat room accounts were closed down and their remarks removed or blocked. Websites across the board were controlled and censored. Google and others who chose to operate in China were rumoured to have allowed policing of the sites their searches pulled up. Liu Di, the 'Stainless Steel Mouse', her web 'nom de plume', was tracked down and jailed for two years for her hard-hitting, opinionated remarks.

The Party proved that it could take on modern technology, but perhaps most remarkably, allow it reasonable freedom, even while it ensured that strategically key areas were not challenged. Far from being a harbinger of greater freedom, the Internet in fact became a wonderful means of back-engineered propaganda, with innocuous participants in chat rooms actually proving to be government supported contributors, there to strengthen the Party line, and influence public opinion in their favour.

Self-censorship proved a potent tool. The Party allowed a whole range of areas where comment was reasonably free. Those that raged about the environment, or foreign politics, or the economy (up to a point) were given free reign. But those that stepped into areas outside of these were looking for trouble – and an amazing number managed to find it. In its work in becoming a modern Communist state, China had also modernized the methods of repression. Hu Shuli, editor of the Chinese *CAIJING* (Finance) *Magazine* was able to publish hard-hitting material on corruption. Li Datong of *Freezing Point* (*Bing Dian*) was able to do the same, before his magazine was closed down. Even so, he continues to post freely, in English and very critically, on the Open Democracy site. The *Southern Weekend* (*Nanfang Zhoumu*) in both web and print form is remarkably candid. Nevertheless, a famous list it produced in 2004 of those it claimed were China's fifty most influential intellectuals was removed quickly. But there was no such largesse for the Internet activities of Hu Jia, who, despite his case being heard so near the Olympics, still got sentenced to three years for material he had put on the Internet. There were no set rules for those the Party chose to take in – but the most practiced activists and intellectuals worked out pretty quickly that they had to speak in a certain way and only about certain things to avoid trouble. In that sense, at the moment, the Party has won the first skirmish of the war. But there can't be complete complacency about the day that this war is no longer one it can fight. For just as was the case in the 1920s and 1930s, when the enemies of the Party are all around, so that remains true, in a very different context today. And in its heart, the Party knows that it is engaged in a battle against time. The final step to political reform needs to be taken. Then the Party's Long March will indeed be over.

A Few Words about Nationalism

There is one great indeterminate in the complex equation that the Party is working out about its role in China's future at the moment, and one that could be increasingly prominent and potentially decisive. Nationalism is a powerful force. It appears most strikingly in popular reaction to Japan. When there was talk of Japan joining the UN Security Council Permanent Five in 2005 (a logical enough move, as it had been the world's second-largest economy, by a long way, for most of the last thirty years) Chinese students took to the streets in Beijing. There was clear evidence of government collusion in this, with a huge crowd gathering outside the Japanese embassy in Beijing, a place they would never have been able to congregate without official collusion. Similarly, powerful displays of nationalism occurred when the Chinese football team was beaten by the Japanese during the Asian Games in 2003. Former Japanese Prime Minister Koziumi's annual visits to the controversial Yakasuni Shrine where Class A War Criminals are buried in Tokyo was to sour relations between the two countries, despite their massive and highly interreliant economic links, for over five years. Internet chat rooms and conversations with countless Chinese are proof that the relationship with Japan, because of the historical sense of grievance on the side of the Chinese over what happened from 1931 onward, has the capacity to stir up deep levels of national feeling. Japan's reaction does not help. With so much at stake for both sides, it is highly unlikely this could ever lead to a complete breakdown in relations. But it is a massively complicating element. And it is only the most obvious and striking of the forms of nationalism in the country.

Nationalism is an easy card for a political leader in China to play. There are many places in the world where that is true. But the Party has been very successful since 1949 in presenting itself as the only body that speaks for the national interest. The health of the Party, therefore, is often equated to the health of China. And the interests of the Party are aligned, sometimes to the point of being indivisible, with the nation. This is why those with what are deemed 'anti-Party beliefs' or who conduct 'anti-Party activities' are also accused of weakening national unity and therefore acting against China's interests, rather than just against the political party ruling China.

Nationalism appeared most dangerously when the Belgrade embassy was bombed by the US in 1999, leading to a major glitch in the relations with the US and the EU. The British and US embassies were besieged and stoned in Beijing. Foreigners were abused and in some cases even attacked in the streets. Some even went around with T-shirts declaring that they were Australian or New Zealanders and, therefore, as nonmembers of NATO, had not been involved in the bombing. Even the Chinese government realized it had to be careful. After a few days of busing students in, reportedly at their own request, to take part in demonstrations in Beijing, Shanghai and elsewhere, it then sent out reports, the most prominent of which was given by then Party deputy leader Hu Jintao, asking for people to calm down. A similar wave of indignation occurred during the spy plane crisis in 2001, over Hainan, where a US surveillance plane brought down and killed a Chinese PLA pilot. American officials were amazed to find that despite all their contact, for a worrying length of time at the beginning of the crisis, the Chinese would not speak or respond at all to their calls. Jiang Zemin showed considerable courage in 1996, during the elections in Taiwan, in facing down the jingoistic calls of his own army and many people in going for the Taiwanese, even though it would almost certainly have failed as a military exercise.

Chinese nationalism, like nationalism anywhere, is no joke. But it is a fatally alluring card to play in a country where the potential fractures and social divisions run so deep. From putting a satellite into space to winning 51 gold medals at the Beijing Olympics, each event is seen as a statement of China's power and strength. Natural pride sometimes gives way to a visceral mixture of resentments stored up from history to a brutal, blind xenophobia. And every now and again observers spot, just out of sight, a sort of Chinese agenda, an unspoken desire to accrue greater and greater power and influence and to start to impose its values and systems and ideas on the rest of the world. This even became an issue in the elections held in Zambia, Africa, in 2006, when what was seen as over-reliance on Chinese investment, aid and workers, and their perceived inability to assimilate, operating almost as an ominous fifth column, became an election issue.

The Party's Communication Problems

As a latecomer to internationalization, perhaps the Party should be accorded some sympathy. It has had to learn the language of international PR late, and quick. In the early years of its time in power, when the Cold War was at its peak, all it needed to do was chuck stentorian, shrill denunciations at 'the enemies of the proletariat revolution', translating its internal discourse into a variety of languages and then unleashing this on the world, with no real care for its reputation (it had nothing to lose, it considered, as it was already deemed the enemy).

Early attempts to do something about the way it talked to the rest of the world happened in the 1990s. But the rejection of China's bid to hold the Olympics in 1993, by a mere two votes to Sydney, and the residual disgust at what had happened in China in June 1989, meant that the 'them against us' language persisted. About Taiwan, Chinese diplomats and the state media trooped out lines like 'Taiwan was an indivisible and inseparable part of China,' and anyone who thought otherwise was a 'separatist and enemy of the PRC'. The Falungong got a particular rhetorical drubbing, as there were – inexplicably for many in the upper levels of the Party – many foreign sympathizers of this esoteric and, in their eyes, sinister movement. The UK experienced a rich period of this state-rhetoric, when Chris (now Lord) Patten, last Governor of Hong Kong from 1992 till the handover in 1997, attempted to introduce limited democratic reforms. Famously called a 'tango dancer' and 'a whore', he was also castigated as a 'criminal for ten thousand years'. There were many times when his actions were interpreted as 'hurting the feelings of all Chinese people'. This encouraged one wag in the British Foreign Office to ask, after one outburst like this, if having annoyed the feelings of 1.3 billion people, the British might ask for an entry in the Guinness Book of Records.

The Chinese government and the Party did care about their reputation, though. And perhaps more than outsiders thought. They wanted to be seen, admired and looked up to. The long and finally successful campaign to host the Olympics and the widespread joy it was to give rise to in 2001 when it was announced (joy largely absent when the event itself actually happened seven years later) was only the most prominent example of the Party, the political elite and indeed, many Chinese people wanting their achievements over the last quarter of a century to be recognized. The Chinese government took on PR agents like Ogilvy, taking advice from them about how to present its arguments. Sometimes this paid off. The central government kept its mouth shut in early 2008 during the Taiwanese presidential and government elections, unlike on the occasions before when it had waged active campaigns against Democratic Progressive Party (DPP) leader Chen Shuibian. The net result of these was to deliver him two election victories. Its silence in 2008 meant that the KMT, under Ma Ying-jeou, got back in – a far more palatable partner for the PRC.

Problems in the buildup to the Olympics over Tibet, Xinjiang and human rights only showed how much the Party does care about its own and China's image. It sent out delegations to explain China's position on Tibet more.[5] The language they used was more conciliatory. They half-disowned the angry attack on the Dalai Lama by the Party Secretary of Tibet who called him, after the worst of the troubles, a 'jackal with a wolf's heart'. This was explained away by one delegation coming to London from the National Minorities Institute as language aimed at the local population, who had been the main sufferers of the surge of ethnic violence during that period. Even so, the Party realized that it had to find better language with which to speak to the outside world. The Party School looked at ways it would be able to do more effective translations of its slogans into English, realising that 'The Three Represents' and 'Scientific Development' weren't quite hitting the spot for a foreign audience. It appointed a very experienced and able ex-diplomat, Liu Guijin, to be its special rapporteur on Africa, setting out the benefits of Chinese involvement there and trying to calm down western fears that it was colluding with repressive regimes like Mugabe's in Zimbabwe or Bashir's in Sudan. This met with mixed success. China's positive moves to be involved in peacekeeping forces in troubled areas and the real benefits its investments brought to many African and other developing countries were little known. As the Olympics was to prove, in some quarters China was to remain fair game to those who wanted to hit it over two or three key issues – treatment of dissidents, freedom of speech and transparency. It was often found guilty even before it had opened its mouth.

This was not helped by the fact that China had as its most visible leader, General Secretary Hu Jintao, a man who had given no one-to-one interviews to the Western press, and who must rank as one of the world's most wooden performers for the media. Hu's inscrutability has nothing to do with him being Chinese; many Chinese find him deep and unreachable. His smile remains in place no matter what context, and there are some wonderful pictures of him being bear-hugged by leaders like Bush, a momentary look containing a mixture of shock, horror and distaste plastered across his face. Unlike Jiang, who famously exploded in rage in front of a group of journalists in Hong Kong in 2000, giving rise to much merriment to those in Hong Kong and China who saw this event on TV or online, Hu lacks the human touch. This is ironic, as he has a humble, grassroots background. Former President Jiang was keen to speak in English, Russian and any other tongue he could master a few words in. He was also famously keen on karaoke, belting out songs at state dinners and formal occasions. This evident curiosity and love of life did positive things for China's international image, even if his visits abroad were usually greeted with trepidation that a stray egg, or a badly placed demonstrator, would stimulate the great man's sense of noblesse oblige and stir the flames of his volatile temper. One poor diplomat in Switzerland was to memorably provoke the rough edge of Jiang's tongue when he confused him over which chair to sit in during a signing ceremony.

Many Chinese, however, interpreted this as face-losing buffoonery. They disliked his evident like of travel, and his gallivanting about on the international stage. He was accused of being a foreign lackey. Hu is a more severe case and could hardly be accused of compromising national dignity. He never uses any language but Chinese. His body language at least maintains the same controlled dignity. But he is patently not the right person to put in front of the cameras of CNN or BBC to explain the ways of China to the rest of the world. The Party's, and China's, inability to justify its priorities and actions in a way that translates well remains a problem. Its search continues for a spokesperson who can at least set out its stall well for the rest of the world. There is no lack of eloquent, witty and intelligent Chinese diplomats, economists and officials. But none of them has been entrusted with the sacred task of justifying the ways of China to foreigners.

In the early days, the Party were masterly propagandists. They honed their message perfectly for their target audience. They created stirring narratives of national liberation that haunt the PRC collective consciousness to today. They need to rediscover those formidable communication skills in the twenty-first century. So far, this part of their campaign has totally eluded then.

Did Someone Just Say 'Democracy'?

Democracy is the great elephant in the room no one dares talk about much in modern Chinese politics. This is despite the fact that leaders like Jiang Zemin and Hu Jintao had said that China's final aspiration is to be a democracy. They have even set a time scale on this. By 2050, according to Jiang, China will have democratized. Hu Jintao, during his visit to the United States in 2006, said clearly that 'Democracy is the common pursuit of mankind.'[6] In the Government White Paper, 'Building of Political Democracy in China', they had stated:

> Democracy is an outcome of the development of political civilisation of mankind. It is also the common desire of people all over the world. Democracy of a country is generally internally driven, not imposed by external forces.[7]

It is not an issue for the Party leadership about the value of democracy. The real issue is that it is their profound conviction that the groundwork necessary for democracy to flourish in China is currently lacking. China is still developing towards this. It will need more time. Overnight introduction of democratic processes and demands would, on this account, create great instability and return China to its pathetic, weakened position of the 1930s, from which it has taken so long, and through such a painful process, to emerge. As the 2005 White Paper makes patently clear – in its formulaic and somewhat wooden presentation of the revolutionary progress of the Chinese people in the last century – what is meant by 'democracy' (at least in this internal discourse) is not something that western liberal democracies would recognize as such, and equates more to Maoist notions of 'democratic centralization' (i.e., in the hands of one all-powerful man), and 'new democracy' (i.e., power monopoly by the CCP after 1949). The paper even brazenly talks of already practicing 'socialist people's democracy'.

More cynical commentators might say that, after all, the Party would say these sorts of things about the 'd' word, trying to anesthetize and 'decontaminate' it. Democracy, as carried out in the West, would carry with it the very real likelihood that sometime in the near or distance future, the Party would lose its power. Competition would be very unwelcome. The idea that the Chinese people, and China, are somehow at the moment intrinsically not yet developed enough or ready for democracy is a highly convenient one for the Party. All the early talk of reform, and village elections, and gradual steps towards openness and accountability are interpretable, on this basis at least, as clever moves, usually as late as possible, for the Party to quieten down more impatient reformists in its fold and members of Chinese society that it needs to keep on board. There are many willing servants of this 'culturist' approach in the West – people who say that the main developed governments, particularly those in the G8 group, just want to return to their old habits of controlling and weakening China by forcing on it an inappropriate and alien political system. They say that 'we' (meaning the so-called liberal democracies) should let China alone, stop banging on about human rights, and realize that every country needs to find its own path towards the best system that suits it. Such apologists rarely stray, in their brief visits to Beijing, from the five-star hotels and government guest houses they are pampered in, and carry on a quaint tradition kicked off in the era of high Maoism of foreigners sometimes being the most passionate defenders of things that most Chinese themselves find indefensible.

Perhaps the most objectionable thing about this approach today is that doesn't honour the many within China who have agitated for, and sacrificed much for, a more representative political system. Many of them point to a history of broken promises the Party has made in this area. If democracy along the lines practiced in much of the West was so awful, why would the Party have had such a long hard look at what it had to offer? And why does the Party remain so defensive? It was playing with ideas of reform in the 1980s – but these were broken in 1989. Even earlier, Deng seemed to countenance a full review of the Party's hold on power in 1979 – but the Beijing Democracy Wall activists at the time badly misinterpreted his objectives, and they were all rounded up and put into jail. Can we really say that the Party is trustworthy? Many were lured out to speak openly in the Hundred Flowers campaign in the 1950s, only to be incarcerated as being leftists. Those that spoke out against the Party, and particularly Mao, were never quite forgiven till the day he died. This process of relaxation and then repression continued for the next three decades. Strike-hard campaigns in the 1990s and 2000s saw newspapers closed down, and those who had spoken out on subjects finally judged subversive clamped down on. Activists in China are right to be wary. The Party has a long history of saying great things, promising the earth – and then completely forgetting these and turning on people when convenient or expedient, or, worst of all, when it gets frightened.

I believe that China will be a democracy and that it will happen before 2050. I think that China will become a democracy in the years immediately after 2020. It might become one before, but there would have been major and potentially destabilizing shocks that would have provoked this, and bloodshed may well have been attendant upon them. China's democratization will occur at about the same time as it is predicted to become the world's largest economy. This process will be one that the Party will grudgingly cooperate with, with the enlistment of some of its most senior leaders. They will do this for the pragmatic reason that it offers the only sustainable future for their Party, even if it carries risks. It will not be the kind of smooth, controlled transition that China's current leaders and ideologues still talk about. Nationalism will play a major part. The Party will aim to end up something like the LDP (Liberal Democratic Party) in Japan, with an almost continuous hold on power for most of the last half a century. There will be some difficult and rocky moments, both for China and the rest of the world, during this process. The key reason, and a very simple reason, why I believe that democracy will happen in China is that it is the only form of government that can adequately reflect, and has a chance of accommodating, the hugely different aspirations, needs and priorities of China's increasingly complex society. The CCP till now has managed to change its political model from one serving one kind of society (largely agricultural, equal, undeveloped in terms of industry and economy) to a wholly different society. It is stretched to its limits. The day will come when it can no longer continue this balancing act. The kind of democracy China will end up with will be more representative, but it will not be a carbon copy of Western liberal democracies. In that sense, the Party is right. China needs to find its own way. But the Party will need to make some big, and often painful, compromises. That is when the trouble could occur.

Here is how I think it will happen.

Understanding on the Ledge

China's transition to the next generation of leaders in 2012 will be the first without the clear mandate of a CCP senior leader with massive political credibility like Deng Xiaoping. The smoothness of this transition will be critical. Xi Jinping and Li Keqiang might look well set (although there are mutterings of potential outside candidates like Wang Yang, current Party Secretary of Guangdong or Vice Premier Wang Qishan), but things can go wrong in three years. And somehow, in a way utterly without transparency or clarity to the outside world, this new generation of leaders will need to demonstrate that they have some kind of mandate, both within the Party, and, more critically, in the country and the general population. With no real proper tests for this, the Party will need to know somehow by 2012 that it has the right man (no women at the moment are realistically in the frame). A back room deal won't do this time. No one has the clout. And in terms of work record, fidelity to the Party and ability, these leaders are all much the same. In a system with no real rules, one of them will need to win and at the same time let the Chinese people, and the Party, feel that they have won. Building this kind of consensus will be a process fraught with dangers, and although the Party is already part of the way there, there are many potential upsets till they can be confident that they are home and dry, and the new leaders can be announced and have credibility.

Such a leader will be grappling with problems that will be almost intrinsically global in their nature. Those of the environment, and energy, and economic sustainable development, outlined in Chapter Five, are the most pressing. They will only get worse by 2012. But there are other ticking time bombs. The demographics of China look bad. In some areas in rural Guangdong there are 145 men to 100 women. Even at the moment, the national imbalance is striking, with 106 men to 100 women. By 2020 there will be over 100 million men who are likely never to marry. Then there is the worst side result of the one child policy – the aging population. By 2020, for every two people of working age, there will be one who is retired. Relying on family care when there is only one child to live off won't work. China has only a primitive social security system in many places at the moment, and would need massive capital injection to change this. Its pension provisions are even worse than the West's.[8]

Rising expectations towards government and the Party will not help. The middle class is increasingly less likely to accept arguments that it has to allow for the primary stage of socialism to develop. They will want to see their government more sensitive to their needs. Media and information flows are only likely to increase and get more sophisticated by 2020. China will need to come up with, in partnership with the rest of the world, technologies that are energy efficient and less polluting. It will need to regain all the famous innovativeness and creativity British sinologist Joseph Needham, author of the multi-volume *Science and Civilisation in China*, imputed to ancient Chinese scientific culture (though some have questioned this so-called forgotten tradition). And more than ever before, it will need technical assistance from the West.

By 2020, the largest process of urbanization in history will be well advanced. Well over half of China's population, probably by that time in excess of 1.6 billion, will live in the cities. The issues of infrastructure, communicable diseases and planning will have to be faced head on throughout the decade from 2010 onward. Some of the magnificent buildings that China has thrown up in mega-quick time in the 2000s will look very different after 15 years of wear and tear and will offer a very visible symbol of the underlying fragility and sustainability of what China has been trying to achieve in the last few years.

Any one of these questions could pose massive challenges that could potentially bring a government down. Mishandling of public healthcare could bring people out on the streets. So could a massive economic downturn in the housing market (already the high end of the property market in Shanghai and Beijing in early 2009 is hurtling towards a nasty-looking crash). The four million estimated to be involved in public protests in 2005 will be as nothing compared to country-wide flaring up of discontented crowds that then, somehow, form a link, and start to look ominously like the widespread disturbances in 1989. But this time, people will not so easily be hushed into a compliant silence by the use of troops and hard-edge tactics. The Party had a difficult enough time in 1989 dragooning troops into operation. It relied on two crack regiments in Beijing, especially after the failure of the People's Armed Police, formed in 1982 to deal with just this sort of civil disturbance, to perform well. In the next turmoil, if it happens, the Chinese PLA, after years of professionalization and discipline, might see it as in its long-term interests to go against the Party. And then the many members of the Party itself, some of them very high up, will make their own calculation. The splits that had run underground till then will appear, like slashes across the front of a broken ship's hulk, sinking it. The Party, as the narrative of its past given in Chapters

One to Three shows, has a history of violence. But playing this card will be a last gasp call.

There is one landmark that must weigh heavy on the minds of the Party leadership even now. The USSR Communist Party lasted from 1917 to 1991 – 74 years in power. It still ranks as the world's longest Communist Party in power, along with the Mexican Institutional Revolutionary Party. The CCP is now standing at its sixtieth anniversary. Every day as it travels towards this 73-year benchmark, it will know it is getting closer to a journey into the unknown. And it will also know of how many ruling dynasties in the past were felled by small spurts of popular uprising that then spread across the body politic. The peasant rebellions that led to the falling of the Yuan, and then the Ming and finally the Qing will weigh heavy on their minds. One can accuse modern Chinese leaders of many things, but not lacking a sense of the importance of history. And with its frequent, overwhelming bursts of turbulence and upheaval, Chinese history is far from reassuring.

There are many who are pessimistic about China's chances of political reform. Minxin Pei is representative of these, in his *China's Trapped Transition: The Limits of Developmental Autocracy*. To him, China is frozen in a moment it can't seem to move from, of the Party knowing it needs to reform, and needs to revise its hold on power radically, but being simply unable to do this. It is trapped in its own power paradigm. The Party may look strong now, but its power is brittle. While at the moment, at least, it is not likely, but nor is it impossible with China's recent history of political instability, that it could be blown away by an unfortunate series of events. Perhaps this explains the very slight frown on Hu Jintao's brow from time to time as he stands, otherwise impassive, before ceremonial troops of kowtowing visiting heads of state and dignitaries. Who saw the collapse of the USSR or even the Shah's Iran before it actually happened? We should not be complacent about the stability of the Party and its hold on power. Hu, and Wen and the other Chinese senior leaders certainly aren't.

The stumbling and possible fall of the CCP in China would cause immense problems for the rest of the world. We need a stable China. We may not like its political system, but in the last half century at least, this has delivered stability. And in the era of globalization, we are now reliant on China's economic performance, and its being a stable part of the international economy and political system.

A fragmented, weakened China would be a massive problem. It is a nuclear power. Even the possibilities of millions of displaced people would pose an unwanted challenge. Its borders with Russia, North Korea, Pakistan and India are highly sensitive. The fall of stable government would be a political tsunami, raising the horrific possibility of the sort of divisions and implosion that China tragically saw in the early twentieth century. This would be the worst-case scenario, and one the rest of the world, whatever shape it is in in the decade after 2020, would need to do everything it could to stop. In that sense, continuation of one Party rule, after many years of opposition, would be something the rest of the world might want to see fully maintained.

The Party has thought through all of these scenarios. It knows what might be in store. In the next few years, it will become progressively more daring and more open in its attempts to reform. It will not do this because it wants to, but because it has to, just as it did not want to change into a party championing the role of violence in social and political transformation after 1927, but did this because it had to just to survive. There is one unique feature of the CCP that marks it apart from any other Communist Party. Its apprenticeship was long, and savagely bitter. It earned an astonishing mandate in 1949. It has demonstrated again and again that this period has given it an amazing instinct for self-preservation. Even its main shaper and former, Mao Zedong, was unable to undo a creation whose rise to power was so much due to his work. If the Party can survive Mao, it can survive anything.

This process of reform towards democratization will be interrupted by some very nasty bumps. Its path towards democratization as envisaged by Bruce Gilley in *China's Democratic Future,* where it neatly sets up a proper federal system with proportionate representation for each of China's provinces, and something like a US- or UK-style bicameral system, is more ideal than likely.[9] There more likely might be an abrupt change in leadership, the breaking away of a prominent splinter group and social disruption. The Party will be challenged more and more vehemently. It may even try the boldest move of in fact changing even its public commitment to Marxist ideology to something like social democracy, an idea it played with very superficially in the past. It will then claim that it has, in fact, transformed to a democratic party, but a party that keeps democracy within itself.

People will not be so easily fooled. As in Taiwan, there will come a time around 2020 to 2025, when the Party has leadership that will do what until then had been unthinkable and lift the restrictions on organized political opposition. They will sanction, and live with, a free press. And they will do this because the sort of input that they need from society will be utterly critical if they are to survive – and the country maintain its integrity – the massive challenges facing it. China's democratic transition will take about a decade to a decade-and-a-half. But by the end of this process, China will have become a great power and will have effectively replaced the United States as the most important and prominent leader of the twenty-first century. One of the most remarkable historic transformations ever will have happened. And it is very likely that the leader of the Communist Party will win at least the first election. Beyond that, it is hard to say what will happen!

Being a Good Communist in the 21st Century

Liu Shaoqi's rehabilitation in 1980 was also the occasion to make one of his most famous texts more widely known again. He had written *How to be a Good Communist* in the 1940s, as a primer for Party members. It was a text that was to be thrown back at him during the CR. But these days, the sort of moral qualities and sense of public commitment espoused in this book are the kinds of things the Party publicly wants its members to sign up for. And Party members in the twenty-first century can at least hold their heads high, no matter what horrors the past may have held. They are now members of the world's most successful and largest political organization, in terms of the number of years it has been in power, its membership, the size of the territory it rules over and the importance it holds for the rest of the world.

To enter the Party in the twenty-first century is not a straightforward process. Those browsing through the political sections of bookshops throughout China will see the usually red-covered 'Party Handbooks', often with the yellow hammer and sickle, symbol of the CCP, on the cover. Inside are the rules, regulations, required reading and ideological knowledge and background necessary for applicants who are even thinking about entering the Party. Only 10 per cent of those applying get in. They need to take written tests, have interviews and then make a formal commitment. Perhaps the hardest part of this process is to show that political 'X factor', the sort of attitude and understanding that shows those who are assessing your application that you have what it takes to be a Party member. This is not based on knowledge (many of the most knowledgeable about Party history and structure are not Party members), nor an understanding or even necessarily a belief in Marxism. Nor is it total fidelity to Deng Xiaoping thought, or the latest enunciation of Hu Jintao's 'Socialist Scientific Development'. It is much more about attitude and bearing. More often than not, these are ineffable qualities that are bestowed rather than acquired. A surprisingly high number of senior party officials seem to be able to pass them on to their offspring.

In theory, anyone can join the Party. In the Cultural Revolution, there were clear restrictions. Those with bad class backgrounds were doomed. In a twentieth century form of Augustinian predestination, some were preordained to be Party members and some, no matter how much they tried, could never cross the great divide. There were elaborate theories in the late 1960s of blood-lineage, with Party membership linked to your parentage, and your being in the right social class.

These days, entrepreneurs, members of national minorities, even former prisoners who have been incarcerated for thought crimes in the past, can apply to join. The Party wants to build a broad church, where it combines all the capacities of the vast constituency that it embraces for what it articulates as the common good.

To be a good member of the CCP in the twentieth century is to subscribe to a highly heterodox ideology in which you ostensibly look up to both Mao and Deng, but at the same time passionately support the market economy. You stand by one-party rule of China on the grounds that China's people are currently not yet ready for universal suffrage democracy, and believe in a strong, rising but peaceful China that does not look to interfere in the affairs of other countries but has not renounced war as a means to win back Taiwan. You believe in intra-party democracy but know that in the end the final choice over who will be the General Secretary after 2012 will be made by a tiny clique right at the top of the Party tree. You stand by the wisdom and correctness of your organization, while either being, or daily dealing with, members of a non-state sector whose wealth creation you know your country's economy fundamentally relies on. You pay your dues each month to an organization whose finances are shrouded in mystery. And you are aware that while you are able to speak freely about economic policy or the environment or even international affairs, there are some key issues, like democratization and party reform, about which you had better be careful. You are one member of an organization that covers a territory making up the world's third-largest country, controlling the destiny of a fifth of humanity, with an economy ranking third-largest in the world. Those are the reasons in the end why you join and stay a member of the only surviving Communist Party in charge of a major country in the twenty-first century.

Conclusion: Gambling with the Devil: Why the Fate of the CCP Matters to Us All

In 1998 the late Gerald Segal, an academic specializing in China, wrote a piece for the US foreign policy periodical, *Foreign Affairs*, that bluntly asked 'Does China Matter?'[1] His point was simple. Observers, and especially foreign governments, had a habit of greatly overstating the importance of China in the modern world. In terms of China's economy, for instance, it was still, at that time, less than 5 per cent of the global total and trailed massively behind Japan, which seemed to provoke far less excitement in people. Its market opportunity for foreign companies was probably no greater than tiny Belgium in Europe. Its army was ill-equipped and had last seen real combat experience two decades before. Its political system was riddled with corruption, ineffective and backward. It suffered from problems of lack of good governance and rule of law. Its industrial efficiency was poor, and its banking system riddled with nonperforming debts and about to go under. Did China really matter as much as so many claimed?

Segal was right to ask these questions. But after ten years, we know a lot more. China's banks caught a terrible cold in the Asian Financial Crisis; but ten years later, they are doing better than anyone expected. China's army cleaned up its act soon after Segal's article appeared. Good or bad, it's now one of the best-resourced and most-professionalized military forces in the world.[2] It's entry into the WTO in 2001 pushed its economy further into the global first rank. Chinese consumers might not spend as much as foreign companies want, but no one denies their importance, and most companies now work there. Corruption and political reform remain issues, but the Party's hold on power, as this book has tried to show, remains perhaps even firmer now than when Segal was writing. There is simply no meaningful opposition outside the Party to speak of.

And in areas like energy, global economic development and the environment, solutions to problems are simply unthinkable without China being a partner. Carbon emissions targets are senseless without China signing up. So, too, are international agreements on energy efficiency. Chinese state funds have gone into Western companies like Blackstone, Prudential, BP and Total. China has become the third largest investor in Africa almost overnight. China does matter now – more than ever before. Its problems, by their size and complexity, are global problems. Its political leadership, at the top of the CCP, are therefore by definition global leaders. We need to work with them and understand them and their background and the organization they work within, more than ever before.

The template of globalization may well have been created in the West. But now that China has opened up, it has the capacity and the right to challenge and remould that template more in its own image. Some argue that, in fact, China's authoritarian political system offers a sustainable alternative to democratic systems that are themselves undergoing crisis and self-doubt. They point to low turnouts in elections in the US and Europe, low trust placed in politicians, and the difficulties that these countries have in delivering large-scale projects and issuing judgements. They point to the way in which China was able to deliver the USD40 billion investment in the 2008 Olympics and hold such a massive event without evident logistic mishap. They compare this to the political bickering already surfacing in the London 2012 Olympic organizing committee.

Whether in fact China is any more or less efficient than other countries in delivering outcomes is a mute point. Spectacularly bad decisions that waste billions of dollars can be cited the length and breadth of China. The Formula One track for which China lobbied for so many years and is now located in Shanghai, is a case in point. A beautiful circuit with some of the best facilities in the world, it was evidently built with massive government collusion, and contributed in part to the fall of Shanghai Party Secretary Chen Liangyu and hundreds of his officials and cohorts in 2006. As a commercial project, it is totally unviable at the moment. In a proper market economy, such a project is far less likely to get built.

Because China remains with the political system it has, it is far easier to dismiss or excuse it. In the end, on this one point, it remains fundamentally different to most of the other countries in the world – at least the developed ones. It is extremely unlikely that, in terms of political systems, China will influence the rest of the world. But the interesting question comes when one sees a reformed China, a China with a political system that at least allows greater participation and is visibly representative of its people's attitudes and beliefs.

At that point, we will not have the self-asserting Party standing between us. It will be us looking at the Chinese people, and what they want and aspire to. China's impact on almost every area of global policy, once this has been achieved, becomes massive. The desire of Chinese people to own their own cars will, as stated earlier, have a fundamental impact on the world's environment. Their aspiration, rightly, for a life style similar to the West will only be able to happen if we have succeeded in finding a development model that is different from the one that most developed countries have used till now. The sort of use of energy, production of waste, and side effects that the average American or European have grown up on, if translated to the 1.3 (and probably nearer 1.5) billion Chinese would cause a resource meltdown. Some time by 2030, we would need to either find many more energy resources or shift our supply to another source. The age of oil will be coming to an end. We might then be entering a nuclear or solar age, and China will be leading us into it.

China is already inspiring talk of an alternative development model – one that is more state-led. If the Party were to reform, this would become a much more powerful inspiration. China could well redefine the role of the state in the coming century. It would stand in opposition to the reign of the free market and the kinds of inequalities and disequilibrium that has brought. Strong state leadership will become more viable with the example of China. We can be sure of one thing. Whether the Party continues to have a monopoly on power in China or not, the very structure of the modern PRC means that it will need a strong state at its heart, or it will simply fall apart. The State will need to survive, the Party not necessarily. This is something the Party must know in its darker moments.

China as it evolves will then begin to deploy the massive intellectual resources and the human power that it evidently has. After the continuing mystery of why it did not participate in the first industrial revolution in the eighteenth century till far too late, it will then be at the forefront of the second revolution to clear up the mess created by the first and to create a sustainable future for itself and the world. It won't be a case, then, of the West having the answers and passing them on. The West, China, and others, will need to work together as they have never done before. It won't be a matter where there will be a choice. As Mao himself said, there is the road to oblivion, and the road to success. And for either, we will need to go together, not alone.

For that reason, China will fundamentally change our world, and its impact from now on will become something that marks our lives. It will be a stakeholder in globalization and a shaper of the forces of globalization as we go forward. Negatively or positively, the CCP will be a key player in all of this. And that is an extraordinary thing for a Party that started life with a dozen people, lost thousands of its membership in a purge in 1927, was nearly wiped out in global and civil war in the 1930s and 1940s, destroyed by its most important founder in the 1960s, and ostracized by much of the rest of the world after an internal uprising that shook it to its core in 1989.

Notes

Introduction

1. 'Deng Xiaoping Tonzhi zai guanjian shoudu jieyan budui jun yishang ganbu shide jianghua' [Comrade Deng Xiaoping's speech to capital martial law troops at the corps level] quoted in David Shambaugh, *China's Communist Party, Atrophy and Adaptation*, University of California Press 2008, p 42–43.
2. Andrew J. Nathan and Perry Link, Eds., *The Tiananmen Papers*, Little, Brown Book Group London, 2001.
3. In *The Gate of Heavenly Peace*, documentary film produced by Richard Gordon and Carma Hinton, in 1995.
4. Timothy Brook, '*Quelling the People. The Military Suppression of the Beijing Democracy Movement*' (Stanford: Stanford University Press, 1999), offers a comprehensive background, and account, of what is so far known about the 4 June events.
5. See Andrew Scobell, *China's Use of Military Force: Beyond the Great Wall and the Long March* (Cambridge: Cambridge University Press, 2003).
6. Deng's last formal position was the Chair of the powerful Central Military Commission, which he had resigned from in 1989. Ironically, despite his enormous power in the 1980s, he never formally occupied the position of president or head of the Party during this period, although he was the third ranking member of the Standing Committee of the Politburo for most of this time until his retirement from that at the 13th Party Congress in 1987.
7. For a beautifully written history of Beijing, which covers well the despoliation of the great city after 1949, see Jasper Becker's *The City of Heavenly Tranquillity: Beijing in the History of China* (London: Allen Lane 2008).
8. Harrison Salisbury, *The New Emperors: Mao and Deng, a Dual Biography* (London and New York: Harper Collins 1993).
9. See the full list at <www.cecc.gov/pages/victims/20080807_PPD.pdf?PHPSESSID = 6bb415261903f11b764a306531fd624.d> (accessed 9 September 2008).

10. Kerry Brown, *Struggling Giant, China in the 21st Century* (London: Anthem Press 2007).
11. See Canadian historian Margaret MacMillan's entertaining account of the build up, and then the taking place, of this momentous meeting, in *Seize the Hour: When Nixon met Mao* (London: John Murray 2006).
12. According to Yongnian Zheng and Sow Keat Tok, in Wang Gungwu and John Wong (eds) *Interpreting China's Development* (Singapore: World Scientific Publishing 2007), pp 20 to 24, membership of the CCP in the past was dominated by farmers and workers. They made up 83 per cent of the Party in 1956. Deng Xiaoping, as in so many other areas, proposed reforms that increased the constituency the Party could reach out to. Workers and farmers now only make up 29 per cent of the CCP membership. As of 2005, the membership of the CCP is as follows:

Self employed	1.4%
Students	29.7%
Government officials	8.1%
Military	8.8%
Workers	9.1%
Farmers	19.9%
Mangers of enterprises, and professionals	23.0%

As of 2005, therefore, the Party has become the essence of a middle class, professional organization. It has travelled far from its roots.
13. The Mexican Revolutionary People's Party was also in power for over 70 years.

Chapter One. A History of Violence: The Rise to Power of the CCP

1. See for instance Hans van de Ven's use of these archival materials in 'New States of War, Communist and Nationalist Warfare and State Building 1928–1934', in *Warfare in Chinese History*, Hans van de Ven, ed. (Leiden: Brill Academic Publishers 2000), 321–98.
2. See F. W. Mote, *Imperial China, 900–1800* (Cambridge: Harvard University Press 1999), 137–138.
3. *1587, A Year of No Significance* (New Haven: Yale University Press 1981).
4. Huang, 93–94.
5. Immanuel C. Y. Hsu, *The Rise of Modern China*, Sixth Edition (Oxford: Oxford University Press 2000), 45–46.
6. There are, in addition, issues over islands and international sea boundaries, that China still disputes and claims special interests in. For China's treatment of its border disputes, see Bates Gill, *Rising Star* (Washington: Brookings Institute 2007).
7. John King Fairbank, Albert Feuerwerker, Denis Twitchett, *The Cambridge History of China: Republican China 1912–1949, Part 2*, (Cambridge: Cambridge University Press 1986), 2.
8. Frank Dikotter, *The Age of Openness, China Before Mao* (Hong Kong: Hong Kong University Press 2008), 3.

9. Jacque Guillermaz, *A History of the Chinese Communist Party 1921–1949* (London: Methuen Press 1972), 12.
10. The first recorded mention of Marx in a Chinese language publication that has survived was in March 1899, in the *Wanguo Gongbao* produced in Shanghai. Sun Yat-sen, while based abroad, seems to have been aware of Marx since 1896.
11. Ishikawa, *Zhongguo Gongchandang Chenli Shi* (Beijing: Chinese Academy of Social Sciences Press 2005), 6.
12. The intellectual origins of Communist in China are described in Michael Y. L. Luk, *The Origins of Chinese Bolshevism: An Ideology in the Making* (Hong Kong: Oxford University Press 1990). Marx on the Taiping is referred to in Immanuel Hsu, *The Rise of Modern China*, Sixth Edition (Oxford: Oxford University Press 2000), 253.
13. It is true that there were many millions of people engaged in 'handicraft' industries and other non-agricultural occupations in China, in the centuries preceding twentieth-century mass industrialization. Substantial numbers were engaged in manufacture and commerce, but working within structures not classified as 'proletarian'. That does not make them all farmers.
14. These are the figures from the official Chinese history of the Communist Party, *Zhongguo Gongchandang Lishi* (History of the CCP), Volume 1 (Beijing: Central Party School 1991), 19.
15. Hans van de Ven, *From Friend to Comrade, the Founding of the Chinese Communist Party 1920–1927* (Berkeley: University of California Press 1991), 73.
16. Quoted in Lucien Bianco, *Origins of the Chinese Revolution 1915–1949* (Palo Alto: Stanford University Press 1971), 115–116.
17. The full membership, dates, and key discussion and decision points of each Congress, are given in '*Zhongguo Gongchandang Lici – Quan Guo Daibiao da hui*, Chen Feng and Gao Mei, Eds. (Beijing: China Party School Publishing House 2008).
18. Quoted in Jonathan Fenby, *The Penguin History of Modern China, the Fall and Rise of a Great Power 1850–2008* (London: Allen Lane 2008), 189.
19. *Cambridge History of China*, Volume Twelve (Cambridge: Cambridge University Press 1983), 526.
20. Mao Zedong, *Selected Works*, Vol. 1 (Peking: Foreign Languages Press), 23.
21. Van de Ven, 'New States of War', 53.
22. Mao Zedong, 'Strategy on China's Revolutionary War', in `Selected Works' (Beijing: Foreign Languages Press 1975), 182–3.
23. Van de Ven, `New States of War', 70.
24. Van de Ven, `New States of War', 76.
25. Van de Ven, `New States of War', 77.
26. Van de Ven, `New States of War', 77.
27. Mao evidently had more grandiose views of himself, as not just a political leader, but a philosopher, and while it sits oddly with the unbridled violence of the period in which he came to power, he was keen to stress, as were others on his behalf, his interest in Daoism and in marrying this ancient form of Chinese philosophy to imported Marxism. In that sense, he was able to justify waging a long war against foreign influence and control of China that sought its intellectual justification in an imported ideological system (Marxism-Leninism).

For him, he was just taking the best of both worlds, and using them for national purpose.

28. Jacques Guillermaz, *A History of the Chinese Communist Party 1921–1949* (London: Methuen 1972), 284.

Chapter Two. Revolutionary Administrator: The Party in Power

1. This fascinating and understudied period is dealt with in *Dilemmas of Victory, The Early Years of the People's Republic of China*, Jeremy Brown and Paul G. Pickowicz, Eds. (Cambridge Mass.: Harvard University Press 2008).
2. See, for instance, *Chinese Intellectuals Between State and Market*, Merle Goldman and Edward Gu, Eds. (London: Routledge 2003) and Anne Thurston, *Enemies of the People: Ordeal of the Intellectual in China's Great Cultural Revolution* (Cambridge, Mass.: Harvard University Press 1988) on this vexed relationship.
3. Franz Schurmann, *Ideology and Organization in Communist China* (Berkeley: University of California Press 1966), 61–62.
4. John Wilson Lewis, *Leadership in Communist China* (Ithaca: Cornell University Press 1963), 137.
5. Bao Ruowang and Rudolph Chelminski, *Prisoner of Mao* (Harmondsworth: Penguin 1976).
6. The system that has existed in the Democratic People's Republic of Korea from the 1950s onward is perhaps more completely repressive, but exists only for a population of 21 million.
7. John Wilson Lewis, op cit., 108.
8. John Wilson Lewis, op. cit., 2.
9. The establishment of these national Party structures, right down to the County and village level, are set out comprehensively in A. Doak Barnett, *Cadres, Bureaucracy and Political Power in Communist China* (New York: Columbia University Press 1967).
10. Though he was, in fact, incarcerated slightly earlier than the Hundred Flowers Campaign, in 1955, as the result of a campaign by central literary apparatchik Zhou Yang in 1955. Zhou was to get his just deserts, becoming himself one of the earliest victims of the Cultural Revolution a decade later.
11. See R. J. Lifton, *Thought, Reform and the Psychology of Totalism: A Study of "Brainwashing" in China* (Chapel Hill: University of North Carolina Press, reissued 1989).
12. See Jasper Becker, *Hungry Ghosts: Mao's Secret Famine* (London and New York: Simon and Schuster 1997).
13. See Ralph A. Thaxton Jr, *Catastrophe and Contention in Rural China: Mao's Great Leap Forward Famine and the Origins of Righteous Resistance in Da Fo Village* (Cambridge: Cambridge University Press 2008).
14. See Yao Mingle, *The Conspiracy and Murder of Mao's Heir*, (London and New York: Collins 1983), which is reputedly an internal account of this conspiracy. And for a narrative of Lin's fall, see Frederick C. Teiwes and Warren Sun *The Tragedy of Lin Biao* (London: Hurst and Co 1996).
15. From discussion with Mr Lord in the UK in 2007.

16. His doctor gives the most exhaustive account of Mao's ailments in his twilight years. See Li Zhisui, *The Private Life of Chairman Mao* (London and New York: Random House 1994).
17. It was, in fact, titled 'On Socialist Democracy and the Legal System'.
18. For the full story of Li, see Patrick Lescot, *Before Mao: the Untold Story of Li Lisan and the Creation of Communist China* (New York: Harper Collins 1999).
19. See Jung Chang and Jon Halliday, *Mao, the Untold Story* (London and New York: Vintage 2005), for the most exhaustive, and exhausting, expression of this. For a decent biography of Mao, see Philip Short, *Mao: A Life* (London: Hodder and Stoughton 1999).

Chapter Three. The Party in the Reform Era

1. 'Resolution on Certain Questions in the History of Our Party Since the Founding of the PRC', adopted at the Sixth Plenary Session of the Eleventh Central Committee of the CCP, 27 June 1981. Available at <www.idcpc.org.cn/english/maozedong/comments.htm> (accessed 29 August 2008).
2. 'In the rural reform our greatest success – and it is one we had no means anticipated – has been the emergences of a large number of enterprises run by villages and townships. They were like a new force that just came into being spontaneously.' Quoted in Yasheng Huang, *Selling China* (Cambrindge: Cambridge University Press 2003), 308.
3. Roger Garside, who worked in the British Embassy at the time of the Democracy Wall, wrote a good near-contemporary account of this period, *Coming Alive: China After Mao* (London: Andre Deutsch 1981). Wei Jingsheng's writings are contained in the collection *The Courage to Stand Alone: Letters from Prison and Other Writings* (Harmondsworth: Penguin 1998).
4. In Ba Jin, *Random Thoughts* (Hong Kong: Joint Publishing 1984).
5. Harry Wu and Kate Saunders, *Eighteen Layers of Hell: Stories from the Chinese Gulag* (London: Continuum Publishing 1996) .
6. See Yasheng Huang, *Capitalism with Chinese Characteristics* (Cambridge: Cambridge University Press 2008).
7. It had changed its foreign policy behaviour, though, placing politics in second place as it immediately recognised all the new states from the former USSR and in Easter Europe.

Chapter Four. The CCP from 1992 to 2008

1. See Zhang Jiangjin, *Marketization and Democracy in China*, (London: Routledge 2008) for a lively comparative study of Wenzhou and Wuxi in neighbouring Jiangsu province.
2. For a good account of these debates, see Gloria Davies, *Worrying about China*, (Cambridge, Mass.: Harvard University Press 2007).
3. Randall Peerenboom, *China Modernizes* (Oxford: Oxford University Press 2007).

4. For the calculation of this, see Kjeld Eric Brodsgaard in Wang Gungwu and John Wong, Eds., 'Interpreting China's Development', *World Scientific*, Singapore, 2007, 46.
5. Data from Carter Centre 'China Election Project', quoted on Council For Foreign Relations, <www.cfr.org/publication/13616/> (accessed 28 August 2008).
6. See <http://www.defenselink.mil/pubs/pdfs/China_Military_Report_08.pdf> (accessed 15 September 2008).
7. W. F. J. Jenner, *The Tyranny of History: The Roots of China's Crisis* (London: Allen Lane 1992).
8. Susan L Shirk, *China: Fragile Superpower* (Oxford: Oxford University Press 2007).
9. See Chen and Wu, *Will the Boat Sink the Water* (London: Public Affairs 2006), 174.
10. This is available in English as *Yangtze! Yangtze!* (London: Earthscan 1994)
11. Karl Wittfogel, *`Oriental Despotism'* (Oxford: Oxford University Press 1957) and Mark Elvin, *The Retreat of the Elephants* (New Haven: Yale University Press 2004), Chapter 6.
12. Andrew Mertha, *China's Water Warriors: Citizen Action and Policy Change* (Ithaca: Cornell University Press 2008).
13. In a talk on NGOs in China at Chatham House, London in early 2007.
14. Qiusha Ma, *Non-Governmental Organizations in Contemporary China: Paving the Way to Civil Societ*, (London: Routledge Contemporary China Series 2006).
15. It is a good question to actually ask what Chinese people think, one that should be obvious were it not so often ignored. Defenders of their position, both inside and outside China, are fond of stating that 'Chinese people believe…' But in the absence of elections, it is hard to offer empirical evidence for this. Public surveys, while they do occur, are few and far between and need to be undertaken with a Chinese, state-supported and state-sanctioned partner. One of the few studies based on empirical surveys, Jie Chen's *Political Support in Urban China* (Palo Alto: Stanford University Press 2004), makes clear that there are, at least in his survey base, high levels of dissatisfaction among urban Chinese at the performance of their government. His surveys were conducted, however, in the mid-1990s. Maybe things have improved since then, but in the absence of any clear evidence, it is hard to know how certain one can be about this.
16. See William Hinton, *Hundred Day War, Cultural Revolution at Tsinghua University* (New YorkL Monthly Review Press 1972) for a first-hand account of the CR at Qinghua.
17. Chen Guidi and Wu Chuntao, Zhu Hong, Trans.,*Will the Boat Sink the Water: The Life of China's Peasants* (London: Public Affairs 2006).
18. All information from BBC Monitoring China Social Unrest Briefing 14–20 August 2008.
19. See Joseph Fewsmith, 'An Anger-Venting Mass Incident Catches the Attention of China's Leadership', from the China Leadership Monitor, <http://www.hoover.org/publications/clm/issues/27770829.html> (accessed 18 October 2008).
20. Carin Zissis, 'China's Slow Road to Democracy', 7 March 2008, at US Council for Foreign Relations, <www.cfr.org/publication/13616/> (accessed 28 August 2008).

21. See Yasheng Huang, *Capitalism with Chinese Characteristics* (Cambridge: Cambridge University Press 2008).
22. For the full story of Lai, see Oliver August, *Inside the Red Mansion: On the Trail of China's Most Wanted Man* (London: John Murray 2007).
23. The definition of 'princeling' is anyone directly related (as son or daughter) to a Vice Minister or above.

Chapter Five. The Challenges Facing China and What They Mean for Rule by the CCP

1. Yasheng Huang, *Selling China* (Cambridge: Cambridge University Press 2003), 308.
2. See especially Peter Nolan, *China and the Global Economy* (Basingstoke: Palgrave 2001).
3. Barry Naughton, *The Chinese Economy* (Cambridge, Mass.: Massachusetts Institute of Technology Press 2007), 396.
4. OECD, Economic Survey of China 2005, <http://www.oecd.org/document/21/0,2340,en_2649_34571_35331797_1_1_1_1,00.html> (accessed 28 March 2006).
5. Bruce J Dickson, *Red Capitalists in China: The Party, Private Entrepreneurs, and Prospects for Political Change'*, (Cambridge: Cambridge University Press 2003).
6. James Kynge, *China Shakes the World: The Rise of a Hungry Nation* (London: Weidenfield and Nicholson 2006).
7. Yasheng Huang, *Selling China* , particularly p. 122 onwards: 'Among all the constraints on the growth of private firms, the low political and legal statuses of private firms are most fundamental and most blatant.'
8. Elizabeth Economy, *The River Runs Black: The Environmental Challenge to China's Future* (Ithaca: Cornell University Press 2004).
9. See <www.worldbank.org>.
10. See Qiusha Ma, *Non-Governmental Organizations in Contemporary China: Paving the Way to Civil Society* (London: Routledge Contemporary China Series, 2006).
11. Barry Naughton, *The Chinese Economy*, (Cambridge, Mass.: Massachusetts Institute of Technology Press 2007), 337.
12. Bill Emmott, *Rivals: How the Power Struggle Between China, India and Japan will Shape our Next Decade* (London: Allen Lane 2008), especially chapter 6.
13. *The Cambridge History of China*, ed Dennis Twitchett and John K Fairbank, Volume 13, *Republican China 1912–1949*, Part 2, in particular chapters 2, 4, and 9.
14. Frank Dikotter, *The Age of Openness: China Before Mao* (Hong Kong: Hong Kong University Press 2008).
15. Bates Gill, *Rising Star: China's New Security Diplomacy* (Washington: Brookings Institution Press 2007).
16. Bates Gill, *Rising Star*, 7.
17. Joseph Kurlantzik, *Charm Offensive: How China's Soft Power is Transforming the World* (New Haven: Yale University Press 2007).
18. For instance, in my own *Rise of the Dragon: Chinese Inward and Outward Investment in the Reform Process* (Oxford: Chandos 2008), especially Chapter Five.

19. A good, comprehensive roundup of China's involvement in Africa can be found in Ian Taylor, *China's New Role in Africa* (Boulder and London: Lynne Rienner Publishers 2008).
20. See *Financial Times*, 12 September 2008, 1, 6.

Chapter Six. The Chinese Communist Party as it Moves into the 21st Century

1. David Bonavia, *The Chinese* (London: Allen Lane 1980).
2. Liu Xiaobo was taken by police after being one of several intellectuals to issue an '08 Charter' commemorating the 60th anniversary of the Universal Declaration of Human Rights. At the time of writing (December 2008) he is still in detention.
3. Julia Lovell, *The Politics of Cultural Capital: China's Quest for a Nobel Prize in Literature* (Honolulu: University of Hawaii Press 2006).
4. This is set out in Joshua Cooper Ramo's 2005 leaflet, issued by the UK Foreign Policy Institute, 'The Beijing Consensus', available at <http://fpc.org.uk/fsblob/244.pdf> (accessed 15 September 2008).
5. The particular challenges of China's role in Tibet are well presented by Dibyash Anand, in *Geopolitica Tibet* (Minneapolis: University of Minnesota Press 2008), which shows the equally self-deluding and self-serving myths about Tibet and its mysterious otherness promoted by some key sectors in the West. There is no doubt, though, that in terms of the PR battle, the Dalai Lama has so far won hands down, whatever the nuances. At the heart of this is perhaps, to many foreigners, the baffling desire of the Chinese government to not only be judged winners of the political argument in Tibet (which says that it would not work as an independent country any longer, something largely accepted, even by some Tibetans), but also the moral one (that the Chinese are doing good things there and are morally justified in their actions, something far harder to concede).
6. John L Thornton, 'Long Time Coming: The Prospects of Democracy in China' in *Foreign Affairs*, January–February 2008, 2–3.
7. See <http://english.peopledaily.com.cn/whitepaper/democracy/preface.html> (accessed 3 September 2008).
8. These statistics are from Tony Saitch, 'China:Socio-Political Issues' in *China Into the Future*, W. John Hoffman and Michael Enright, Eds. (Singapore: John Wiley and Co 2008), 142–143.
9. Bruce Gilley, *China's Democratic Future* (New York: Columbia University Press 2004).

Conclusion: Gambling with the Devil: Why the Fate of the CCP Matters to Us All

1. Gerald Segal, 'Does China Matter' in *Foreign Affairs*, September/October 1999.
2. See *Civil Military Relations in Today's China*, David M Finkelstein and Kirten Gunness, Eds. (Armonk: M.E.Sharpe 2007), for a range of perspectives on how the Chinese military has developed in the last two decades.

Further Reading

The most comprehensive history of the rise of the party, along with the historical context in which it was born, through to how it governed in the first part of its life, is contained in *The Cambridge History of China*, Volumes 12 to 15 (Cambridge 1983 onward). I have drawn on this heavily for the first chapter, especially the history of the nationalists. Rana Mitter's *China: A Bitter Revolution*, (Oxford University Press 2004) offers a well-presented argument on the contributions of the Nationalists to China's development, doing something to change their generally negative historic reputation. An elegant and succinct summation of similar arguments is contained in Frank Dikotter's *The Age of Openness: China Before Mao* (Hong Kong University Press 2008). Jonathan Fenby's *Penguin History of Modern China* (Allen Lane 2008) covers the narrative of the general history of China from 1850 onward well and describes some of the travails of the late Qing reforms, the Republican period, and on into Mao, Deng, Jiang, and even part of Hu. For the purists, there is Immanuel C. Y. Hsu's monumental *The Rise of Modern China* (Oxford 2000, 6th Edition), which tells the story from the start of the Ming in 1644.

For the foundation of the Party, I have benefited from looking at *Zhongguo Gongchandang Chengli Shi* (History of the Foundation of the CCP), published by the Chinese Social Sciences Academy Publishing House, (Beijing 2006). The official story is contained in the two-volume *Zhongguo Gongchandang Lishi* (History of the Chinese Communist Party) issued by the Party School Research Department, and published by the People's University Press, Beijing in 1991. I was also grateful for descriptions of the attendees of the first Congress, and their various different destinies after this meeting, to the guidebook *The Site of the First National Congress of the Communist Party of China*, edited by Lin Weiguang and published by the Shanghai Arts Book Publication Company, 2001. Any of the works of Hans van de Ven are also important in understanding this period, especially *Comrades and Strangers*, (University of California Press 1991), his excellent account of the first years of the Party. Although belonging to a different age, General Jacques Guillermaz's two-volume *History of the Chinese Communist Party 1921–1949* and *History of the Chinese Communist Party 1949–1967*, Translated by Anne Desteney (Methuen 1971) is detailed, elegantly told and, unsurprisingly for a man with a military background, very strong on the battle tactics used by the Communists for final victory in the Civil War. Arif Dirlik focuses on the intellectual currents and contexts in which the very earliest Communists operated in China, prior to the 1st Party Congress, in *The Origins of Chinese Communism* (Oxford University Press 1989). The tragic tale of Li Lisan, sporadic leader of the Communists till his unsuccessful military adventures in 1931, is told in highly purple fashion, in French journalist Patrick Lescot's *Before Mao: The Untold Story of Li Lisan and the Creation of Communist China* (Harper Collins 1999). Lucien Bianco's concise *Origins of the Chinese Revolution 1915–1949* (Stanford University Press 1971) does not conceal its political sympathies, but is nevertheless highly readable, and offers a strong, accessible interpretation.

For the structure of the Party from 1949, and its evolution in government, readers might wish to look at the very early *Leadership in Communist China* by John Wilson Lewis (Cornell University Press 1963). His first words, 'The distinguishing characteristic of Chinese communism is the leadership doctrine by which the party elite rules China', is as relevant today as it was when written almost half a century ago. Jeremy Brown and Paul G Pickowicz's *Dilemma's of Victory: The Early Years of the People's Republic* (Harvard University Press 2007), deals with the first few years of Communist rule in China and covers the continuities, and breaks, with the nationalist period, along with fascinating insights into the rebellions against the Party in southwest China, and the slow withdrawal of the Soviet army from the Northeast.

Analysis of the various congresses, along with dates and personnel, all of it very much in terms currently accepted as orthodox in Mainland China, is contained in *Zhongguo Gongchandang Lici Quanguo Daibiao Dahui* (Meetings of the Congresses of the Chinese Communist Party), published by the Party School Publishing House in Beijing, 2008.

The finest history of the Great Leap Forward can be found in Ralph A. Thaxton, Jr,'s *Catastrophe and Contention in Rural China: Mao's Great Leap Forward Famine and the Origins of Righteous Resistance in Da Fo Village* (Cambridge University Press 2008). His meticulous account shows Mao's complete complicity in this tragic period of modern Chinese history. For the buildup to the Cultural Revolution, the key source remains Roderick MacFarquhar's monumental three-volume *The Origins of the Cultural Revolution*. For the Cultural Revolution itself, his single volume, *Mao's Last Revolution* (Harvard: Balknap Press 2006), co-authored with Michael Schoenhals, stands as the best English-language narrative and explanation of this confusing period. Mobo Gao's *The Cultural Revolution and the Battle for China's Past* (Pluto Press 2008) offers a rousing argument both for the good that the Cultural Revolution brought to China and the crimes that need to be laid at Deng Xiaoping's door.

For current analysis of where the Party stands, David Shamburgh's *China's Communist Party: Atrophy and Adaptation* (Routledge 2008) offers a good overview. Minxin Pei's *China's Trapped Transition: the Limits of Development Authoritarianism* (Harvard University Press 2008) is a passionate argument for the failure of political reform by the CCP in China in the last decade. Plotting the rise and fall of careers within the Party, few have done this in such detail, and with such access, as Hong Kong-based Willy Lam, whose *Jiang Zemin Era* and *The Hu Jintao Era* (M.E. Sharpe 2006) all give good, detailed and very readable assessments. Dr Lam also writes extensively about the Party in the press. The work of Joseph Fewsmith also offers excellent background here. The China Institute at Nottingham University has, over the last few years, as the UK's only think-tank solely devoted to research on China, produced a series of very informative papers. Those by Yongnian Zheng repay particular attention.

For Chinese leaders, in the third and fourth generation, Cheng Li of the Brookings Institution in the US had produced detailed analysis of their backgrounds and the various compositions of the Politburo and the Central Committee. He has set this down for the likely makeup of the fifth generation, yet to come, in a volume edited by John Hoffman and Michael Enright, *China into the Future* (John Wiley 2007). Bruce Gilley's *China's Democratic Future* (Columbia University Press 2004) is a bold look into the next two decades.

Index

CPSIA information can be obtained
at www.ICGtesting.com
Printed in the USA
BVHW071734170919
558653BV00001B/60/P

9 781843 317814